Global Adventures on Less-Traveled Roads:

A Foreign Service Memoir

For Trey and Kristina Sklar, with warm regards and best wishes. It was a pleasure to meet you and your impressive children during your visit to Patriots Colony, where we are happy to have your father, Dick, as a good friend.

Jim Bullington

April 30, 2019

1

JAMES R. BULLINGTON

Cover oil painting by

Eva Bullington Gustafson

JAMES R. BULLINGTON

GLOBAL ADVENTURES

ON LESS-TRAVELED ROADS:

A FOREIGN SERVICE MEMOIR

2017

Additional books by James R. Bullington

Adventures in Service with Peace Corps in Niger, CreateSpace (Amazon), 2007

Expeditionary Diplomacy in Action: Supporting the Casamance Peace Initiative, with Tuy-Cam Bullington, CreateSpace (Amazon), 2015

Official Disclaimer

The views expressed in this book are those of the author, and not necessarily those of the Department of State or the U. S. Government.

ABOUT THE AUTHOR

James R. Bullington was a career Foreign Service Officer with the U.S. Department of State for 27 years. He was Dean of the Department's highest level training program, the Senior Seminar; and he served as Ambassador to Burundi and in other diplomatic positions in Vietnam, Thailand, Burma, Chad, and Benin as well as at the State Department and National Security Council in Washington.

After retiring from the Foreign Service, Jim was Director of International Affairs for the City of Dallas, Texas, working with the Mayor, business executives, and civic leaders to promote the city's international development. He left Dallas to become Director of the Center for Global Business and Executive Education at Old Dominion University in Norfolk, Virginia.

In 2000, Jim became Country Director for the Peace Corps in Niger, where he led a 120-Volunteer program providing assistance in agriculture, health, education, and the environment. He remained in Niger until 2006, when he retired. He was called out of retirement by the State Department in 2012-14 for assignment in Senegal as a special envoy to help end a 30-year secessionist insurgency.

Born in Chattanooga, Tennessee, Jim received a B.A. in English from Auburn University and a Master in Public Administration from Harvard. He is also a graduate of the U.S. Army War College and a Senior Fellow at the Joint Forces Staff College in Norfolk.

Jim has been married since 1968 to Than-trong Tuy-Cam, a native of Hué, Vietnam. She accompanied him on his subsequent Foreign Service assignments and post-retirement jobs in the United States and abroad, while raising two daughters. She also worked in Widener Library at Harvard, as a Vietnamese teacher at the CIA language school in Washington, and as a case worker for Catholic Relief Services in Arlington. She is an avid cook and homemaker.

In retirement, the Bullingtons live in Williamsburg, Virginia.

TABLE OF CONTENTS

PREFACE

I shall be telling this with a sigh
Somewhere ages and ages hence:
Two roads diverged in a wood, and I --
I took the one less traveled by,
And that has made all the difference.
Robert Frost, *The Road Not Taken*

From my youth, I've taken less-traveled roads: Being the first in my family to go to college. Publicly advocating desegregation in 1961 Alabama. Joining the Foreign Service. Marrying an Asian. Choosing assignments in remote posts in Southeast Asia and Sub-Saharan Africa. Becoming an Ambassador. Retiring from the Foreign Service at age 48. Continuing an international career with city government and in academia. Returning to Africa with Peace Corps. Arranging recall to active duty in the Foreign Service at 72.

There have been lots of adventures along the way. I hope this professional and personal memoir will prove interesting, perhaps even instructive, not only to family and friends but also to a broader audience, particularly those with international inclinations.

Sources include documents, journals, letters, and pictures I have kept over the years, as well as memories. I have also drawn on books, articles and other published materials, which are footnoted if not mentioned in the text. I have aimed for accuracy, together with a balance between brevity and thoroughness.

I dedicate the book to Tuy-Cam, my loving wife, dear companion, and fellow traveler since 1968 on all these less-traveled roads. I'm grateful to her, daughters Kim and Eva, and William & Mary MBA student Emily Anding for their help in editing and proofreading.

1.

Deep Southern Roots and Redneck Childhood, 1940-57

The Bullington family tree is deeply rooted in southern American history, but not the South of plantations and the aristocracy that lived on them; nor were my forebears educated professionals or political leaders. They were yeoman farmers and, later, working class people. I didn't attempt to trace the genealogy farther back than the immigrants who crossed the Atlantic, but an analysis of my DNA by *23andMe* shows that my more distant ancestors were all Europeans, with 2.8% of my DNA coming from Neanderthals.

Jamestown Beginnings

My ancestor Nicholas Bullington, born in 1605, arrived in Jamestown in 1623. This was the first permanent English settlement in North America, founded in 1607. He must have been an adventuresome young man to undertake such a journey at the age of 17 or 18, especially with no other family members accompanying him. I would like to think some of his risk-taking genes got passed along to me.

Nicholas married Cynthia Clarke in 1624, and the couple moved up the James River to Henrico County, near present-day Richmond. They produced seven children and many grandchildren, including Robert Bullington, who moved to Pittsylvania County, near present-day Danville, in the early 18th Century. The family line continued there for a century, until John Bullington and his family moved to northwest Alabama.

John's son, Henderson, settled in Limestone County, Alabama, near the town of Athens, in 1836. This is where my father was born in 1910, and where I lived for part of my childhood.

My paternal grandmother's family can also be traced back to colonial Virginia, as can the families of both my maternal grandparents. For genealogical details, see Annex 1.

The only remarkable thing about my ancestry is the depth of the family roots in American history, especially Nicholas' arrival in Jamestown only 16 years after its founding. All of my ancestors seem to have been small-scale family farmers or, in later generations, working-class urbanites. There is no indication that any of them achieved substantial wealth, fame, leadership positions, or a college education. Nor is there evidence that any of them were other than law-abiding citizens. I'm happy to note that forebears served honorably, though without known distinction, in both the Revolutionary and Civil Wars.

Perhaps because of this unremarkable history, I have no interesting family traditions or stories to pass along. I don't recall having any family discussion of ancestors earlier than my grandparents' generation.

In the Beginning...

I was born in Chattanooga on October 27, 1940, the firstborn child of Mike and Elizabeth Bullington, and I remained an only child until the birth of my brother Mike in 1951. There was nothing unusual about my arrival, and I was a reasonably healthy baby.

My father was a farm boy from just outside Athens, a town of perhaps 5000 people and the county seat of Limestone County, in the part of Alabama that lies north of the Tennessee River. His given name was Iris Nell, a name his mother took from some long-forgotten novel she was reading during the pregnancy. Understandably, Daddy hated that name. Although in Athens he was always known as Iris, as soon as he left home he adopted the name of Mike. He refused to reveal his real name even to close friends, and on legal documents he would use only his initials, "I. N."

After graduating in 1926 from Athens Agricultural School, a vocational high school, Daddy worked on the family farm and had some menial jobs in town before getting hired as a laborer to work on construction of Wheeler Dam, an early project of the Tennessee Valley Authority. The TVA, which brought flood control and electricity to the Tennessee Valley, was one of the Roosevelt Administration's most successful efforts to fight the Great Depression. In due course Daddy became a journeyman welder and lifelong member of one of the American Federation of Labor trade unions: the United Association of Journeymen and Apprentices of the Plumbing and Pipefitting Industry.

With the end of the Wheeler project in 1936, Daddy got another TVA job working on construction of Chickamauga Dam, just outside of Chattanooga. He was boarding at a house in town when he met my mother, Esther Elizabeth Justice. They were married in 1937.

Mother's parents, James Fred and Jessie Florence Justice, had been living in Chattanooga for many years. Granny was born there, and Granddaddy came there as a young man from a farm in Middle Tennessee, to work for Southern Railroad. At first he was a switchman, but he lost his right hand in a work accident. Southern then trained him to operate the control towers in its freight yards, a job he kept until he retired. Mother was born in 1917, and had only one sibling, Frances, born two years later.

Shortly after their marriage, Daddy was transferred to work on Hiwassee Dam, in the Smoky Mountains near the North Carolina line, and subsequently to Fort Loudon Dam, between Chattanooga and Knoxville. Largely because of my childhood asthma, in 1943 the family moved to Miami, Florida, where we lived in a trailer park. I don't know where Daddy worked, but it must have been a construction job. My asthma went away (never to return), and after about a year we moved back to Tennessee.

By the time of Pearl Harbor Daddy was 31, with a wife and child, and consequently was not drafted into the military. As draft calls reached ever deeper into the manpower pool, he might well have been called up, and at one point he planned to volunteer for the Seabees (Navy engineer/construction units). However, after our return from Miami in 1944, he got work on construction of a secret government project. This turned out to be the Oak Ridge National Laboratory, part of the Manhattan Project, which produced highly-enriched uranium for the atomic bomb. That job assured his deferment through the end of the war. During this period, we lived in Lenoir City, a small town near Oak Ridge, southeast of Knoxville.

After the end of the war and his job at Oak Ridge, Daddy decided to try his hand as an entrepreneur, launching a business selling and repairing water heaters. He and Mother moved back to Chattanooga, where we lived with my grandparents in a working class neighborhood. I began the first grade a year early, at the age of five.

Within months, the water heater business was failing. On a Christmas visit to Chattanooga in 1946, Mother's sister, Frances, and her husband, George Otto, told about the good life and job opportunities in the Los Angeles area. Inspired by their experience and pushed to action by the failure of the water heater business, Mother and Daddy loaded up our Studebaker in the summer of 1947 and headed west.

While I have a few dim memories of the first grade in Chattanooga, my coherent recollections only begin in Maywood, a Los Angeles suburb where we lived in a tiny three-room house with an enclosed porch that became my bedroom. Daddy found a job with a big utility company, Pacific Gas and Electric, but the high cost of living in California (compared to the South) kept us near the poverty level. Despite the efforts of Aunt Frances and Uncle George to help them adjust, Mother and Daddy were never comfortable with the lifestyle and culture in Los Angeles. They decided to leave after only a year, and in the summer of 1948 we drove back east.

Redneck Roots on the Farm in Alabama

We moved to my grandparents' farm near Athens. The farmhouse was large, and had a three-room apartment that had previously been rented out. I suppose there was not much else my parents could afford after losses in the water heater business and the near-poverty experience in California. I'm sure they had no savings to draw on, as lack of money was a frequent topic of conversation.

The 40-acre farm was a subsistence operation. Cotton was the only cash crop, which brought in enough money for necessities such as clothes and tools, but life was hard and luxuries few. There was a large garden for vegetables and an orchard for apples and peaches, which were canned and stored in a "storm cellar" (a covered trench used to keep canned goods cool as well as to provide shelter from the tornados that are a threat in that region). Two cows provided milk and butter, which my grandmother made with a hand churn. There was a hog pen with a dozen or so pigs that were turned into ham and bacon to be cured and stored in the "smokehouse." A flock of chickens provided eggs and an occasional Sunday dinner. I recall how my grandfather would kill the victim, by wringing its neck, i.e., grabbing it by the head and swinging it round and round until head and body were detached. After the body stopped flopping around, which usually took a couple of minutes, it was put into a pot of boiling water to loosen the feathers for plucking.

Plowing and hauling were done with the aid of two mules. Water was drawn from a well on the back porch. Food was cooked on a wood stove supplied from a patch of woods on the farm from which trees were cut and chopped into kindling logs that had to be carried to the house every day (one of my chores). A large pasture and a corn field supplied food for the livestock. There was electricity, thanks to the TVA, and an old pre-war radio for entertainment, consisting mostly of network comedy shows such as "Amos and Andy" and "The Jack Benny Program," plus gospel music every morning and the Grand Ole Opry on Saturday nights. A single bathroom with a flush toilet had recently been added to the house, but Pa insisted on keeping the old outhouse as well, which he preferred to the indoor plumbing.

I relished life on the farm for the two years we were there, and on frequent weekend and summer visits thereafter. I had a dog named Bess and a pet pig, Lucy, who was the runt of a large litter and would have perished had I not adopted her. She was much smarter than Bess, and I persuaded the family to let her to sleep under the house. However, she soon grew too big to be left at liberty, as she took an improper interest in the vegetable garden. So, she had to be returned to the hog lot to await her ultimate transformation into ham and sausage. My pleas for her pardon were not heeded.

I spent lots of time fishing in the creek that ran through the farm and playing in the fields and barn. I learned to milk the cows and "slop the hogs" (i.e., take them the bucket of table scraps from our meals), as well as to shuck corn and pick cotton for a penny a pound. The Athens schools had a two-week vacation during cotton-picking time, so the children would be free for this purpose.

The farm fronted a dirt road called North Hine Street. My grandfather's brother had a farm on the other side of the road, and another brother had a farm about two miles distant. Yet another brother had a small general store near the courthouse in Athens. Much of our social life involved visits with them and their families, plus occasional visits "across the river" (Elk River), where the Alabama Bullingtons had originally settled after moving from Virginia. Pa's two sisters, Aunt Vee and Aunt Vona, lived there. Uncle Irvin, Daddy's brother, lived in a small house on Pa's farm, about a quarter of a mile from the main house. He and his wife, Lillian, had a daughter, Mary

Helen, two years older than me, and a son, Robert Mack, two years younger than me; and the three of us often played together.

Other than farm and family, our lives were centered on the church. The Bullingtons of Limestone County were devout members of the Church of Christ, a fundamentalist sect that regarded Southern Baptists as theological liberals. The Bible, all of it, Old Testament as well as New Testament, was held to be the literal, inerrant, revealed Word of God. There was no organ or other instrumental music allowed in the church, nor was there a choir; but there was lots of *a cappela* singing by the congregation -- simple hymns and "gospel songs" that I came to love and still enjoy. Drinking and dancing were considered sinful, and evolution was regularly denounced as the doctrine of atheists inspired by the Devil. Regular attendance at Sunday school and worship services was required.

I accepted this religion as my own, at first willingly, but with increasing reluctance by the time I was in high school. After I left home for college, my shadow never again darkened a church-house door except for ceremonial occasions such as weddings and funerals, and I have not been a religious believer since those childhood years.

I did well in school, so much so that when I had completed the fourth grade in Athens, I was promoted directly to the sixth grade. Thus, having begun school at the age of five and skipping the fifth grade, I was a couple of years younger than my classmates and graduated from high school at 16. This was probably one reason for my shyness and other social limitations during those years.

In Athens, I lived the good life of a redneck Alabama farm boy.

Back to Chattanooga

Although I have fond memories of living in Athens, the situation was not so good for my parents. Mother was a city girl who had never lived on a farm, and she was not comfortable there. And though this was

15

Daddy's home, he found it hard to make a living. The only job he could get was at a blacksmith and farm implement repair shop that paid low wages for piece work, not the modest but adequate union-scale hourly wages he had been used to. Many weeks he would earn only $12 or $15, an extremely low income even in the late 1940s.

Consequently, in the summer of 1950 we moved back to Chattanooga, once again living on the second floor of my grandparents' house. Daddy had gotten a welding job on construction of a DuPont plant that was to produce nylon, a new synthetic fabric then becoming popular. I was enrolled in the sixth grade and continued to do well academically, but I found it hard to make new friends and always looked forward to our frequent weekend and summer visits to Athens.

After the DuPont project ended, Daddy worked at TVA's Hales Bar Dam, about 20 miles west of Chattanooga, and finally at the TVA steam plant (for production of electricity from coal) at Widow's Creek near Scottsboro, Alabama, about 40 miles west of Chattanooga but within commuting distance. This assured geographic and financial stability for the rest of my childhood. However, our standard of living remained modest. He made decent wages for that era, but Mother (like most women of her generation) never worked outside the home, and it was difficult to accumulate any savings. We stayed in the small house with my grandparents, even after the birth of my brother, Mike, in 1951. It was only after I had gone away to college that my parents were able to afford a home of their own.

Yet, I never felt like we were poor, since our relatives and the kids I knew in the neighborhood were in more or less similar circumstances. On the other hand, I did yearn for some luxuries, like a bicycle and eventually a motorcycle, fishing gear, stamps for my hobby of philately, and a hi-fidelity stereo music system. To get them, I realized I was going to have to earn my own money.

I got a newspaper route at the age of 11, delivering the *Chattanooga News-Free Press* to about 50 customers. From then on, I have never been without some sort of paying job for more than brief periods. Before graduating from high school, I had a longer newspaper route (which required a motorcycle), a job tending the scoreboard for the Chattanooga Lookouts (a Southern Baseball League farm-team for the Washington Senators), holiday work as a sales clerk at the National Shirt Shop, and a job washing dishes in the Hotel Patten. Of my many weaknesses, reluctance to work was never among them.

In junior high school (grades 7-9), I continued to excel academically, but I was socially awkward and didn't adjust well. Part of the problem was being overweight and unathletic. I became a voracious reader, and in addition to classics such as *Huckleberry Finn*, by the ninth grade I was devouring books by Ernest Hemingway, William Faulkner, Victor Hugo, and other authors not normally on reading lists for children. But I was not happy, and twice I tried to run away from home, together with friends in the neighborhood. On the first occasion, we managed to hitch-hike as far as Scottsboro, Alabama, before calling our parents. The second time we got as far as Atlanta before getting arrested and spending the night in a juvenile detention facility. The first time we had a vague idea about going to the West and working as firefighters in a national park; and the second time we were heading for Florida to find work as deckhands on a fishing boat. With maturity, my ambitions became higher.

As an only child, I felt jealous of friends who had siblings, and I welcomed the birth of my brother Mike in 1951. Mother and Daddy had wanted another child, but it was only after settling permanently in Chattanooga in 1950 that they felt enough financial and geographic stability to have one. They also thought it would be good for me to have a sibling. However, because of the difference in our ages – I left home for college the same year he started first grade – Mike and I were never as close as most brothers. After I completed college, geographic distance became another constraint on our relationship, as I was overseas or in Washington, while Mike stayed near home. However, we remained in contact and enjoyed good relations until his death in 2016.

On to High School...with Polio

After completing Northside Junior High, in the summer of 1953 I contracted polio. This was before the Salk vaccine (introduced in 1955), and polio epidemics were common every summer. Many people died, and many others were left severely crippled (most famously, President Franklin Roosevelt). Although I was hospitalized in the "isolation ward" for several weeks, I was fortunate that the only permanent damage was a weakened left leg and foot. This resulted in a slight but lifelong limp, as well as even further limits on my already mediocre athletic abilities. It also put an end to my plan to go to West Point or Annapolis and have a military career, or failing that, to enlist and go to college on the GI Bill after completing my service. I was sorely disappointed when my doctor told me I could never meet the physical requirements for the military.

My experience at Chattanooga City High School was happier and less troubled than in junior high. Socially, I participated in school activities and clubs as well as the Church of Christ youth group; but I was not a leader. I remained shy and awkward, particularly with girls. Not until my senior year did I manage to find a girlfriend, Dottie, and begin dating. Though this romance became serious (we were eventually engaged to be married during my second year at college), Dottie abruptly left me for someone else. It didn't seem so at the time, but this was one of the most fortunate things that ever happened to me: It freed me to find success as a student leader in college, to undertake a career in the Foreign Service, and eventually to find the right wife. Had I married Dottie, I would likely have been stuck in an industrial job in Chattanooga for the rest of my life, and the marriage would probably have been unsuccessful.

Even though Chattanooga City was an excellent public school with high academic standards, I found I could make good grades (though not all A's) with little application and almost no homework. I continued to do lots of outside reading, including novels by authors such as Tolstoy and Dostoyevsky, and multi-volume histories such as Freeman's *Lee's Lieutenants* and Churchill's *History of the English Speaking Peoples*. One of my classmates, Jim Bishop, introduced me to ham radio, which was to become a lifelong hobby. My grades put me in the top 20% of my 420-member graduating class. More importantly, my Scholastic Aptitude Test (SAT) score made me one of only a dozen National Merit Scholarship semi-finalists in the class. Thus I was assured of acceptance into a good university.

My parents and teachers had always encouraged me to go to college, and I had always assumed I would do so. As I approached high school graduation, however, the problem of how to pay for a college education became pressing. My grades and SAT score, while very good, were not sufficiently elevated to gain an academic scholarship at a competitive university. Scholarships were much more limited in the 1950s than they are now, and student loans were rarely available. There was no way my parents could afford to pay for my college education, or even contribute to it more than marginally.

The technological competition of the Cold War, particularly the space race and the launch of the Russian *Sputnik* satellite in 1957, and the perception that the United States was lagging behind the USSR, produced pressure during my high school and college years to steer young people into science and technology careers. I had good grades and test scores in math and science, so teachers and counselors encouraged me to take that direction. When I learned about the co-op program for engineering students, I saw this as my best – probably my only – opportunity to finance a college degree.

The co-op program, in which students alternated semesters or quarters at school and in full-time work, was offered for engineering studies at most major universities, at least those in the South that I was considering. I examined the programs at the University of Tennessee in Knoxville, Georgia Tech in Atlanta, and Alabama Polytechnic Institute (as it was then named, before changing to Auburn University in 1960) in Auburn. I visited these campuses, along with two classmates, Dick Barnwell and Jim Bishop, who also planned to study engineering via the co-op route. Jim chose Georgia Tech; Dick and I picked Auburn.

I preferred Auburn because it was cheaper, with tuition at only $75 per quarter and lower living costs than in cities such as Atlanta and Knoxville. Moreover, I found Auburn's small college town atmosphere more appealing than the urban campuses of Tennessee and Georgia Tech.

Jim

My first grade class in Chattanooga.

***

Ida and Mack Bullington, on the farm near Athens, c. 1948.

James and Jessie Justice, on their 50th wedding anniversary, 1961.

Mike, Elizabeth, and Jim Bullington, 1942.

Justice home in Chattanooga, where we lived upstairs, 1950-57.

****

2.

Transitions and Transformations:

Auburn and the Foreign Service, 1957-65

Toward the end of my senior year at City High in 1957, I connected with a Chattanooga company, Tennessee Products and Chemical Corporation, which was interested in taking on a co-op student in chemical engineering. They had a factory near the foot of Lookout Mountain that produced industrial chemicals. This was ideal for me, since I could live at home during work quarters and save enough money to pay for the following quarter in school. Moreover, they agreed to let me start work right after graduation, so I would be able to begin college in the fall, along with the "regular" freshman class. The co-op office at Auburn endorsed this arrangement.

My job that summer was as a supply clerk in the chemical plant warehouse. It wasn't very interesting, but the pay, $1.25 an hour, was far more than I had ever earned before, and I relished the leap toward independence and grown-up status the job represented. I needed transportation to work, so with $250 I had saved from part-time jobs plus $150 Daddy gave me as a graduation present, I was able to buy my first car, a 1949 Plymouth. It was a basic, plain-Jane, 8-year-old vehicle, but a source of pride for me.

Now, with a serious job, a car, and status as a college student, I began to feel more like an adult than the 16-year-old kid I remained.

In September, my classmate Dick Barnwell (who had gotten a co-op job with TVA) and I drove to Auburn in my car and found a room in a private house near the campus. Auburn was (and remains) a small town, where life is centered around the university. I felt at home there from the beginning. Everyone was friendly, and the pace was unhurried. Classes were more interesting than in high school, but I didn't find them too difficult and was able to maintain a B+ grade average without a lot of effort. Football was (and remains) an important part of life at Auburn, and that fall Auburn's team won the national championship.

The most important development of my first quarter at Auburn was "pledging" Sigma Pi fraternity, along with Dick Barnwell. The fraternity became the center of my social life. I ate all meals there, and joined in the frequent parties and long evenings at local beer joints. I had never experienced anything like this drinking and partying, and it became a big part of my life at Auburn. I had a great time, but managed to keep up with my schoolwork, making the Dean's List more often than not, and avoided getting into serious trouble.

The fraternity remained my social anchor even after I began taking on student leadership roles. Without the friendships and network it provided, I doubt my college experience would have been successful, and it certainly wouldn't have been as much fun. A few fraternity brothers (Dick Barnwell, Tom King, Paul Hall, Joe Ed Voss, Carl Myatt) have remained my close friends into our retirement years.

Career Shift and Leadership Beginnings

After three years of co-op experience, and after the end of my engagement to Dottie, I had doubts about a career as a chemical engineer and developed aspirations for a future beyond the confines of Chattanooga.

At work, I progressed from stock clerk in the warehouse to technician in the quality control lab, doing chemical tests on incoming raw materials and outgoing finished products to assure that they met established standards. Next, I became an assistant to the plant's chief engineer, helping design new equipment and buildings. I was then made a "shift foreman," a front-line supervisor of the dozen or so operators of the mixers, stills, and other production equipment. As I began to understand more about the work I was likely to be doing as a chemical engineer, I decided that was not what I wanted for the rest of my life.

At the same time, education was broadening my horizons. I enjoyed my classes in English, history, and philosophy more than those in calculus, chemistry, and engineering drawing. I also became a sports reporter for the student newspaper, *The Plainsman*, and discovered that I had some talent for writing. And intensifying an interest that began in high school, when I became a regular reader of the newspapers I was delivering as well as of Granddaddy Justice's *Newsweek* magazines, I read more and more about current events, politics, and international affairs.

Consequently, I decided to change my major from chemical engineering to English. A friendly professor's effort to steer me toward a Ph.D. was helpful only in convincing me that I didn't want an academic career. I began to lean toward journalism, and dreamed of a romantic life as a foreign correspondent. At the same time, I was inspired by John F. Kennedy's call to "ask not what your country can do for you, but what you can do for your country," along with his creation of the Peace Corps, and I started to think of an international career in government. By 1961, my aspirations focused on the Foreign Service, with journalism as a back-up plan, perhaps beginning as a Peace Corps Volunteer.

The first problem with this change in direction was how to finance completion of my college education if I left the co-op program. The solution was an increased availability of long-term student loans through federal government programs plus a part-time job at Auburn with the University News Bureau. I was able to get this job because of excellent grades in English, experience writing for *The Plainsman*, and (most importantly) a connection with the University Publicity Director and News Bureau chief, L. O. Brackeen. He was a native of Athens, and his wife, Lilla, was Daddy's first cousin. The family connection got me a try-out; I did well, and I was able to earn $20 a week while learning writing and reporting skills. The job involved preparing press releases about interesting happenings at the University, and I enjoyed it.

At the end of my summer work quarter in 1960, I told my employers at Tennessee Products that I was leaving the co-op program, and I changed my major to English, with minors in philosophy, history, and journalism.

Even more important than my change of majors that fall was my emergence as an active student leader. First, I moved up to Sports Managing Editor for *The Plainsman*, a position from which I could make a bid to become editor the following year. I also became editor of the *Tiger Cub*, the guidebook for all new freshmen, that needed to be updated every year.

Another leadership role was as publicity director for the Auburn Conference on International Affairs, an annual student-organized event that brought distinguished speakers to the campus. One of the speakers that year was Ambassador Clare Timberlake, a career Foreign Service Officer then serving as Political Advisor for the Air War College at Maxwell Air Force Base in Montgomery. Ambassador Timberlake, a patrician gentleman and "old school" FSO who had entered the Service prior to World War II, had been Ambassador to the newly-independent former Belgian Congo. The first FSO I ever met, he was kind enough to take an interest in my aspiration for a Foreign Service career. He helped me refine that goal, heightened my enthusiasm, and gave me much-needed practical advice. He even invited me to his home on the Air War College campus, where he introduced me to pink gin, a drink then popular among diplomats (and a major change from the Pabst Blue Ribbon I normally drank). He wrote a recommendation letter for my Foreign Service application, which was a principal reason for my success in the Foreign Service examination process.

Looking back on that school year, 1960-61, I'm surprised I was able to manage so much: a part-time job (15-20 hours per week); lots of work as *Plainsman* managing editor and in my other student leadership roles; heavy partying at the Sigma Pi house (where I lived); regular visits to the War Eagle Club, Archie's Bar-B-Q, Tommy's Beauty Rest Motel, and other beer joints; and fairly consistent class attendance (clearly not my highest priority, even though my grades remained good). The final months of that year, April and May of 1961, were especially intense, even dramatic.

Civil Rights Epiphany and Landmark Editorial

The *Plainsman* editor for the coming school year was chosen in a campus-wide election held every April from candidates deemed qualified by the student-faculty Publications Board. The president of the student body and other student leaders were elected at the same time. This was my first taste of political campaigning, with posters, speeches, and mobilization of supporters. Even though I didn't like campaigning, with the help of fraternity brothers and other friends, I won the election. I was not supposed to take office until the following September, but the current editor, Jim Phillips, had to leave school because of health problems, so I became editor in early May.

Like most white Southerners growing up in the 1940s and 1950s, I had accepted segregation as a given, a legal and cultural norm, the way things were and ought to be. No one in my family or among my friends or teachers questioned this Jim Crow system, at least not openly, as it was long-established, strongly supported by the white community, and well enforced by state and local governments. In the South, segregation was not even perceived by most white people to be a political issue until the Supreme Court's *Brown vs. Board of Education* decision in 1954. The process of desegregation and the civil rights movement that promoted it did not develop much traction until the late 1950s. Even in 1961, there had been essentially no progress on implementing school desegregation or other civil rights measures in

26

Alabama and most other Southern states. That spring, as I assumed my duties as *Plainsman* editor, I had not given much thought to the matter. It had not come up during the election, and it was not publicly discussed on campus.

The events that prompted my civil rights epiphany were the "Freedom Rides" and what happened when they came to Alabama. Several groups of young people, black and white, mostly students, rode interstate busses into the South and attempted to integrate local bus stations. In Anniston, Birmingham, and Montgomery, the Freedom Riders were attacked by ugly mobs, while state and local police stood by approvingly. These attacks were massively covered in newspapers and on television. I found them appalling. Moreover, with my new position as editor, I felt obliged to say so publicly. So, the night of May 22 I took a six-pack of Blue Ribbon to the *Plainsman* office and wrote an editorial denouncing not only the attacks on the Freedom Riders but also the political leaders who let them happen and the whole systemic culture of segregation in which they were rooted. The editorial ended with a call for the peaceful desegregation of Auburn University. I put it on the front page. (See Annex 2 for the text.)

When the *Plainsman* was distributed across campus the morning of May 24, the reaction was immediate, massive, and overwhelmingly hostile. Everywhere I went I was cursed, confronted, and threatened with violence by angry students. A group of them collected copies of the paper and built a large bonfire to burn them along with an effigy of me. The president of the university and the dean of student affairs called me in to denounce my "poor judgment," threaten expulsion, and demand that all future editorials be submitted for censorship before publication. The Ku Klux Klan burned a cross, about seven feet high and wrapped in oil-soaked rugs and burlap bags, on the front lawn of the Sigma Pi house, where I lived.

This uproar caught the attention of the local press, and the AP sent out a wire story that was widely published, especially in Alabama and

27

neighboring states, but also in the *Washington Post* and *New York Times*. Advocacy of integration by the student newspaper of a major state university in the deep South was big news in those days, and the cross burning and other hostile reaction made it even bigger news. After the story appeared in the Chattanooga newspapers, my parents got several hostile phone calls.

In writing the editorial, I didn't expect such a vigorous reaction. Insofar as I can recall, I didn't even think about the likely consequences. Nor do I recall ever being frightened by the hostility it evoked. (I probably should have been, but like many young people, I felt somehow invulnerable.) My feelings were at first simple amazement that the reaction was so strong, growing into disgust and anger as the threats and insults continued, accompanied by a strong conviction that I was right and my attackers were bigots on the wrong side of both morality and history. Before long, I came to relish my new-found notoriety.

Since Auburn is a state university, both the governor, John Patterson, and members of the state legislature were quick to get involved. They demanded that the university administration take action to control me and any like-minded "radical agitators" on the campus, and they threatened to cut Auburn's state funding if this were not done. Governor Patterson was especially vocal, both publicly and (I was told)

in calls to the university president, Ralph Draughon.

In 1958, Patterson had defeated George Wallace (who later became the country's most famous leader of resistance to racial integration) in Wallace's first run for governor, largely because he was perceived as more militant than Wallace on preserving segregation. In his post-election analysis of the reason for his

Gov. John Patterson

defeat, which was stated publicly and widely quoted in Alabama, Wallace said, "No other son-of-a-bitch will ever out-nigger me again!"[1] (In subsequent campaigns, Wallace made good on this pledge.) Thus Patterson's reaction to my editorial was not surprising. I've often told the story of my first meeting with him:

> In 1978-79, the State Department sent me to the Army War College for senior training. As part of the graduation festivities, the Army invited a number of distinguished citizens from around the country to visit Carlisle Barracks. On the guest list for the reception to welcome them, I was astonished to see the name of former Governor John Patterson, now a leading lawyer in Montgomery. At the reception, I recognized him in the crowd, made my way across the room, and presented myself, saying, "Governor, we never met, but when you were governor of Alabama I was editor of *The Plainsman* over there at Auburn." Patterson immediately drew himself back, pointed his finger at my chest, and exclaimed, "So you're the son-of-a-bitch that wrote that editorial!"
>
> I was proud to acknowledge that I was indeed that son-of-a-bitch; and I was enormously pleased that he had remembered the editorial and it had bothered him for all those 18 years.

I'm still surprised that I wasn't expelled from Auburn or at least forced out of my position as editor. Partly, this was because of the national support I received, including a telegram to President Draughon from the American Association of University Professors. The administration probably realized that any action against me could result in more trouble for Auburn than it would be worth. Moreover, they likely thought I could be sufficiently intimidated to comply with their demand to submit future editorials for censorship. I remained editor

---

[1] Trest, Warren, *Nobody but the People* (biography of Gov. Patterson), New South Books, Montgomery, 2008, p. 240.

throughout the following school year, 1961-62, and continued to publish commentary supporting civil rights, never submitting anything for censorship.

Integration did not come to Auburn until 1964, when a lone black man was enrolled as a graduate student. A small group of students, including some who were *Plainsman* staff members when I was editor, tried to welcome and support him, but he was isolated and made to feel sufficiently uncomfortable that he transferred to another school after only a year. Nonetheless, the barrier had been broken, and other black students came to Auburn. At first only a handful enrolled, but they continued to do so in ever more substantial numbers. The football team got its first black player in 1970, and that marked a tipping point in white acceptance of integration. By the early 1980s, it was no longer an issue at Auburn.

There was no violence associated with Auburn's desegregation, nor was there any political theater such as George Wallace's famous gesture of "standing in the schoolhouse door" to block federal agents forcing integration at the University of Alabama. Segregation ended quietly at Auburn. Perhaps my advocacy of civil rights and peaceful change in 1961 contributed to that outcome.

The Spades Drama

Spades was the top student leadership honorary organization at Auburn, composed of the 10 most outstanding seniors – the president and vice president of the student body, the editors of *The Plainsman* and the *Glomerata* (yearbook), the president of the Inter-Fraternity Council, etc. Each Spades group selected 10 rising seniors near the end of the school year who would serve for the following year.

Spades was much more than an honorary organization. In reality, it was a secret society, with an elaborate initiation ritual, clandestine meetings in isolated locations late at night, belief in its mission "to promote the betterment of Auburn," and a history dating to the beginning of the 20th Century. It also had a strong alumni group that included men in leadership roles at Auburn and throughout the state.

As *Plainsman* editor, I was "tapped" for Spades, and I was elated by the honor. However, I soon learned disturbing things about the organization from my friend and predecessor as editor, Jim Phillips. He revealed that a principal tool it used "to promote the betterment of Auburn" was the rigging of student elections, so as to assure that only the "best" people, as determined by the 10 members of Spades, would be elected. This was done for all elected positions, including Miss Auburn and the homecoming queen. The method was simple: They arranged that only Spades members would count the votes. Moreover, Phillips told me that although I had actually won the vote as *Plainsman* editor, the election for student body president had really been won by the candidate not selected by Spades, and the votes were miscounted so as to produce the "correct" result.

I found this revelation shocking, since I believed in American democratic principles and felt offended by the blatant dishonesty and injustice of rigged elections. Moreover, it had a special emotional impact for me, because the losing candidate for student body president, who had actually won the election, was a Sigma Pi fraternity brother, Bill McKnight. I wrestled with conflicting loyalties, but decided that I couldn't remain silent or accept continuation of this practice by Spades. I told Bill what had happened, and also told my nine fellow Spades that there could be no more rigged elections and that a new, transparent vote-counting system had to be adopted that would preclude it from happening again. They agreed.

We turned for advice on next steps to two prominent Spades alumni, the vice-president of the university and the editor of the Auburn weekly newspaper. Together with Bill's older brother, who was a Spades alumnus, they persuaded Bill and me not to go public with the information, on the grounds that it would do disproportionate damage to Auburn. They also promised us that the university would institute a new system to assure an honest vote count in student elections (which was in fact done the following fall).

I still wonder if not going public, and possibly destroying Spades as an organization, was the right decision. However, this drama was unfolding at the same time as publication of my Freedom Riders editorial and the reaction to it. I was already under a great deal of stress, and perhaps I realized that another major public upheaval with me at the center might be more than I could endure. I really did love Auburn in spite of its faults (and still do), so I didn't want to do it more harm than necessary. The problem of election rigging was corrected, I reasoned, so perhaps it would be best to put the past behind and move on.

The challenges of this spring quarter, 1961, were intense, especially for a 20-year-old kid who had never experienced anything remotely similar. Meeting these challenges contributed to my self-confidence, maturity, and ability to function under pressure.

At the end of the quarter, I went home to Chattanooga to begin a summer job at the *Chattanooga Times* as a copy editor, making corrections in stories, cutting them to fit the allotted space, and writing headlines. I also worked at the *Times* the following summer, 1962, as a reporter covering local news. The *Chattanooga Times* was owned by the *New York Times*, and it maintained similarly high journalistic standards. My two summers of experience there honed my writing and reporting skills, which proved useful for my coming Foreign Service career.

Of more immediate importance was the income from these summer jobs. Combined with student loans and the $20 per week I was paid as *Plainsman* editor, it financed completion of my degree at Auburn.

When I graduated in December 1962, my total debt was just over $8,000, which would be equivalent to $63,000 in today's money. My initial annual salary as an entry-level FSO was $5,600 ($44,000 in 2016 dollars). It was 1972 before I was able to repay all my student loans, but except for mortgages to buy homes, I was never again in debt.

Becoming a Diplomat

On a cold December Saturday in 1961, I drove 50 miles from Auburn to the federal courthouse in Montgomery to take the Foreign Service written exam, which was only offered once per year. It was a day-long challenge, somewhat comparable to the Graduate Record Exam. There were lots of questions on history and economics, plus a substantial number on science, math, music, art, and philosophy. Most of the exam was multiple choice, but there were also essay questions and a composition to write. Scoring was on "the curve," i.e., participants were competing with all the other exam-takers throughout the country that year. We were told that only the top five percent would "pass" and be invited to go on to the oral exam. Moreover, I noted that nearly all my competitors were older than me, and many had advanced degrees plus military and work experience. I was astounded a few weeks later to receive a letter from the State Department telling me I had passed and should contact them to schedule the oral exam.

The first available slot was in April. A couple of days before the appointed date I took a train from Auburn to Atlanta and a flight on to Washington. This trip marked the first time I had ever been on an airplane as well as the first time I had ever been north of Tennessee. I had been invited to stay with the parents of one of my friends on the *Plainsman* staff, Jim Dinsmore, whose father was an FBI agent. They lived in Alexandria and were gracious hosts, even setting up a dinner date with an interesting young lady.

The oral exam was simpler in that era than the multi-task, day-long assessment it has become in recent years. Then, it was just a three-hour intensive grilling by a panel of three or four senior FSOs, designed to assess how well the candidate could articulate responses, defend positions, make persuasive arguments, and hold up under pressure. I remember only one of the specific questions I was asked: "Should we open an Embassy in Ulaanbaatar?" Fortuitously, on the flight from Atlanta I had picked up a *National Geographic* magazine with an article by Supreme Court Justice William O. Douglas about his recent explorations in Mongolia (of which Ulaanbaatar is the capital). Otherwise, I wouldn't have had the foggiest notion of where Ulaanbaatar was, much less whether we should have an Embassy there. Armed with the information provided by Justice Douglas, I was able to offer a reasonable response, based on the need for a listening post to monitor the then-emerging Sino-Soviet conflict.

The panel members had read my reference letters, especially the one from Ambassador Timberlake in Montgomery, which I'm sure included information about my Freedom Riders editorial and the reaction to it. This was the subject of a substantial part of the interview, and it was a matter on which I could be articulate. I think I did OK on the other subjects raised in the exam, but I suspect this experience and my discussion of it were decisive in the panel's deliberations. As I left the room at the end of the interview, I was told to wait in a nearby office. In half an hour the chairman emerged to tell me I had passed, and subject to medical and security clearances, I would be invited to join the Foreign Service.

I was elated and astonished. I had recently turned 21, had not yet even graduated from Auburn, had no international experience, and came from a redneck background sharply different from the upper class origins of the vast majority of FSOs in that era. The trip back to Auburn was like a dream. I was really going to be a diplomat!

It was the following September before the medical and security clearances were done, and I was scheduled to join the A-100 basic officers class that was to begin December 27, 1962. This was perfect timing for me, since I needed another quarter to complete my degree at Auburn. That fall quarter was enjoyable, since my post-college job and career were already secured, classes were easy, my term as *Plainsman* editor had ended, and student loans were sufficient to preclude the need for a part-time job. It was like a three-month vacation with frequent parties and a chance to decompress from what had been an exciting but stressful experience for the two previous years.

Reporting for Duty

After a long drive from Chattanooga on the day after Christmas, I checked in at the Washington YMCA, which I had been told was the cheapest place to stay in the downtown area. The next day I reported for duty at the State Department and met my 13 A-100 course classmates (12 men and one woman – a typical gender ratio in those days). We bonded quickly, and on New Year's Day, three classmates and I moved into a two-bedroom apartment in Arlington Towers. Located in Rosslyn, just across the Potomac from the State Department, Arlington Towers was a high-rise apartment complex that was home to many FSOs because the Foreign Service Institute, the Department's training facility, was housed in its basement. This was where we took the eight-week A-100 orientation course, which in my case was followed by 16 weeks of intensive French.

Almost all of my classmates were graduates of Ivy League or other prestige universities such as Georgetown or Stanford. Most had advanced degrees, military service, international experience, and other qualifications that I lacked. As the youngest and least experienced member of the class, despite my classmates' friendliness I felt out of place and wondered if I could ever fit in with the elite culture of the Foreign Service. But I soon learned that even then the State Department was beginning to proclaim its dedication to increased diversity, so I laid claim to being that year's token redneck.

Later, in talks about the Foreign Service, I've often told this story about the reaction back home to my new career:

> After several months in training programs in Washington, I went home to Chattanooga for a brief visit over the July 4 holiday. At a gathering of family members and friends hosted by my parents, people were curious about what I was doing now that I had graduated from college. "Why, I've joined the Foreign Service," I proudly announced to the first couple that asked. Their eyes widened and their jaws dropped in consternation. "Now why in *HAIL* would yew go and do a thaing like that?" asked the husband. Further conversation revealed that they mistook the Foreign Service for the Foreign Legion (about which they had recently seen some old Hollywood movies on TV), and they couldn't imagine why I would want to go and fight for the French Army in the Sahara Desert.

> When one of my parents' neighbors asked a similar question, I re-formulated my answer. "I've gone to work for the State Department," I declared. "Oh," the man exclaimed, "so I reckon yer fixin' t'move up thar t'Nashville!" It was difficult to convince him that the State Department had nothing to do with state government.

> Asked about my employment yet again, this time by an elderly great-aunt, I reverted to the Foreign Service formulation. She smiled brightly, and for an instant I felt good that someone had recognized my accomplishment. But then she said, "Well, you're gonna look mighty good in one of them thar Smokey B'ar hats." I was totally perplexed by this comment until I realized she had heard "Foreign Service" as "Forest Service."

First Assignment: CENTO Desk

Two weeks before the end of the A-100 course, a man came from the personnel office to announce our assignments. This was before a

36

reform of the system in the 1970s that made it possible to see a list of upcoming job openings and submit a "bid list" of preferences. The assignment process was opaque, especially to us neophytes, and we had no input into it. Unlike all of my classmates, who were sent to posts around the globe, I was assigned to the State Department in Washington, as Assistant Desk Officer for CENTO (the Central Treaty Organization) in the Bureau of Near Eastern and South Asian Affairs. I was disappointed. My personnel counselor explained that I was kept in Washington to give me the opportunity to take French and get off "language probation." (New FSOs remained on probationary status until they had demonstrated fluency in a foreign language.) He added that in view of my exceptional youth, it would be good for me to have some "seasoning" before going abroad. I suppose this made sense, and in any case there was nothing I could do about it.

CENTO was created in 1955, primarily at the instigation of Eisenhower's Secretary of State, John Foster Dulles. It was a military alliance, a less-robust version of NATO, conceived as a Cold War instrument to deter Soviet aggression in the Middle East. It was never very strong, and under the Kennedy Administration it had already begun a long, slow process of fading into irrelevance. (It was formally dissolved in 1979.) Nonetheless, there was a secretariat and staff, annual meetings of the foreign ministers, and military and economic committees that met regularly to issue reports and pass resolutions.

The organization had begun life as the Baghdad Pact, but the name had to be changed when a military coup in 1958 took Iraq out of the alliance. The remaining members were Turkey, Iran, Pakistan, and Great Britain, with the United States officially an "observer" but in practice a full participant. My job was to assist the CENTO desk officer in providing back-up and guidance for the U.S. permanent representative at the CENTO secretariat in Ankara and for U.S. delegations to committee meetings and the annual Ministerial Council meeting. This involved writing instruction cables, position papers, and briefing books, and getting them cleared through State Department offices, the Pentagon, and other parts of the government.

One project I remember from my CENTO assignment involved construction of a rail link from Van, in eastern Turkey, to connect with the Iranian rail system at Tabriz. CENTO was involved because the project was presented by Turkey and Iran as an important piece of strategic infrastructure that would link the two countries militarily as well as economically, and thus enhance their common defense while promoting trade and development. It was an agenda item at upcoming committee and Ministerial Council meetings, and I was assigned to write a position paper on it, with instructions that the U.S. could not provide the requested support.

As I researched the project's history, I discovered that at previous meetings U.S. representatives had endorsed it, urged Turkey and Iran to commit to building it, and promised our support. I also found a forgotten three-year-old feasibility study, financed by CENTO, which found the rail link would be a sound economic investment that would promote development of a long-neglected region at relatively low cost. Thus, I concluded that the project deserved our backing if we were serious about strengthening the alliance, and that a negative position on it would be seen by our allies as failure to keep our promises. My bosses were persuaded I was right, and the U.S. agreed to include a contribution to the project in our foreign assistance budget. Eventually, the rail link was built, and it continues to function today.

This experience demonstrated to me that even a very junior FSO could sometimes have an impact on important international decisions.

The highlight of my two years on the CENTO desk was being a member of the U.S. delegation at the 1964 Ministerial Council meeting, held in Tehran. This meant I got to fly with Secretary of State Dean Rusk and other senior people in the Secretary's Boeing 707 jet, provided by the

Air Force. This was the first time I had ever been outside the United States. It was thrilling to actually talk to the Secretary.

Life in Washington

This initial Washington assignment served its purposes in allowing me to remove my language probationary status and to gain experience in the ways of the State Department and Foreign Service. However, I didn't join the Foreign Service to live in Washington, nor did I much enjoy the bureaucratic paperwork of the CENTO desk. Also, after my A-100 classmates left for their assignments, I was lonely.

This loneliness was relieved the second year, when two Auburn friends – Jim Phillips, my predecessor as *Plainsman* editor, and Bobby Boettcher, a Spades brother who had also worked on the *Plainsman* and had been one of my few supporters during the Freedom Riders episode – moved to Washington. Jim began work as a reporter at *Congressional Quarterly*, later moving to the *Washington Post*, and Bobby began a masters degree program at Georgetown's School of Foreign Service (he eventually joined me as Auburn's second FSO). The three of us got an apartment together near the State Department.

Also during this second year in Washington, I acquired a serious girlfriend, the first since my unhappy experience with Dottie. Margie had just begun work at the Interior Department after graduating from the University of North Carolina. The relationship flourished; we visited each other's homes in Greensboro and Chattanooga; and by early 1965, we were planning marriage. These plans were delayed by my assignment to Vietnam, and the engagement did not survive my first six months there. I returned to Washington for a brief visit in early 1966, to discover that she was dating someone else and no longer wished to marry me. As with my previous rejection by Dottie, this was at first painful; but I came to regard it as another stroke of good fortune, since it cleared the way for two additional assignments in Vietnam during which I found my true love and lifelong wife.

Washington was an exceptionally interesting place to be during the 1960s, in many ways the most turbulent and transformative decade, at least for Americans, in the 20th Century. During my time there in 1963-65, especially notable were the assassination of President Kennedy and the emergence of civil rights as the dominant national issue, particularly with the "March on Washington for Jobs and Freedom" on August 27, 1963. The State Department was closed for the day, so my Auburn friend Bobby Boettcher and I decided to participate. We made a cardboard sign proclaiming ourselves "Alabamans for Jobs and Freedom." Even though there were a substantial number of white people in the March, we drew lots of curious looks. We soon fell in with a small group of black students from Alabama, and shared a few drinks with them after the March. Hearing King's "I Have a Dream" speech live, while sitting alongside the reflecting pool near the Lincoln Memorial, amidst that great throng of people, remains one of my most memorable experiences, even though at the time I didn't fully recognize its historic significance.

In spite of an improved personal situation and all the excitement of the 1960s in Washington, I was eager to get overseas as the end of my assignment approached.

On to Vietnam

After the French defeat and withdrawal from Vietnam in 1954, the United States had assumed the role of principal sponsor and protector of newly-independent South Vietnam. The emerging insurgency instigated by North Vietnam and supported by China and the USSR was seen as an integral part of the Cold War. The insurgency gained strength, slowly at first and then more rapidly in the period of political instability following the overthrow and assassination of President Ngo Dinh Diem in 1963. By 1964, the United States had more than 16,000 military advisors in South Vietnam. In March 1965, the first U.S. ground combat units arrived: three battalions of Marines assigned to protect the Danang airbase. They were followed in July by an Army division, and the build-up continued until there were half a million U.S. troops in Vietnam by 1968. Along with this military build-up, the State Department and other U.S. civilian agencies began augmenting their staffs in Vietnam to support the war effort.

To follow my assignment on the CENTO desk, I had been scheduled for Farsi language training and assignment to the Consulate in Tabriz, Iran, where I was to spend a year as a student at the local university, with the objective of becoming a specialist on Iran and Afghanistan. This was a coveted assignment, and I was pleased to have it. In early 1965, however, it was abruptly cancelled and replaced with posting as Vice Consul in Hué, Vietnam, via 10 weeks of Vietnamese language training at the Foreign Service Institute.

The Vietnam War had not yet become a major story in the United States, and I knew little about it. I recognized that we were becoming increasingly engaged, and the conflict was already regarded as a hot spot in the Cold War. I considered it my duty to go, even though it meant delaying my marriage to Margie. The Foreign Service, particularly in those days, was considered a calling, much like the military, and FSOs felt the same obligation as military officers to go where they were sent, including into harm's way. This was part of the Foreign Service culture, and I fully accepted it. I had no idea that the Vietnam War was to become not only a major event in American history but also a transformational experience in both my professional career and my personal life.

I said goodbye to family, friends, and Margie, and took the long Pan-Am flight across the Pacific to Saigon in July, 1965.

***

The Sigma Pi fraternity house in Auburn, where I lived in 1961 and the KKK burned a cross on the front lawn in response to my editorial.

My December 1962 Foreign Service basic training class, plus instructors (standing, far left and far right). I'm standing, in the center. There was one woman and no minorities, typical for the time. Today's Foreign Service is more than 40% female and one-third minority.

****

3.

Warrior Diplomat: Vietnam, 1965-70

The Vietnam War was a life-changing experience: It set the trajectory of my career toward service in unfamiliar, remote, sometimes dangerous places. It brought me from youth to maturity. It gave me self-confidence, a taste for adventure, and a heightened sense of patriotic duty. It showed me both the horror and the heroism of war. It strengthened my ability to perform under pressure and in threatening circumstances. It gave me some lifelong friends and, above all, a lifelong wife.

I was fortunate to have survived the Vietnam War, and I'm proud that I was there.

The war dominated American politics and culture from the time U.S. combat units were committed in 1965 until its end in 1975. It was bitterly controversial, dividing the nation more deeply than any conflict since the Civil War. This was partially because television made it more vivid and immediate than previous wars. Yet, it was poorly understood, even by the participants. Half a century later, it remains so. And for people born after 1970, it isn't even a distant memory -- just a few (often inaccurate) pages in a school textbook, and perhaps an old movie or an occasional story from an aging veteran.

Therefore, before recounting some of my Vietnam experiences, I need to present a brief summary of the context in which they occurred.

***

North and South Vietnam, 1954-75

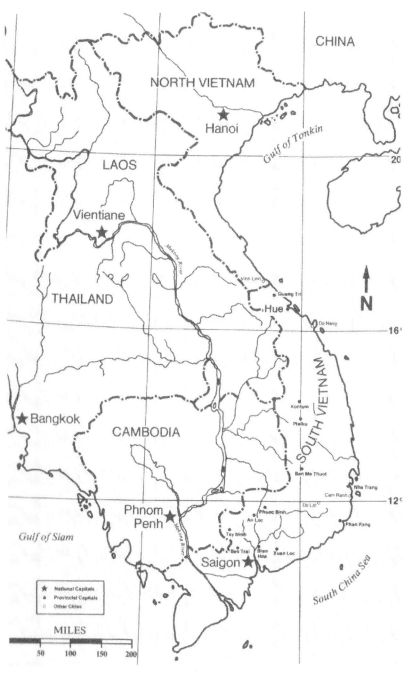

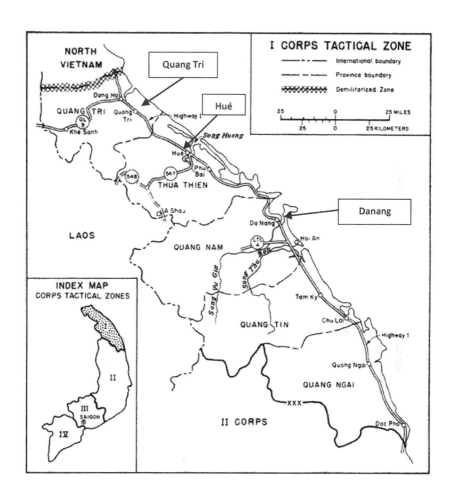

The Cold War Context

Why did the United States fight a war in Vietnam, suffering and inflicting such death and destruction in a far-away place that few Americans had heard of prior to the 1960s? This was a difficult question to answer at the time, and it's still hotly disputed. After a decade of direct professional involvement, and a lifetime of study and reflection, here's my response.

Vietnam, then part of French Indochina, first came to the attention of American policy-makers when it was occupied by Japan at the beginning of World War II. After Japan's defeat in 1945, the French re-occupied the colony, but they were ultimately defeated by a Communist-led insurgency and forced to withdraw in 1954. Many Vietnamese, however, especially in the southern half of Vietnam and among the 20% of the people who were Catholic, were strongly opposed to the Communists. Therefore, the 1954 peace agreement, concluded at an international conference in Geneva, set up two independent countries: a Communist state in the north led by Ho Chi Minh, and a Western-oriented state in the south led by Ngo Dinh Diem. Several thousand Communist supporters in the south moved north, and about a million (mostly Catholic) nationalists moved from north to south, with assistance from the U.S. Navy.

In the years immediately following independence, leaders of both North and South Vietnam were preoccupied with establishing governments and consolidating their rule. A referendum to unify the country, called for in the Geneva Accords, never took place. The Communists were zealous in pursuing their long-term goal of a unified Vietnam under their rule, and when it became apparent they could not achieve it by political means, they launched an insurgency war in the south. It was nominally led by an indigenous southern "National Liberation Front," generally known as the Viet Cong. In reality, this organization was from its inception under the direct control of the Communist Party politburo in Hanoi.

Growth of U.S. Involvement

The United States began providing military and economic assistance to newly-independent South Vietnam in 1954. However, under the Eisenhower Administration, this assistance remained modest in scale, with only a few hundred Americans in Vietnam to deliver it.

After the Viet Cong insurgency became a serious problem in 1960 and 1961, the new Kennedy Administration decided to dramatically increase U.S. assistance to South Vietnam. This policy was guided by the Cold War containment strategy and inspired by the President's pledge in his inaugural address to "pay any price, bear any burden, meet any hardship, support any friend, oppose any foe to assure the survival and success of liberty." New measures included massive economic aid, direct military air, naval, and logistics support, and 16,000 U.S advisors integrated throughout South Vietnam's armed forces.

This effort at first slowed the insurgency's progress, but the Diem government experienced growing internal opposition, especially from a well-organized Buddhist political movement. Political instability undermined the government's counterinsurgency efforts, and its heavy-handed methods of controlling Buddhist demonstrations led to greater unrest and international condemnation.

In November 1963, South Vietnamese military leaders, with at least tacit approval from the U.S. Government, organized a coup in which President Diem and his powerful brother, Ngo Dinh Nhu, were murdered. However, the generals were not unified among themselves, and they failed to restore political stability. The war effort continued to flounder, and the Viet Cong steadily gained strength and territory.

Sensing the government's vulnerability, in 1964 Hanoi began sending increasing numbers of North Vietnamese Army regulars to join the fight in the South. The war's intensity grew. Casualties mounted, there were attacks on U.S. air bases and military barracks, and a car bomb heavily damaged the U.S. Embassy in Saigon. The Johnson Administration was constrained from making any military response by the 1964 election, in which Johnson campaigned on limiting U.S. involvement in the war, as opposed to the more hawkish Republican candidate, Barry Goldwater.

By March 1965, the threat of South Vietnamese defeat had grown sufficiently great that the Administration sent the first ground combat units to Vietnam, to defend the American airbase and port at Danang. After a further policy review, President Johnson decided in July 1965 to send a full-scale American expeditionary force. This force grew rapidly, and it was able to check Communist gains, though not to reverse them, as Hanoi continued to build up its forces in the south as well. With this American support, the South Vietnamese government was able to restore political stability, under General Nguyen Van Thieu as President and Air Vice Marshal Nguyen Cao Ky as Prime Minister.

Why Vietnam?

More than five decades distant from the decisions of the late 1950s and early 1960s that gradually led us into full-scale war in 1965, it can be hard to understand why these decisions were made. Indeed, if we focus only on Vietnam, they can seem irrational. It is only in the context of the Cold War that they make sense.

In those years the Communist threat was very real. The Soviet takeover of Eastern Europe, Mao's victory in China, the unprovoked invasion of South Korea, the installation of Soviet missiles in Cuba – these were recent events at the forefront of policymakers' minds. They put these events into the framework of the lesson drawn from Western capitulation to Hitler's demands at Munich in 1938: Appeasement of dictators is dangerous. Communism seemed to be monolithic, on the march, attractive to the new countries emerging from colonialism, and highly threatening to American security and values. Their perceptions were reinforced by exaggerated assessments of Soviet military and economic strength. Moreover, Soviet leaders proclaimed a new Cold War strategy of "wars of national liberation," involving aggressive assistance to insurgencies in newly-independent countries designed to bring Communist regimes to power.

And now South Vietnam, whose support we had taken over from the French, had come under attack by an insurgency that was inspired, supported, and directed by Communist North Vietnam and ultimately (so it seemed) by its Soviet and Chinese sponsors. Surely, most Americans believed, it was time to draw the line and not let this new method of exporting Communism – insurgency – succeed.

By the late 1960s, some of these perceptions had begun to change. The Sino-Soviet split was recognized, and we were coming to understand that the conflict in Vietnam was not only Communist-led aggression but also a nationalist movement and the continuation of a civil war with roots deep in Vietnamese history. But by then we were fully at war, and we were committed to preserving South Vietnamese independence and avoiding a humiliating defeat that, it was believed, would undermine our ability to support other Cold War friends and allies.

Given this context, the decisions that led to war were not irrational. In fact, they were probably inevitable, even if, with 20-20 historical hindsight, they can be seen as mistaken.

Assignment to Hué

Unburdened by any doubts about the policies that were deepening our involvement in the war, I arrived in Saigon in July 1965 eager to do my duty and contribute all I could to help win it. Although I was to be stationed at the U.S. Consulate in Hué, my principal job was to travel throughout the five northernmost provinces of South Vietnam (which constituted I Corps) to prepare reports on the political, economic, and security situation for the Embassy's political section. Therefore, I spent my first two weeks in an orientation program with experienced political officers. Notable among them were Political Counselor Phil Habib, who later became Under Secretary of State, and John Negroponte, a fellow junior officer who eventually served in several Ambassadorial and Cabinet-level jobs, including Ambassador to the United Nations. John became one of the most distinguished Foreign Service Officers of our generation.

The Hué Consulate, housed in a two-story French colonial-era residence, was staffed by three Americans: Consul Sam Thomsen, me as Vice Consul, and a communicator/administrative support officer, Joe O'Neill.[2]

There were also three "Foreign Service National" (FSN) Vietnamese professional-level staff: political assistant Nguyen Van "Joe" Nghia, communications technician Nguyen Van Binh, and receptionist and translator Than-trong Tuy-Cam. I especially noticed Tuy-Cam, an attractive and unmarried young woman, but at first not as a romantic possibility, because I was engaged to Margie. However, after Margie broke off the engagement, I saw Tuy-Cam in a new light, and courtship began.

There were about a dozen other American civilians in Hué, working for CIA, USAID (U.S. Agency for International Development), and USIA (U.S. Information Agency), along with a couple of hundred American

---

[2] In September, the U.S. Marine commander in Danang, Lt. Gen. Lewis Walt, requested Embassy help in dealing with the Vietnamese government, and particularly with his highly politicized counterpart, Lt. Gen. Nguyen Chanh Thi, the I Corps commander. Sam Thomsen was transferred to Danang to become Gen. Walt's Political Advisor. He was replaced by a political officer from Saigon, Walt Lundy, who remained in Hué until December. Beginning in January 1966, I was left in charge of the post as Acting Consul until late May, when the deputy chief of the Saigon political section, Tom Corcoran, was sent to Hué as Consul.

military advisors to the Vietnamese First Division and local security forces.

Provincial Reporting Officer

During the rest of 1965, my work as a provincial reporting officer kept me outside of Hué half of the time, visiting the five I Corps provinces. Typically, I would spend a week or 10 days in a province, staying with the American military advisory teams in the province capital and in rural districts. I interviewed Vietnamese government officials, military commanders, local politicians, business and religious leaders, long-term foreign residents (mostly missionaries and French business people), and American military and civilian advisors. After each trip, I would return to Hué and prepare a cable to the Embassy covering security trends, internal politics, economic problems, and whatever else seemed important to the war effort.

These reports, from me and the other Embassy provincial reporters working out of Saigon and covering the rest of the country, tended to be more frank and less optimistic than the reporting coming through the U.S. military chain of command or from Vietnamese government officials. Even though the South Vietnamese and newly-arrived American combat forces were winning almost all of the battles and inflicting heavy casualties on enemy forces, the Communists, with an ever-growing flow of supplies and reinforcements from the North, were gradually increasing their control in rural areas. Moreover, refugees were becoming more numerous, attacks on bridges and other infrastructure were disrupting the economy, and non-Communist political opposition to the military government of President Thieu and Prime Minister Ky was mounting.

With my background in journalism, I was comfortable with this provincial reporting work. I also liked living in Hué, which was a popular destination for American official visitors from Saigon and Washington. The city remained secure from enemy attacks; and as

Vietnam's pre-colonial capital, it was historic, exotic, and attractive, with a massive walled city, the royal palace, elaborate tombs of former emperors, and peaceful pagodas. Even though its days of imperial splendor were long past, it remained a major cultural, religious, and educational center.

An important part of our duties at the Consulate was hosting and briefing these visitors. One of them was Henry Kissinger, a young Harvard professor whose books and articles on national security policy were highly influential. He had been hired by the Johnson Administration as a consultant to provide recommendations on Vietnam. In three years, he was to become one of my professors and then my boss.

The Buddhist Struggle Movement

After a period of calm in 1965, internal political tensions within South Vietnam were mounting in early 1966, especially in Hué and Danang. The opposition to the still-military government of President Thieu and Prime Minister Ky was led by Thich[3] Tri Quang. He was a charismatic

Thich Tri Quang

monk based in Hué who had also been a leader in the uprising that led to the 1963 overthrow of President Diem. He directed the radical half of the organized political Buddhist movement, whose strength was predominantly in the I Corps region. Tri Quang was popular among the country's students, especially those at Hué University. He was also politically allied with the I Corps commander in Danang, Lt. Gen. Thi, and he had strong influence

[3] "Thich" (pronounced like "tick") is the new family name, indicating "children of the Buddha," that is applied to those entering the monkhood. It was often translated in English as "the Venerable."

with the Vietnamese troops in the region via his control over the Buddhist military chaplains.

When anti-government demonstrations began in February, as Acting Consul and the only FSO at the post, I had to end my provincial reporting trips to other provinces and remain in Hué, which was Tri Quang's headquarters and the center of the growing political unrest.

This was a heavy responsibility for a young FSO-7, my rank at the time, which is comparable to a first lieutenant in the military. I was reporting from the focal point of what was becoming a major crisis for South Vietnam and for U.S. Vietnam policy. I dealt directly with Thich Tri Quang, as well as with senior government officials and military commanders in the region, many of whom were participants (or at least sympathizers) in what became known as the "Buddhist Struggle Movement." The Struggle drew heavy press and TV coverage in the United States and raised deep concerns at the White House, State Department, and Pentagon, as it increasingly disrupted the war effort.

Next to the 1968 Tet Offensive, the Struggle was the most important event behind the erosion of American public and Congressional support for the Johnson Administration's Vietnam policy.

The Struggle became more intense and dangerous with the dismissal on March 10 of the I Corps commander, Lt. Gen. Thi, who supported Tri Quang. After his dismissal, he came to Hué and stayed for the duration of the crisis. Thi had been well on the way to establishing himself as a warlord, defying or ignoring direct orders from the central government. He was popular in I Corps, and his removal immediately set off massive demonstrations and strikes throughout the region.

By the end of March there was evidence that the Viet Cong had infiltrated the Struggle, and its message became increasingly anti-American, with demands that the U.S. Government remove President Thieu and Prime Minister Ky from power. Ominously, by early April, large numbers of soldiers, policemen, and civil servants were joining anti-government demonstrations in Hué and Danang. On April 6, the Embassy decided to evacuate "non-essential" U.S. Government civilians from I Corps and advised all private citizens to leave. Bob Shaplen, one of the most perceptive American reporters covering the war, wrote in *The New Yorker* on April 16, "In many years here, I have never seen the morale of both the South Vietnamese and the Americans descend so close to a state of panic."

In this situation, my daily cables from Hué to the Embassy received lots of attention, and most were forwarded directly to Washington. Some were read by, or at least summarized for, Secretary of State Dean Rusk and other top-level officials, including President Johnson. An example was the cable I wrote the night of May 17, recounting the dramatic, extraordinary events of that day.

May 17, a Day to Remember

The newly-appointed commander of I Corps, Maj. Gen. Huynh Van Cao, had scheduled a visit that morning to the ARVN First Division in Hué. I went to Division headquarters, together with the senior American advisors to the Division, for the arrival ceremony. Of the whole Division staff, only six officers, the highest ranking of whom was a major, turned out to welcome their new Corps commander. The rest, including the Division commander, refused to appear. At the conclusion of the abbreviated ceremony and briefing, Gen. Cao and his American advisors hurried to their waiting U.S. helicopter. Just as the helicopter lifted off the ground, an ARVN lieutenant began firing at it. The American door gunner on the helicopter returned fire, killing the lieutenant and two other First Division soldiers. It was later established that this was part of an organized plot to assassinate Gen. Cao, which was poorly executed and thus unsuccessful.

After witnessing these events, I got in my car, the official Consulate black Plymouth sedan with a U.S. flag on the fender, to drive back to the office. A few hundred yards outside the First Division compound I encountered a mob of several hundred students, who had been holding a demonstration downtown. They had been informed of Gen. Cao's visit and were on their way to Division headquarters to confront him. The mob filled the street, and I had to stop the car and sit there for a quarter of an hour as they passed by, beating on the car and shouting anti-American slogans. They tried to open the locked car, but didn't break the windows.

When the last of the demonstrators had passed, I returned to the Consulate to pick up Tuy-Cam to accompany me for an appointment with Thich Tri Quang at his pagoda. He did not speak French, and I needed her to serve as interpreter. The previous week, Tri Quang had sent a message through me to President Johnson, asking us to oust President Thieu and Prime Minister Ky and replace them with people acceptable to the Struggle Movement. (We found this more than a little ironic, since one of the principal demands of the Struggle was that Americans cease interfering in internal Vietnamese affairs!) The purpose of my appointment was to deliver President Johnson's response. My instructions in delivering it, as described to a *New York Times* correspondent and reported in the May 18 edition, were: "Mr. Bullington has been told to be neither overly cordial nor overly cool and to tell Tri Quang that the United States hoped he and the Premier would be able to come to some understanding."

By the time we reached the pagoda, Tri Quang had gotten word of the incident at First Division headquarters. According to his version, the American helicopter gunner had, without provocation, fired on and killed pro-Struggle soldiers. He was furious about this, rejected my eye-witness account that the Vietnamese lieutenant had fired first, and found it difficult to listen to my counsel of moderation.

Before our conversation came to an end, prolonged small arms fire broke out near the pagoda, and Tri Quang told Tuy-Cam and me to leave right away for our safety. We did so. A few hundred yards from the pagoda we were stopped by a roadblock manned by armed Buddhist students. They were agitated and pointed their weapons at us. After telling them we had just met with Thich Tri Quang to deliver a message from President Johnson, we persuaded them to let us pass. We later determined that the gunfire was between these students, who had been joined by some soldiers and policemen, and an armed militia group from a nearby Catholic neighborhood.

After finally returning to the Consulate, I wrote a lengthy cable reporting all this -- the assassination attempt on the new I Corps commander, the massive student demonstration I had encountered, delivering the President's message to Tri Quang, and the Buddhist-Catholic firefight in the middle of Hué. It was the most interesting and widely read cable I ever wrote.

By this time the Embassy realized that additional diplomatic representation was needed in Hué, and that a junior officer on his first overseas assignment should no longer be left to handle the situation alone. Consequently, in a couple of days the deputy chief of the political section, Tom Corcoran, arrived to be Consul. Tom had spent two weeks in April on temporary duty in Hué, but now his assignment was to be permanent, or at least long-term. He was a senior officer with extensive Vietnam experience, including as our last Consul in Hanoi, until the post was closed in 1955 following the Communist victory over the French. I welcomed Tom's arrival, and he became a friend and mentor, as well as my boss.

Moreover, Tom brought with him a cable, addressed personally to me, from Secretary of State Dean Rusk. The text of the cable read:

> It is always gratifying to me to learn that our young Foreign Service Officers have the courage to grasp the initiative and respond to situations with intelligence and alacrity. Congratulations to you and your colleagues for your performance in Hué during the period you were at the helm.

It is exceedingly rare for a junior FSO to receive a personal message of any kind from the Secretary of State. I was thrilled.

Burning of the Consulate

There had been a lull in Struggle activities in mid April, following a government-organized national political convention in Saigon. The convention was well attended and representative. It adopted most of the Buddhist demands, including an election within five months for a constituent assembly to write a new constitution, followed by a speedy return to civilian government. At Tri Quang's urging, anti-government demonstrations ceased for a time. However, moves by Struggle leaders to consolidate their extensive power in I Corps, countered by government moves to re-assert its authority, soon re-ignited hostilities.

In Hué, some 2,000 students were formed into a "Death Volunteers Association" and were given weapons by the First Division commander, Brig. Gen. Pham Xuan Nhuan. (It was members of this group that Tuy-Cam and I encountered at the roadblock on May 17.) Throughout I Corps, many government officials and military officers considered loyal to the government were purged. Evidence mounted that the Viet Cong had infiltrated the Struggle leadership. The region was again slipping into a state of open insurrection.

On May 15, the government airlifted 1,500 Vietnamese Marines and paratroopers into Danang. They achieved surprise and quickly occupied most of the city, with only sporadic resistance. However, Struggle fighters were able to regroup around two pagodas, and a lengthy standoff ensued. Tri Quang and other militant Struggle leaders pictured this operation as an unprovoked attack on the Buddhist religion and a betrayal of the agreement to return to civilian government. With most of the First Division on their side, the Strugglers began preparations to defend Hué militarily.

In Danang, after efforts to negotiate the dissidents' surrender proved unsuccessful, the Marines and paratroopers attacked and overran their positions following some sharp fighting. The city was quickly secured, government control was restored, and the Struggle in that part of I Corps collapsed as an organized force.

These developments in Danang made the Strugglers in Hué even more hostile to the government and its American backers. Security in the city deteriorated further, and large groups of students and Buddhist monks and nuns alternated in daily demonstrations in front of the Consulate. Several American reporters came to cover the action, which was front page news in the United States.

On May 26, a student mob attacked and burned the U. S. Information Service library and cultural center, after the police unit assigned to protect it had fled. We immediately decided to evacuate all remaining American civilians in the city except Tom Corcoran and me, Consulate communicator Maurice Brooks, and a couple of CIA officers. When this was accomplished, we all moved into the compound housing the American military advisors to the First Division, from which we did what political reporting and intelligence gathering we could, even though movement about the city was dangerous and hence limited. We continued to maintain contact with our loyal and courageous Vietnamese staff, including Tuy-Cam, who provided vital information about the rapidly evolving situation.

On June 1, the U.S. Consulate was sacked and burned. As described by the Associated Press:

> A mob of about 1000 screaming students attacked the two-story Consulate building just before noon, ripped down portraits of President Johnson and carried off two U.S. flags as the building burned....A company of Vietnamese Army troops fled when the students marched on the Consulate.

Tom Corcoran, Maurice Brooks, and I were safely inside the U.S. military compound, and the only casualties from the incident were several students who were injured by the explosion of some of our propane tanks that were in a storage shed adjacent to the Consulate. We shed no tears for them.

Government Control Restored

After the burning of the Consulate, while the most radical of the Strugglers continued demonstrations and other protest activities, the more moderate elements who had been allied with them, including some Buddhist monks and senior officers of the First Division, as well as former I Corps commander Lt. Gen. Thi, began seeking reconciliation with the government or dropped out of sight. We assessed that Tri Quang and the Struggle Movement had never achieved the support of the majority of the people of Hué, although for several weeks they had clearly become the strongest of several political forces in the city. Moreover, on June 1 the government reconfirmed its commitment to a fall election by requesting United Nations observers to monitor it.

On June 9, a 400-man police unit from Saigon, soon reinforced by elements of the Marine and Airborne troops that had re-asserted government control in Danang, began moving into Hué. There was little resistance, as the most militant student leaders fled to rural areas to join (or in some cases re-join) the Viet Cong, and Tri Quang was taken to Saigon and put under house arrest. One of the leading American journalists, Frances Fitzgerald, wrote in the August issue of *The Atlantic*: "The Struggle dissolved as rapidly as it had taken shape." Although we didn't recognize it at the time, this marked the effective end of Tri Quang and the Buddhist movement as a powerful political force in Vietnam.

In late June, a decision was made not to re-build the Consulate in Hué but to relocate the post to Danang, with Tom Corcoran as Consul General. I was assigned to Saigon as staff aide to Ambassador Henry

Cabot Lodge. Our Vietnamese staff was transferred to Danang, with the exception of Tuy-Cam, who accepted a job in the economic section of the Embassy in Saigon. This facilitated continuation of our courtship.

Both Tom Corcoran and I were given State Department Superior Honor Awards for our service in Hué. The citation on my award reads:

> For extraordinary performance in the best traditions of the Foreign Service during the recent mob action in Hué, in which the USIS library and Consulate were sacked and burned. His response to the situation in which not only was his personal safety gravely threatened but in which also American interests were vitally involved, demonstrated great courage, initiative and intelligence.

Together with the personal commendation cable from Secretary Rusk and positive performance evaluations by my bosses, this assured promotions in both 1966 and 1967, to FSO-5 (equivalent to the military rank of major).

Students burning the American Cultural Center in Hué, May, 1966.

***

Buddhist monks demonstrating at the Consulate, May 1966.

Meeting with student protesters at the Consulate, May 1966.

Students burning the Consulate, June 1, 1966.

The U.S. Embassy in Saigon (above), where I was Ambassador Lodge's aide in 1966-67, was badly damaged by a car bomb in 1965. In late 1967, it was relocated to a new building (below), which was attacked, but never penetrated, by a VC sapper team during the 1968 Tet Offensive.

LEFT: Receiving Superior Honor Award from Ambassador Lodge - August, 1966.

CENTER: Party at Ed Lansdale's house in Saigon - September, 1966. I'm playing the guitar.

BOTTOM: Distributing roofing material to refugees at Cam Lo - April, 1967.

***

Staff Aide to Ambassador Lodge

Only in a few of the largest and most important U.S. Embassies do the ambassadors have personal staff aides, and by 1966 Saigon was at the top of the list in both size and importance. The job of staff aide to Ambassador Lodge was high profile and coveted by all the junior officers in the Embassy, and I was delighted to be selected for it. Although it involved no policy-making or command responsibility, it put me at the right hand of a major American political leader and a principal actor in the country's most vital international engagement at the time. The work was intense, interesting, and important.

Here is how Ambassador Lodge described the job in my performance evaluation:

> This officer screens all cables, memoranda, letters and other papers which come to my office, deciding what I should see, what can be discarded, and what can be taken up with someone else. Similarly, he screens telephone calls and visitors, protecting me from cranks and others whom I need not talk to nor see, and, together with me, making and keeping the schedule of those I do see. He drafts replies, either for my signature or his own, for most of my correspondence; and I sometimes call on him to do substantive drafting, such as portions of my weekly report to the President. He is responsible for maintaining liaison with the Mission Coordinator, the Political Counselor, and other senior members of the Mission on a wide variety of matters with which I am concerned; and he exercises day to day supervision over my secretarial assistant and my receptionist, and over the workings of my office. Finally, he serves as a sort of utility man, taking care of many diverse chores at my direction, such as scheduling the small jet aircraft which is assigned for my use, preparing suggested guest lists, and assisting with representation at large social functions.

The "Boston Brahmin" family of Henry Cabot Lodge was one of New England's wealthiest and most politically powerful, and he had a distinguished career. He was elected U.S. Senator from Massachusetts in 1936, but resigned his Senate seat in 1944 for active duty in the Army, including combat action in France. He remained in the Army Reserve after the war, and eventually rose to the rank of major general. He was again elected to the Senate in 1946, and was Dwight Eisenhower's campaign manager in 1952, but he lost his own Senate re-election campaign that year to John F. Kennedy. Eisenhower appointed him Ambassador to the United Nations in 1953, where he remained until he resigned in 1960 to become Richard Nixon's Vice Presidential running-mate in the election that was narrowly won by Kennedy. His subsequent appointments as Ambassador to South Vietnam, first by Kennedy in 1961-63 and then by Lyndon Johnson in 1965-67, represented both confidence in his ability and desire to consolidate Republican support for the war effort.

I admired and liked Lodge, found him to be a demanding but reasonable boss, and learned a great deal during the seven months I was his aide. He appreciated my service, and wrote in my performance report that I was "an absolutely first-rate officer -- intelligent, courageous and high-minded. He has already rendered distinguished service -- will surely do so in the future. It is inspiring to see young men of his quality entering the U.S. Government service."

In December 1966, Lodge went home for a month of consultations and vacation. This left me with nothing to do, so I asked to return temporarily to my previous work as a provincial reporter. An experiment designed to make U.S. combat units and advisors more effective in supporting long-term "pacification" (the term most commonly used to describe what would today be called counterinsurgency), had recently gotten underway in Long An province, a short distance southwest of Saigon, and I was sent to assess its progress.

The experiment involved putting Army Colonel Sam Wilson, who had been Lodge's military assistant and Mission Coordinator at the Embassy, in command of both the American military and civilian advisors who were responsible for pacification in the province. I spent two weeks in Long An and wrote a positive evaluation of the experiment's impact. When he returned, Lodge forwarded my report to Washington and summarized it in his weekly cable to President Johnson. The Long An experiment influenced the President's March 1967 decision to extend this structural model for the pacification program nationwide, in the joint civil-military organization eventually named CORDS (Civil Operations and Revolutionary Development Support), of which I was soon to become a member.[4]

My personal life in Saigon was marked by continuing courtship of Tuy-Cam, who was working at the Embassy and living with her Uncle Thuan, a senior South Vietnamese judge and former Governor of the Central Highlands region. However, in early 1967 our relationship was temporarily broken off when she backed away from my attempt to intensify it with a good-night kiss after bringing her home from a dinner date. I turned instead to intensified partying with a couple of colleagues from Hué who had also been transferred to Saigon, CIA officer Joe Murphy and U.S. Information Agency officer Bill Stubbs, who were to become two of my closest lifelong friends. We were regulars at "Mimi's Flamboyant" and other bars along Tu Do Street.

Ed Lansdale, and Songs of the Vietnam War

An important relationship that developed during my time as Lodge's staff aide was with Ed Lansdale, one of the leading American practitioners and theorists of counterinsurgency warfare during the 1950s and 1960s. As a young Army officer in World War II, Ed had served in Europe with OSS (Office of Strategic Services, the predecessor

---

[4] Hunt, Richard A., *Pacification: The American Struggle for Vietnam's Hearts and Minds*, Westview Press, Boulder, CO, 1995, pp. 86-87.

to CIA), and following the war he was assigned to the Philippines as an intelligence officer. He was integrated into the newly-formed U.S. Air Force, from which he retired as a major general in 1963. In the early 1950s, he became the principal advisor to Philippine Defense Minister (later President) Ramon Magsaysay in the successful counterinsurgency campaign that defeated the Communist-led Hukbalahap rebellion. Then, in 1954-57, he was transferred to Vietnam, where he helped President Ngo Dien Diem launch the new South Vietnamese government and provided guidance for its initially successful counterinsurgency and nation-building efforts. It was in the Philippines and these early years in Vietnam that Lansdale developed his basic theory that Communist revolution was best countered by democratic revolution, which required emphasis on political, social, and economic development as well as military and police operations.

After several jobs in the Pentagon, including as Assistant Secretary for Special Operations, Lansdale was sent back to Vietnam in 1965-68 as an assistant to Ambassador Lodge. He was influential in strengthening South Vietnamese pacification programs, which had deteriorated following Diem's overthrow in 1963. However, with the arrival of U.S. combat units in 1965, pacification became increasingly marginalized by strategic focus on attrition of enemy forces in conventional "search and destroy" operations. Lansdale became marginalized as well.

During this period, Lansdale regularly hosted parties in his Saigon home, at which Prime Minister Ky and other senior Vietnamese leaders were frequent guests. I was invited to many of them. Since Lansdale believed that music could make an important psychological contribution to national morale and the war effort, entertainment for these events was often provided by Pham Duy, a famous folksinger and composer of patriotic songs. Along with a few other Americans, I had written some songs about our perspectives on the war, and we sometimes performed them to supplement Pham Duy's programs. A member of Lansdale's team made a recording of these songs, with background narration, which Ed sent to Washington as a sort of musical report on the war's progress (or lack thereof).

I continued this relationship with Lansdale when we were in Washington after 1968, until his death in 1987. He became a friend and mentor as well as one of my professional heroes and an inspiration for much of my subsequent thinking and writing about counterinsurgency warfare and expeditionary diplomacy.

It was through Ed that I met Dr. Lydia Fish, a Buffalo State University (New York) professor of anthropology and folklorist specializing in folksongs of the military, primarily during the Vietnam War. In addition to collecting hundreds of these songs, Lydia had put together a group of several of the people who had written and sung them, which I was invited to join. I did several performances with this group during the 1980s and 1990s, including at the Smithsonian in Washington, Hampden-Sydney and other colleges and universities, and the officers club at Fort Myer. [5]

Back to Washington, Very Briefly

My tour of duty in Saigon ended in February 1967, and I returned to the U.S. for assignment to Porto Alegre, Brazil, via six months of Portuguese language training. After a few days in Chattanooga, I arrived in Washington just in time for a major snowstorm. I was cold, lonesome, and unenthusiastic about Brazil. The more I thought about it, the more I wanted to return to Vietnam. That was where the action was, and that was where I really wanted to be.

In this case, my personal desires were consistent with State Department priorities and the need to staff a still-growing presence in Vietnam. When I informed friends at the Saigon Embassy that I wanted

---

[5] Two of my songs were included in *Next Stop is Vietnam: The War on Record, 1961-2008*. This is a 13-CD "anthology of the Vietnam War's musical legacy" that was published in 2010 by Bear Family Records in Germany.

to return for a field assignment in pacification operations, their request for my re-assignment was promptly approved. By mid March, I was back in Saigon.

North to Quang Tri

Because of the senior-level contacts I had made as Lodge's aide, I had an unusual opportunity to choose among several available positions. I wanted an operational job in the field, not staff work in Saigon or at a Corps-level headquarters, and I decided on a position as deputy USAID representative in Quang Tri, the province immediately to the south of the border with North Vietnam[6]

My professional reasons for choosing this position were: (1) it would give me program implementation, management, and supervisory responsibility; and (2) Quang Tri was one of the country's most strategically important provinces, where the war was especially intense, so there was likely to be a good deal of excitement. Today, at age 76, it seems strange to say that, but then, at 26, it really was the way I felt.

Beyond the professional reasons, moreover, I had a personal motivation for wanting to work in I Corps. Shortly before I had left Saigon, Tuy-Cam had been recruited for a job at the U.S. Consulate General in Danang. I found that I was missing her, and I wanted a chance to renew the romance. Quang Tri was the closest place to Danang with an appropriate job opening, and since the I Corps pacification program headquarters was in Danang, I knew I would be able to visit frequently. I stopped in Danang on the way to Quang Tri;

---

[6] South Vietnam was administratively divided into 44 provinces, each of which had American military and civilian advisory teams -- in the case of Quang Tri, about 150 people in all -- to work alongside South Vietnamese military and government "counterparts" in pacification, i.e., counterinsurgency, operations.

we had lunch, and the flame was rekindled. By November, I had asked her to marry me, and she had agreed.

When I arrived in Quang Tri in late March, 1967, the provincial capital (where most of the U.S. advisors were located) had been attacked the previous night by an enemy raiding force. Though none of the Americans had been hurt, there were several casualties among the South Vietnamese defenders, and parts of the provincial offices were badly damaged. It seemed I was going to have all the excitement I wanted, and perhaps more.

I also found that my assignment as deputy USAID representative had been suspended. Instead, I had been detached to work directly under Ambassador Barney Koren, the civilian deputy to the Marine commander in Danang, on a special project to relocate some 15,000 Vietnamese civilians from the southern half of the "Demilitarized Zone" (DMZ) along the border. They were to be moved to Cam Lo, on Route 9 west of the town of Dong Ha, where a site would have to be prepared to house them. ARVN Colonel Do Khien Nhieu, who had previously been Mayor of Saigon, was put in charge of the relocation project, and I was to be his American counterpart.

**

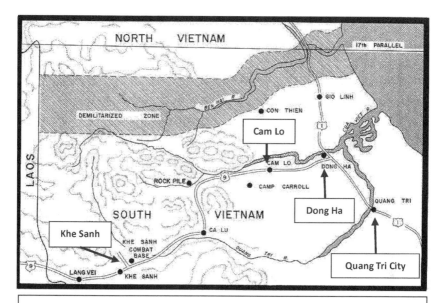

DMZ and Northern Quang Tri Province

The 1954 Geneva Accords established the Ben Hai River as the border between North and South Vietnam, with a "demilitarized zone" 3-5 km in width extending along the river from the sea to the border with Laos. By 1959, the North Vietnamese had built part of the Ho Chi Min trail through the western end of the DMZ, and thereafter neither side observed its nominally demilitarized character. Note the bomb craters in this 1968 photo of the DMZ.

***

The McNamara Line

The reason for relocating these civilians out of the DMZ was the imminent construction of what came to be known as the "McNamara Line," since its principal champion was Defense Secretary Robert McNamara. This was to be a barrier across South Vietnam from the sea to the mountainous area near the Laos border, designed to block the infiltration of North Vietnamese troops and supplies. Based on an idea sold to McNamara by Harvard and MIT academics, it was to consist of a bulldozed 500-meter strip with mine fields, ditches, and barbed wire, supplemented by high-tech electronic devices that would detect movement and alert defensive units stationed in a series of strongpoints just behind the line. These units could then destroy the infiltrators with artillery and airstrikes. It was thought that intensified airstrikes in the mountainous area to the west, extending across Laos, could interdict North Vietnamese efforts to simply go around the barrier and continue infiltration down the Ho Chi Minh trail.

U.S. military leaders, from Washington to the Marine commanders in I Corps, were skeptical of this plan throughout its development, and they had recommended against it. They felt there were insufficient ground troops available to support it, and they wanted to use their forces in mobile operations, not static defense. McNamara overruled their objections and ordered implementation of the plan. Marine units and Navy Seabees (engineers) were directed to begin construction of the barrier in the summer of 1967.

As things turned out, very little construction was accomplished, because of heavy NVA attacks throughout northern Quang Tri province beginning in September and continuing through the Tet Offensive in early 1968. By the summer of 1968, the barrier project was deemed impractical and was abandoned in favor of mobile operations. An official account published by the Defense Department in 2011, called the McNamara Line:

> ...a metaphor for the Secretary's arbitrary, highly personal, and aggressive management style that bypassed normal procedures and sometimes ignored experts to get things done. He had adopted an idea from civilian academics, forced a reluctant military to implement it, opted for technology over experience, launched the project quickly and with minimum coordination, rejected informed criticism, insisted available forces sufficed for the effort, and poured millions of dollars into a system that proceeded by fits and starts.[7]

Those of us on the ground in Quang Tri in the spring of 1967 could not foresee that the McNamara Line project would be a failure, and we were barely (if at all) aware of the controversy surrounding it. Our orders were to prepare for it, including by relocating the 15,000 people then living along the Ben Hai River in the southern DMZ to the relative safety of Cam Lo, south of Route 9.

These people were almost all Catholics originally from the North, who had fled south of the Ben Hai River in 1954 ahead of the Communist takeover. Led by a dynamic Vietnamese priest, they were well-organized and strongly anti-Communist, and they readily agreed to relocate to Cam Lo. The first problems we faced were to organize transportation, secure the move from North Vietnamese attack, and arrange for water, food, and housing in Cam Lo. Both Colonel Nhieu and I realized that this was well beyond the capacity of the South Vietnamese provincial authorities and their available military forces, so we had to turn to the U.S. Marines for transportation and security, and to USAID for food, roofing material, a well-drilling machine, and other supplies and equipment. The Marines assigned a colonel to work with Colonel Nhieu and me, and the three of us directed the move until its successful completion in late May. Prime Minister Ky came to visit the Cam Lo site and presented us with medals for our work.

---

[7] Drea, Edward J., *McNamara, Clifford, and the Burdens of Vietnam, 1965-69*. Historical Office, Office of the Secretary of Defense, Washington, DC, 2011.

Because my boss for this project, Ambassador Koren, was in Danang and communication with him was limited, I operated with almost total independence, a role that I relished. Together with my time as Acting Consul in Hué and my experience as editor of *The Plainsman*, this reinforced my inclination to seek out leadership positions in which I had considerable autonomy as well as responsibility. I was convinced that this was my best path to both job satisfaction and career success.

After the Cam Lo project, I returned to Quang Tri in June to work in what had the previous month become CORDS (Civil Operations and Revolutionary Development Support), the reorganized American joint civil-military pacification program.

CORDS in Quang Tri

Prior to the CORDS reorganization, all the American civilians in the field, outside Saigon, reported to their home-agency section of the Embassy, primarily State, CIA, USAID, and USIA. All of the American military advisors to the Vietnamese regulars (ARVN) and territorial units (militia-like RF, PF, and PSDF -- Regional Force, Popular Force and People's Self-Defense Force), as well as the U.S. combat units, reported to MACV (Military Assistance Command, Vietnam) in Saigon through four corps headquarters headed by three-star generals. In Saigon, there was some coordination on pacification between the Embassy and MACV, but it was very limited. In the field, outside Saigon, there was no organized, structural linkage between the American military and civilians. In practice, there was some civil-military cooperation, but it was informal and *ad hoc*, often developed over a few beers at the officers club.

Under CORDS, the MACV commander, General Westmoreland, was given a new civilian deputy who was to be in charge not only of the American civilians in the field, but also of the U.S. military advisors to the Vietnamese territorial forces, who were primarily responsible for providing security at the village level. Moreover, each of the three-star

U.S. corps commanders was given a new civilian deputy for CORDS. Thus, they now had three hats: commander of the U.S. combat units in the corps area, senior advisor to the Vietnamese Corps Commander, and commander of the civil-military CORDS teams in each province and district. Half of the CORDS team leaders, called Province Senior Advisors (PSAs), were Army colonels with civilian deputies; the other half were civilians with Army lieutenant colonels as deputies.

In Quang Tri, our CORDS team had about 150 total staff. The PSA, Bob Brewer, was a CIA officer who had served in the 101st Airborne in World War II as a member of the unit immortalized in Stephen Ambrose's *Band of Brothers* book and the TV miniseries of 2001. Bob's deputy was an Army lieutenant colonel, Joe Semoe (killed in combat during the 1968 Tet Offensive). I was a second-level deputy, in charge of most of the civilian aspects of pacification.

In a scholarly book about pacification,[8] CORDS was described as:

> ...a mixture of civilians and military, from headquarters in Saigon to the districts....Each level would have a single manager to establish a single chain of command as well as designate one official voice at each level for dealing with the South Vietnamese government. That manager would integrate civilian and military planning, programming, operations, evaluations, logistics, and communications.

This integration even included writing official performance evaluations. For example, my 12-person staff in Quang Tri included not only State and USAID civilians, but also two Army captains and three sergeants. I wrote the captains' performance reports, and I was evaluated by the PSA, a CIA officer. He was evaluated by the I Corps Deputy for CORDS, a State Department Foreign Service Officer, who was in turn evaluated by a Marine general.

---

[8] Hunt, Richard A., *Pacification*, Westview Press, 1995, p.88.

Now, all U.S. programs and activities outside Saigon, except American combat units and some clandestine operations, came under the operational control of CORDS, which was an integral part of MACV. This included the American military advisors to the Vietnamese territorial forces (RF, PF, PSDF), the Phoenix program to attack the Viet Cong political-military and administrative infrastructure, the Chieu Hoi program to encourage and re-integrate VC defectors, agricultural and other development programs, the care and feeding of refugees -- in other words, the full range of counterinsurgency efforts.

This was true civil-military integration, of a sort never achieved by the U.S. government before or since. It was the only time in U.S. history that civilians in a wartime field organization actually commanded U.S. military personnel and resources. Most importantly, after several months of civilians and military working closely together in CORDS, we became unified, not just on the organization chart, but in spirit. It was no longer "us and them," but just "us." This unification was especially evident at the province and district levels, the "tip of the spear," where it mattered most.

A new and more effective pacification strategy was implemented following the 1968 Tet Offensive, emphasizing population security rather than enemy attrition and body counts, and replacing "search and destroy" operations with the concept of "clear, hold, and build." The CORDS structure facilitated its effective implementation and the ultimate success of the counterinsurgency part of the war.

From June 1967 to March 1968, I was a counterinsurgent with CORDS/Quang Tri, working with Vietnamese military and civilian officials on small development projects such as schools and clinics, psywar operations to encourage enemy defectors, refugee relief and resettlement, technical support for agricultural and public health programs, and monthly reports assessing security in the countryside. This was primarily field work, not office work, and I enjoyed it. I also enjoyed visiting CORDS regional headquarters (and Tuy-Cam) in Danang once a month.

However, Quang Tri was the scene of intense fighting during this period -- in fact, the most intense of any of the country's 44 provinces (as measured by casualties, frequency of enemy attacks, tonnage of bombs dropped in airstrikes, etc.). This pervasive combat limited the scope and effectiveness of our counterinsurgency efforts, sometimes destroying the province's physical and organizational infrastructure faster than we could build it.

The Battle of Hué, Tet 1968

The 1968 Tet Offensive, which began January 30 and continued until the end of February, was the most dramatic, intense, and important event of the Vietnam War. The Battle of Hué was the bloodiest, most destructive, and most decisive of the dozens of battles that were part of the Tet Offensive. Tuy-Cam and I were both there, in Hué, during the battle. It was the most memorable experience of our lives, an experience we are fortunate to have survived. To tell our story, I first need to outline the background of the Tet Offensive and describe the Battle of Hué. [9]

From its beginning in the late 1950s as an insurgency, fought primarily by South Vietnamese Communists with the direction and support of the government of North Vietnam, the war had escalated with the introduction of regular North Vietnamese Army (NVA) units in 1964 and American ground combat units in 1965. There was increasingly heavy fighting, but neither side had been able to achieve decisive advantage. By 1967, the war had become a bloody stalemate.

In the spring of 1967, the Communist Party politburo in Hanoi decided to break this stalemate, and began sending additional forces

---

[9] For a detailed account of the battle, see *Fire in the Streets* (1991), by Eric Hammel. He includes our story in the book.

southward down the Ho Chi Minh Trail. The plan was to draw U.S. units to the peripheral areas of South Vietnam and then attack and occupy the major cities and population centers. This, the Communist leaders believed, would induce much of the South Vietnamese military to defect or desert and spark a popular uprising of the South Vietnamese people against their government, thus bringing the war to a speedy and victorious conclusion.

At the same time, in response to waning domestic support for the war, the Johnson Administration launched an effort to convince the American people that its policies were succeeding. In a National Press Club speech in November, 1967, the U.S. commander in Vietnam, General Westmoreland, said that the Communists were: "...unable to mount a major offensive....I am absolutely certain that whereas in 1965 the enemy was winning, today he is certainly losing."

As a result of this good-news campaign, the American public as well as the U.S. military and political leadership were profoundly shocked by the Tet Offensive. As with many other intelligence failures, there were ample warnings of a massive enemy attack, but they were either disbelieved or ignored. The dots were not connected.

Also contributing to the surprise was that the attacks came at Tet, the Vietnamese New Year celebration, an important family and religious holiday that began January 30. For all Vietnamese, Tet is like Christmas, New Year's Eve, and Thanksgiving all combined in one massive holiday. As in past years, both sides had declared a three-day Tet truce, and in the past such truces had been fairly well observed.

But in 1968, on January 30 and 31, Communist forces struck more than 100 South Vietnamese towns and cities. In spite of the surprise they achieved, the attacks were contained, primarily by South Vietnamese forces, and were soon beaten back with massive casualties inflicted on the attackers. Nowhere were there South Vietnamese military defections or the popular uprisings expected by the Communists.

One exception to this pattern of quick Communist repulses was Saigon, where the attack included the spectacular but unsuccessful effort to occupy the U.S. Embassy, and fighting continued in parts of the city for nine days.

The other exception was Hué.

Hué was South Vietnam's third largest city, but it had no particular economic or military importance. Although there had been much heavy fighting nearby, Hué had heretofore been left in peace. It had been the capital of the Vietnamese emperors, and it was still the historical, cultural, educational, and religious heart of the country. Its symbolic and psychological importance made Hué a potentially decisive target for the Vietnamese Communists.

Hué was physically two adjacent cities, bisected by the Perfume River. On the north bank was the old, traditional city, mostly within the Citadel, a huge, square fortress nearly two miles on each side, surrounded by a moat and a 20-foot-high wall that was 60 to 200 feet thick. In addition to crowded homes and small shops along narrow streets, the Citadel contained the imperial palace and the headquarters of the ARVN First Division. On the south bank was the modern city, built mostly during the French colonial period, containing attractive villas, government offices, medical facilities, Hué University, and U.S. civilian and military offices, notably the MACV compound. This was a converted hotel housing some 200 American military advisors to the First Division and other South Vietnamese forces in the region.

***

A painting of Vietnamese women and schoolgirls in traditional dress (*ao dai*) strolling by a lotus pond inside the grounds of the imperial palace.

The MACV compound in Hué. During the Tet attack, about 200 resident advisors and administrative personnel defended it from NVA attacks.

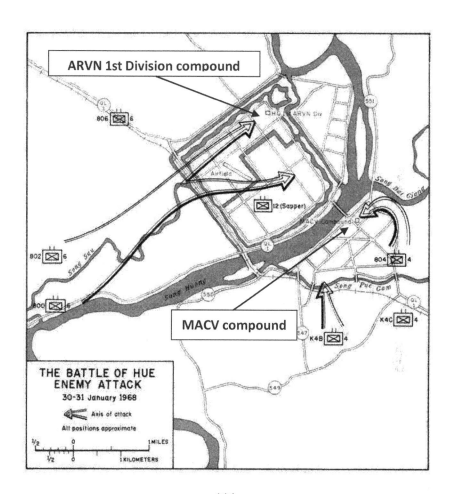

***

Initial Attack

Approximately 8000 Communist troops, mostly regular NVA units, attacked Hué in the predawn hours of January 31, beginning with a rocket and mortar barrage. [See map, previous page.] Since there were almost no combat forces in Hué to resist them, they quickly occupied the entire city, both north and south. However, there were two critical exceptions, where their repeated attacks were repulsed.

In the Citadel, ARVN First Division commander Ngo Quang Truong was the only South Vietnamese or U.S. general both to foresee the Tet attack and to prepare for it as best he could. Although all his combat maneuver battalions were stationed well outside of Hué and couldn't be relocated to the city in time, on January 30 Truong had cancelled all leaves, placed the division on full alert, and assembled all available troops at the division headquarters compound. These were mostly clerks, trainees, and rear-echelon logistics types, plus the Division reconnaissance company with about 100 combat-ready soldiers. One of the best generals on either side in the Vietnam War, Truong managed with this motley force to hold off the entire NVA 6th Regiment and keep open a route by which he could be reinforced.

On the south side, the 200 Americans in MACV were able to prevent their surrounded compound from being overrun by an attacking NVA force of two battalions, about 1,000 men. But it was clear they could not hold out long without reinforcement.

The approximately 20 American civilians in the city were isolated in their houses, and most were gradually killed or captured in the next few days.

U.S. reinforcements would have to come from Phu Bai, a large base five miles south of Hué. However, on January 31 the situation in Hué was obscured not only by heavy clouds and a cold drizzle but also by the fog of war, which took a week to clear sufficiently for the U.S.

higher command to have a realistic understanding of the situation. Although physically nearby, Phu Bai was separated from Hué by a wall of misinformation and disbelief.

Consequently, only one Marine company was sent to the city on January 31, with orders to reinforce the First Division and MACV compounds. No one at Phu Bai realized that all of Hué had been occupied by 8,000 North Vietnamese. The company barely managed to fight its way into MACV, taking heavy casualties along the way.

On February 2, two additional Marine companies were sent to Hué from Phu Bai, and on February 4 two more were sent, all of them having to fight their way into MACV and its expanding defensive perimeter. By this time, General Truong had managed to call in three of his battalions from rural areas and to stabilize the situation around First Division headquarters, so it was decided in Saigon that the task of retaking Hué would be divided, with ARVN forces responsible for the Citadel and U.S. Marines responsible for the south side of the city.

Thus five Marine companies, organized in two small battalions, began the arduous task of clearing southern Hué of a determined, dug-in enemy that greatly outnumbered them, fighting street by street and house by house. This was deadly, destructive urban combat of a sort the U.S. military had not engaged in since the Battle of Seoul during the Korean War, and for which the Marines were not trained. But they improvised, learned quickly, and broke the back of North Vietnamese resistance by February 10, although serious fighting continued until late February.

General Truong's fight in the Citadel had not been progressing as well as that of the Marines on the south side of the city. This was because the NVA had been able to bring in as many or more reinforcements as had the ARVN high command. In spite of their determined attacks, after two weeks the ARVN forces were essentially stalemated. So, with the south side battle largely won, it was decided to send U.S. troops to help them. A fresh Marine battalion from Phu Bai arrived in the Citadel February 13.

The Marines found the fight to be just as difficult as had their South Vietnamese allies, and over the next two weeks they took heavy casualties. But with help from the Third Brigade of the U.S. Army's First Cavalry Division, which in fighting west of the city managed to cut off the flow of NVA reinforcements and supplies, the Marines and ARVN forces prevailed.

On February 24, ARVN troops replaced the giant VC flag that had flown over the Citadel and dominated the Hué skyline since January 31 with the South Vietnamese flag. Hué was declared secure on February 26, and the beaten remnants of the NVA attacking force withdrew into their base areas along the Laotian border.

Impact of the Battle

During the Battle of Hué, friendly forces suffered more than 600 killed and nearly 4,000 wounded. About two-thirds of these casualties were South Vietnamese. The U.S. Marine casualty rate was nearly 50% in each of the three battalions committed.

Of the 8,000-man NVA attacking force, approximately 5,000 were killed. This estimate was thought by the mistrustful American press to be exaggerated, but after the war it was confirmed by North Vietnamese leaders to be accurate.

As for the people of Hué, during the course of the war no city in either North or South Vietnam suffered so much bloodshed and destruction for so long as did Hué and its 140,000 residents. By the end of the battle, much of the city was in ruins, and 116,000 people had to leave their homes as refugees.

About 6,000 civilians were killed during the Battle of Hué, but only half of them lost their lives to what in more recent years has been called "collateral damage," as an unintended result of the combat. The rest, nearly 3,000 people, were executed by the Communists, usually shot in the back of the head, but often bludgeoned and buried alive, in the war's worst atrocity. The victims were political leaders, city officials, civil servants, teachers, priests, policemen, and several Americans and other foreigners.

Both the Tet Offensive and its greatest battle, Hué, were disastrous military defeats for the Communists. The Viet Cong insurgency never recovered, and it took four years, until 1972, to rebuild the North Vietnamese Army to the point of mounting a comparable countrywide offensive. Far from defecting, as the politburo had expected, South Vietnamese forces fought valiantly; instead of sparking a popular uprising against the government, the attacks strengthened opposition against the Communists.

But the American and South Vietnamese military victory within South Vietnam was historically insignificant compared to the impact of Tet within the United States, particularly the prolonged combat in Saigon and especially in Hué, which was massively covered by the press and generally portrayed as American and South Vietnamese failure if not outright defeat. For example, after CBS News anchor Walter Cronkite visited Hué, he said in an hour-long special broadcast:

> We have been too often disappointed by the optimism of the American leaders, both in Vietnam and Washington, to have faith any longer in the silver linings they find in the darkest clouds....We are mired in a stalemate that can only be ended by negotiation, not victory.

On hearing this, President Johnson exclaimed, "If I've lost Cronkite, I've lost the American people!"

The psychological and political impact of the Tet Offensive, and especially the Battle of Hué, on the leadership and people of the United States was decisive in determining the outcome of the war.

Father Jim, Behind Enemy Lines

Tuy-Cam and I had long planned to meet at her family home in Hué for what was to be her last Tet before our marriage and departure for the United States. So, on January 30 I flew from Quang Tri to Hué on the Air America shuttle flight and proceeded to her home for a Tet dinner with the family. Joining us was Steve Haukness, a Foreign Service communicator and one of Tuy-Cam's colleagues at the Danang Consulate General who was visiting Hué as a tourist, and one of my Foreign Service Officer classmates, Steve Miller, who was working in Hué as a "psywar" officer with the U.S. Information Agency.

After dinner, Haukness and Miller went to Miller's house, and I went to the municipal power plant, where I had been invited to stay in a guest cottage by a French friend, Albert Istivie, whose company operated the power plants in both Hué and Quang Tri. I was awakened by the NVA rocket and mortar barrage that began at 3 a.m. It was noisy, but I had experienced such attacks before and could tell that the shells weren't falling nearby. I didn't perceive myself to be in any great danger, and after the noise abated, I drifted back to sleep.

When I awoke about 7 a.m., all was quiet, so I dressed and went into the power plant in search of my friend, Albert. When I found him he quickly took me to a window and directed my attention to a group of NVA soldiers in the courtyard I had just crossed. He told me they had occupied the whole city and seemed prepared to stay. This was startling news. There had been attacks on cities before, but only as raids – enemy forces were always gone by dawn to return to their rural sanctuaries.

Albert told me to go back to the guest cottage and wait, and he would try to find a way to move me out of the power plant compound that evening, noting that it would be mortally dangerous for us both if I were discovered by the NVA. I re-crossed the courtyard – the soldiers, if they noticed me, must have thought I was a Frenchman working at the plant – and spent a very, very long day pondering the situation.

About 6 p.m. there was a knock on the door. I was extremely relieved to find that it was Albert and not the North Vietnamese. He told me to await his signal -- scratching his head -- from the far side of the courtyard, and then walk across. The signal soon came. As I crossed I noted the NVA were grouped at one end, eating their supper. They again let me cross unmolested. Albert led me out a back door and over some fences to the home of a French priest, Father Cressonier, who had agreed to take me in.

Father Cressonier had been in Hué for 35 years. He welcomed me and introduced me to his other guest, Father Poncet, a younger priest who had been evacuated to Hué from his post in Khe Sanh, where another major battle was then raging. He gave me a black gown and a set of beads, and told me that if the Communists came to the house, we would claim that I was a visiting Canadian priest. While my French was good, it would have been obvious to anyone fluent in the language that I wasn't a native speaker.

So, for the next nine days I became a Catholic priest in Communist-occupied Hué. For a Tennessee hillbilly raised in the Church of Christ, this in itself was a memorable adventure! We were fortunate that the Communist cadre who were combing the city for enemies never came to the house, so we didn't have to test the Canadian story.

At first, we thought it would only be a day or two before friendly forces re-took the city, but as the days wore on we could always see the huge VC flag flying from the Citadel just across the river. From the sounds of battle, however, we could tell that the fighting was getting closer, a realization that was dramatized by a mortar round that heavily damaged the second floor of the house. We were downstairs at the time it hit and were uninjured.

Rescue by Hotel/2/5

Finally, on February 8, I heard the sound of American voices, moving in our direction. Albert had visited that morning to let us know the NVA troops in the power plant had left during the night, so we didn't anticipate any fighting as the Marines moved in. I climbed to the demolished second floor, and when I spotted the Marines I gave a thumbs-up sign to let them know I was American. It was Hotel Company, Second Battalion, Fifth Marine Regiment. When they got to the house they radioed the company commander, Captain Ron Christmas, to come.

I introduced the Captain and his men to the priests and Albert, and briefed them on all I knew. So as not to advertise to neighbors that the priests had been hiding an American, the Marines wrapped me in a blanket and carried me out as if I were a wounded Marine. They took me to the MACV compound, which was now secure except for mortar attacks, where I spent the next two nights.

While at MACV, I was interviewed by *Washington Post* reporter Peter Braestrup, and he included an account of my rescue in his story about the Hué battle. That's how my parents found out I was still alive. They had been informed by the State Department that I was missing, so they were greatly relieved when they saw the *Washington Post* report, via the *Chattanooga Times*, that I had been rescued.

On February 10, I found space on a medical evacuation helicopter to Danang and reported to the U.S. Consulate General and CORDS headquarters. After a much needed bath, some hot food, and sleep, and writing a report on what I had observed in Hué, I told my bosses I had to go back to look for Tuy-Cam. They said no, as the battle was still raging and it was much too dangerous. I decided to disregard these orders and go anyway. I found a friendly Army helicopter pilot at the Danang airbase and hitched a ride, flying into Hué on February 14.

Tuy-Cam's Ordeal

While I was hiding with the priests, Tuy-Cam was having a more difficult experience. Two of her brothers, both South Vietnamese military officers, were home on leave and hid in the attic when the city was occupied. Tuy-Cam, as a U.S. Government employee, was also in grave danger. NVA soldiers frequently came to the house demanding food, and local VC cadre came to look for enemies and give propaganda lectures. Amazingly, the brothers in the attic were not discovered, and Tuy-Cam was not identified.

Although Tuy-Cam's house was only a few hundred yards from that of Father Cressonier, it was on the other side of the Phu Cam canal, a barrier that the Marines didn't cross until five days after my liberation. When they did cross it, on February 13, the shelling in that neighborhood became intense. After their house was hit by a mortar round, Tuy-Cam and her family decided they had to flee. They went with other refugees to a nearby pagoda, but a group of NVA and VC came and took away her two brothers as well as others among the refugees whom they considered enemies. Tuy-Cam again escaped, because the chief monk of the pagoda, Thich Chon Thuc, hid her under the Buddha altar. The next day, the family fled again, this time to a refugee camp at Hué University, near the MACV compound.

On February 14, Tuy-Cam came to MACV to seek news about me. Learning that I had survived and was evacuated to Danang, she went to the nearby helicopter pad to try to get to Danang as well. She hadn't been there long before a helicopter landed and I got off it. Our reunion was emotional! Appropriately, it was on Valentine's Day.

We stayed on in Hué a couple of days to help take care of Tuy-Cam's family, and then returned to our jobs in Quang Tri and Danang.

***

89

NVA troops in Hué. They were tough opponents.

Attending a wounded Marine during a pause in the battle.

Hué after Tet battle

TOP: Physical destruction.

CENTER: Fleeing refugees.

BOTTOM: Re-burying victims of Communist massacre.

| Tuy-Cam's house | Power plant compound | Fr. Cresonnier's house |

The U.S. Consulate building, left, and Father Cresonnier's house, right, were repaired after the war, and are now used as government offices. These pictures and Google Earth image (top) are from 2007.

***

A Wartime Marriage

We were married as previously scheduled, on March 16, but at the U.S. Consulate General in Danang rather than in a traditional Vietnamese ceremony at Hué, as we had planned. The road between Hué and Danang had just been reopened, so Tuy-Cam's mother and several family members were able to attend. Also included were our colleagues from the Consulate General and CORDS, as well as a few American friends who flew in from Saigon. My best man was Joe Murphy, a CIA officer who had been stationed with me in Hué in 1965-66. To some extent inspired by my example, in 1969 Joe married a Vietnamese woman, Trinh. We continued our close friendship with Joe and Trinh, and served together with them in Burma as well as in Washington. They retired in Williamsburg, and influenced our decision to retire there as well.

The wedding was a happy occasion, but the war and the loss of many friends and relatives in the Tet Offensive was still on everyone's mind.

Tuy-Cam's two brothers were never found, and were doubtless executed by the NVA.

As for the two American friends who had dinner with us the night of the attack, Steve Miller's body was found a few days after the end of the battle, hands tied behind his back and a bullet hole in the back of his head. Tuy-Cam and I delivered his ashes to his widow in Washington after our arrival there in May. Steve Haukness' body wasn't found until many years later.

My French friend, Albert, stayed on in Hué, working at the power plant, but he was forced to flee to France after the Communist takeover of South Vietnam in 1975.

Father Cressonier and Father Poncet, having refused my offer of evacuation by the Marines because they wanted to stay and minister to their flock, were murdered by Viet Cong cadre the next day, after leaving the house to help refugees at a nearby church.

Ron Christmas, the commander of the Marine company that liberated me, was seriously wounded towards the end of the battle, but after two years of hospitalization and therapy he went on to a distinguished Marine Corps career, retiring as a lieutenant general. In retirement, he served as the first president of the Marine Corps Heritage Foundation, responsible for creating the Marine Museum at Quantico. In 2008, Tuy-Cam and I visited the museum and had lunch with Ron, the first time I had seen him since 1968. It was an emotional reunion.

Ron was one of the heroes of the Battle of Hué, for which he was awarded the Navy Cross. Tuy-Cam and I merely survived it. We owe our survival to Ron and the other Marines and ARVN soldiers who liberated the city, and we remain deeply grateful to them, as well as to the three Frenchmen, Albert and the two priests, who sheltered me, and to the monk who hid Tuy-Cam at the pagoda. We can never repay our debt of gratitude to these people.

The day after the wedding, we flew to Saigon, where it took two weeks to get Tuy-Cam's exit visa from the Vietnamese government. We then proceeded to Washington via honeymoon stops in Hong Kong and Tokyo, and a visit with my family in Chattanooga.

Married Life

Our marriage began with many challenges, especially for Tuy-Cam. Two of her brothers had just been captured by the North Vietnamese, and chances for their survival were remote. Her home had been badly damaged, and her native city was in ruins. Now, she was leaving her family and her country for a new life in a place she had never seen and a culture she had never experienced.

In those days, moreover, racism was more common and interracial marriages were rare. Neither of us knew what sort of issues that might bring.[10] While American attitudes were evolving rapidly in the 1960s, State Department policy still required that a Foreign Service Officer who planned to marry a non-citizen had to submit a letter of resignation, which, it was understood, would be accepted or declined depending on the Department's assessment of the "suitability" of the prospective spouse. In my case, the resignation was not accepted (although the official letter informing me of that was not approved until March 22, a week after our marriage). Nonetheless, the policy created uncertainty about my career prospects.

Vietnamese attitudes toward marriage to a foreigner were also negative, particularly in traditional, culturally conservative families such as Tuy-Cam's. However, my status as a professional diplomat helped our case for winning the family's approval, as did the prophecy by a Chinese soothsayer at her birth that she would marry a foreigner and live outside Vietnam.

Beyond the obvious differences in nationality, culture, race, language, etc., our family backgrounds were also very different. In fact, American and Vietnamese definitions of the meaning of "family" are widely divergent. Americans think of a core mother-father-children unit, probably with active ties to grandparents and a few aunts, uncles, and first cousins. Vietnamese, on the other hand, have a much broader concept of family, extending back several generations and with ties, at least in principle and often in fact, to distant relations of whom Americans would typically be unaware. Vietnamese also share the Confucian concept of reverence (early Christian missionaries called it "worship") for their ancestors, and they maintain household altars where they pray and conduct rituals to honor them.

---

[10] It was only in 1967 that the U.S. Supreme Court had invalidated state laws prohibiting interracial marriage (Loving vs. Virginia). However, such laws remained on the books in many states until 2000, when the last of them, in Alabama, was repealed.

Tuy-Cam is the eldest of 10 children in an urban, middle class family. Her father, who had been a mid-ranking officer in the government security service, had died in 1962, leaving the family with very limited resources. His ancestral family, the Than-trong, was well-known and respected from the time of the Vietnamese emperors for service as court mandarins and government officials. Tuy-Cam's mother was a member of the royal family, but since the emperors typically had many wives and dozens of children, by the mid-Twentieth Century the royal family had become so numerous that it no longer had much practical distinction. With the abdication of the last emperor, Bao Dai, in 1954, it became no more than an historic artifact.

I soon discovered that Tuy-Cam's extended family included many distinguished people, including former Ambassadors to the United States and United Nations, the governor of the central bank, and three South Vietnamese generals. We became friends with several of them.

One of Tuy-Cam's sisters was in graduate school on a Fulbright scholarship at Pennsylvania State University when South Vietnam fell in 1975, and on completing her studies she moved to the developing Vietnamese diaspora community (now the largest in the United States) in the Westminster/Fountain Valley area of Orange County, California. She and her husband were joined in 1977 by another sister and her husband, who fled Vietnam as "boat people" and landed in Hong Kong. (We were in Burma at the time, and Tuy-Cam went to Hong Kong to facilitate their onward movement to California.) Tuy-Cam's mother and two unmarried sisters were unsuccessful in repeated attempts to leave Vietnam with the boat people migration, but were able to come to Orange County in 1985 under the "orderly departure program" negotiated between the Vietnamese and U.S. governments. Two married sisters and Tuy-Cam's only surviving brother, who was still a young boy at the time of the Tet Offensive, chose not to emigrate to the United States. They remain in Vietnam, where we visited them in 2007 for the first time since the end of the war.

While we experienced the occasional misunderstandings and need for adjustments that I assume are common to all newlyweds, our marriage proved strong from the beginning, as love and shared values outweighed the cultural and other differences. Moreover, the relationship was forged in war and tempered by powerful mutual experiences, notably including the Tet Offensive, that gave us both self-confidence and confidence in each other.

Tuy-Cam adapted quickly and well to America and the Foreign Service lifestyle. She was soon comfortable in her role as the wife of an American diplomat, while at the same time retaining close ties to her family and Vietnamese culture. The marriage had a positive, not negative, impact on my career, enabling me to achieve a degree of success that would not have been possible without Tuy-Cam and her support as my lifelong partner.

Concerns about racial issues, moreover, proved unfounded. Even my very Southern family in Tennessee and Alabama, as well as my Auburn friends, welcomed and accepted Tuy-Cam immediately and without reservation. There was some initial curiosity, since few of them had ever met an Asian or even seen one except in movies, but it was not negative or in any way hostile. If we ever encountered racial prejudice against Tuy-Cam, it was too insignificant to be noticed by either of us.

***

The groom stands out among Tuy-Cam's family, at our wedding on March 16, 1968, at the U.S. Consulate General in Danang.

Cutting the wedding cake.	Welcome to Chattanooga by my parents, April 1968.

***

Harvard

My next assignment was to a year of mid-career training at Harvard, to get a Master in Public Administration at the Kennedy School of Government. This was one of the most coveted assignments available to an officer of my rank. I had hoped to go to graduate school some day; to do so at Harvard, with tuition fully paid, while continuing to receive my normal salary, was beyond my fondest dreams. On top of that, the Department arranged my selection for a "Career Education Award" from the National Institute of Public Affairs. This amounted to a $1000 grant and a week-long seminar at Williamsburg, together with the 49 other NIPA award winners from across the country.

The Harvard assignment was an unstated reward for my three years of service in Vietnam and a gesture of compensation for my Tet Offensive ordeal in Hué; but it also represented, I'm convinced, an effort by the Foreign Service "system" to remove a bit more of the Tennessee and Alabama red from my neck and make me a better fit for the still-elitist Foreign Service culture. It did give me a great educational credential and increased my social self-confidence, but the red has never faded. I was not comfortable at Harvard and developed no emotional ties to it. I remain an Auburn man and a redneck hillbilly at heart.

We spent the summer of 1968 in Washington, where I worked as a vacation fill-in and extra hand on the State Department Vietnam desk and made a two-week speaking tour for the Bureau of Public Affairs to discuss U.S. policy and the situation in Vietnam at schools and civic organizations. In September we settled in a three-room Cambridge apartment near the Harvard campus. Tuy-Cam got a job cataloging books in the Widener Library, and I began my studies. The MPA curriculum included two required courses on government administration, but I could choose the other six courses from among any of Harvard's graduate-level offerings for which I was qualified.

The most important of my Harvard courses was National Security Policy, taught by Henry Kissinger. I had met him when he visited Hué in 1965 as a consultant. Now, in 1968, in addition to teaching at Harvard he was an advisor to New York Governor (and Republican presidential aspirant) Nelson Rockefeller. His course had well over 100 students, so I had little personal contact with him. After winning the 1968 election, Richard Nixon selected Kissinger as National Security Advisor. I had no idea that he would become my boss in less than a year.

Although I learned a lot at Harvard and enjoyed the intellectual stimulation, my overall experience there was not pleasant. By 1968, the United States was embroiled in the most heated internal political conflict of the Twentieth Century, involving a social and cultural revolution focused domestically on civil rights, and internationally on U.S. participation in the Vietnam War. Along with other universities, Harvard was a principal battleground of that conflict.

Anti-war protests engulfed the Harvard campus throughout most of the 1968-69 academic year, and I was the target of nasty remarks by classmates who became aware of my Vietnam service. In April, radical protesters led by Students for a Democratic Society occupied the main administration building in Harvard yard and forcibly expelled the administrators and staff. Their demands included ending ROTC at Harvard, and they burned books of professors who were seen as supportive of the war, including Kissinger. When the administration finally called in local police to expel them, the students assaulted and spat on the officers, and then claimed police brutality when the officers dragged them out of the building. This incident was followed by a student strike, which effectively closed the university for a week.

I found the protesters disgusting, and I was dismayed by the pusillanimous reaction of the university leadership and most of the faculty to their provocations. (One of the professors, Henry Rosovsky, subsequently called Harvard in the late 1960s "an academic

Munich."[11]) However, there was nothing I could do about the situation, so I grew a hippie-like beard, avoided confrontations, and got on with my studies.

As a student at Auburn, I thought of myself as a liberal and was considered by most of my peers to be a far-left radical. At Harvard, I was called a war-monger and a reactionary, and I saw that I had little in common with the liberalism that dominated the campus. I decided that I was really a moderate centrist, and there I have remained.

Assignment to INR

Following graduation from Harvard in June 1969, we returned to Washington for my assignment as an intelligence analyst in the Vietnam section of the State Department's Bureau of Intelligence and Research (INR). We moved into an Arlington apartment, along with our newly-acquired toy poodle, Ti-Ti. Tuy-Cam got a job as a Vietnamese instructor at the CIA language school, work that she found enjoyable and at which she excelled.

Although at first I liked my job, serious problems soon developed. The head of the INR Vietnam office, my boss, who was a career Civil Service (not Foreign Service) officer, turned out to be the worst supervisor I ever had, before or since. He was woefully lacking in leadership ability or even basic inter-personal skills. Even though he had never spent any significant time in Vietnam, he considered himself an expert whose opinions on Vietnamese matters were not to be challenged. Moreover, those opinions were firmly rooted in the anti-war ideology that had become dominant in academia, and his analysis of developments and trends in Vietnam reflected that point of view. He rejected most of my papers without comment or explanation.

Before long, I discovered that all five of my fellow Vietnam analysts had similar problems with this man. However, our individual and

---

[11] *Harvard Magazine*, January/February 2016, p. 30.

(eventually) joint appeals to senior INR officers for corrective action produced only expressions of sympathy and counsels of patience.

My salvation came in September, when INR received a directive to furnish an analyst for the Vietnam Special Studies Group (VSSG), a newly-created National Security Council project that was to undertake a long-term study of pacification.[12] Because of my experience with CORDS in Quang Tri, plus my connection to National Security Advisor Henry Kissinger as one of his students at Harvard, I was able to get myself assigned to this project.

Pacification Progress and the VSSG

Until 1968, although U.S. and South Vietnamese conventional combat forces won almost all of their battles, the pacification effort had not been successful in wresting control of the countryside from the Viet Cong. In the aftermath of the Tet Offensive, however, enemy forces were weakened by heavy losses, and the U.S. and South Vietnamese commands intensified their focus on pacification. This involved a new population-centric (as opposed to enemy-centric) strategy in which clear-and-hold operations replaced search-and-destroy operations. Progress was now measured by improved security in the villages rather than by body counts following battles, and the previously disjointed U.S. structure for implementing pacification was unified into a much more effective civil-military organization called CORDS. [See the previous account of my 1967-68 assignment to CORDS in Quang Tri.]

Soon, there were signs of progress, and by 1969, the change was noted in Washington. However, there was still mistrust of the official reporting from Saigon, which had long been viewed as overly

---

[12] "Pacification, " or what is today most often called counterinsurgency, refers to unconventional warfare, a conflict that is political and psychological as well as military, a sometimes shadowy struggle with guerrilla forces and small units for control of the countryside and the support of the population.

optimistic, especially after the shock of Tet 1968 made General Westmoreland's 1967 claims of steady progress and diminishing enemy capability look out of touch with reality.

The new Nixon Administration recognized the importance of pacification in successfully implementing its strategy of gradually withdrawing U.S. combat forces, strengthening the government, and achieving a ceasefire that would leave the South Vietnamese in a position to maintain their independence. Thus, Kissinger ordered a thorough study of the situation in the Vietnamese countryside to be undertaken by the NSC, and the VSSG was created for this purpose. Managed by a senior NSC staff member, the study team included two CIA officers, three military officers, a Defense Department civilian, and me, representing State. All of us had Vietnam experience. It was made clear from the beginning that we were to conduct the study and develop our conclusions as independent analysts working for the NSC, not as representatives of our home agencies.

Experienced bureaucrats will recognize that this mandate was problematic, particularly in view of my ongoing conflict with my boss in INR. For the purposes of the VSSG project, which for eight months became my full-time job, he was not in practice my boss, although he didn't see it that way. Forced to choose between his instructions and those of Henry Kissinger, I chose the latter. This worked out fine until my annual performance evaluation, written by my INR boss, which nearly ended my Foreign Service career.

Measuring Population Control

We began the study with a review of pacification-related reporting from Saigon, including the Hamlet Evaluation System monthly reports from each province and district, prepared by American advisors. From this review, we developed a "control indicator" that gave a realistic picture of population control in the countryside. We further validated the analysis and our indicator by in-depth studies of 12 key provinces, including three-to-four-week field visits to each of these provinces by the VSSG analysts. I visited Quang Tri and Thua Thien (the province of which Hué was the capital).

Our study concluded that the VC controlled about 50% of the rural population in 1967, while the government controlled just under 20%. The rest was contested. The government controlled all of the urban population, which was 38% of the total. By mid 1968, the study found, government control of rural areas began to rise rapidly, with corresponding VC losses. And by early 1970, the VC retained control of only 8% of the population, while the government controlled 62% of the rural population as well as all the urban population, or more than 75% of the total.

The final VSSG report, for which I was asked to write the initial draft, was completed on April 15, 1970.[13] The war's trajectory from 1970 to its end in 1975 generally bore out the accuracy of its assessment.

The report lent credibility to the Administration's Vietnamization policy and its hopes that a Korea-like ceasefire agreement could be reached, leaving in place an independent South Vietnam able to defend itself with limited U.S. assistance. These hopes foundered on the erosion of domestic political support for the war, the self-inflicted wounds of Watergate, and the ultimate refusal of Congress to provide continued support for South Vietnam following the 1973 Paris Agreement.

****

---

[13] This now-declassified report, entitled "The Situation in the Countryside," is available in archives of Vietnam War material. I obtained a copy from the library of the Joint Forces Staff College in Norfolk. For a detailed discussion of the VSSG, see my article in *Small Wars Journal*, March 23, 2012, "Assessing Pacification in Vietnam: We Won the Counterinsurgency War!"

4.

Escape to Thailand, 1970-73

After completion of the Vietnam Special Studies Group report in April, I told my personnel officer that I could not endure another year under my INR boss, and he was sympathetic. Consequently, I was able to escape from INR with an assignment as deputy principal officer at the Consulate in Chiangmai, via 10 months of Thai language training to begin in May 1970 at the Foreign Service Institute in Arlington.

I was pleased with the prospect of developing a geographic specialization in Southeast Asia and learning a "hard" (i.e., non-European) language to add to my French. Hard-language fluency was not a requirement for advancement in the Foreign Service, but it was strongly encouraged. Moreover, FSI was one of the two best language schools in the country, along with the Defense Language Institute at Monterrey. Classes were small (in my Thai class there were two of us); the curriculum and teaching methodology were state-of-the-art; and the instructors were native speakers. We had six hours per day of classroom instruction, and we were expected to spend 20 hours per week with recorded tapes in the "language lab" or at home.

My language aptitude, as tested by FSI, was well above the minimum required for hard language training, and I was a diligent student. My final score was a "strong level three," indicating professional-level proficiency in both speaking and reading (with level five being that of an educated native speaker). In an official letter informing me of my selection for the FSI 1971 Honor Roll, I was told that this score put me in "the top five per cent of students who have studied [Thai] at FSI over the past eight years."

I hoped this evaluation would offset the highly negative performance report I had received from INR. It did not. I was "passed over" for promotion in 1971, which would have marked an average time-in-class interval for my grade.

Tuy-Cam was also pleased with the assignment to Thailand, which would facilitate visits to her family in Vietnam. She continued her work with CIA as a Vietnamese language instructor until two days before the birth of our first daughter, Kim, in January 1971. We had both wanted children and were delighted when she came along.

We departed Washington in March on the long flight to the other side of the world with our two-month-old baby, happy to be ending what had been an interesting but stressful three years in the United States. We looked forward to the relative tranquility of Thailand and our first Foreign Service assignment as a family.

Life in Chiangmai

Of all our Foreign Service posts, Chiangmai was the most pleasant in terms of the environment. It was an interesting, exotic place, very Asian in character, but it was at the same time modern or at least modernizing, with reliable electricity, comfortable housing, a good university, adequate medical facilities, an international-class hotel, and several good restaurants. It was Thailand's ancient capital and second most important city, but it was of modest size (less than half a million people), not over-crowded and polluted like Bangkok, and it enjoyed a less-hurried pace of life than either Bangkok or Washington. There were lots of things to see and do in Chiangmai and nearby areas, including the King's summer palace, ancient pagodas, colorful hilltribe villages, and a training school for elephants that worked in the mountainous teak forests.

The Thai people were welcoming, and we developed several good friendships among them. Thai is in the same language family as

Vietnamese, and that, together with her high aptitude and previous experience in language learning, made it possible for Tuy-Cam to become fluent quickly. With both of us speaking good Thai, we were soon well integrated into the community.

Chiangmai also had a substantial and colorful expatriate community, including some Englishmen who had married local women and had lived there for many years. There were also about 25 American missionaries. Most memorable among the missionaries was a family of three brothers and their wives and children who had been working in southern China until they were chased out by the Communists in 1949. They had fled to Burma and re-established their mission among the Kachin hilltribe people who lived in the mountainous region along the border between Burma and Thailand. In the mid 1960s, however, the anti-Western, isolationist Burmese regime expelled all the Christian missionaries, and the family had to flee again. They settled in Chiangmai as a base, and continued their work in nearby Kachin villages. There, they become involved with the Kachin Liberation Army, which was conducting an armed insurrection, financed by opium trafficking, against the Burmese government.

The protection and welfare of American citizens is an important function of all Consulates. Our most interesting protection and welfare case during my time in Chiangmai was when one of the men of this family came in to seek our help. He reported that his wife had absconded with the family's money, together with a Kachin Liberation Army leader who had looted the KLA treasury, and the two of them were apparently headed for the United States. He wanted our assistance in locating them and recovering both his wife and the family money. We sent out an alert and request for information to the State Department and nearby U.S. Embassies, but there wasn't much else we could do. The wife was a very large American woman, around 250 pounds, and her lover was a normal-size Kachin, perhaps 125 pounds, so they must have been a striking couple as they traveled to the United States. Nevertheless, there were no replies to our inquiries, and so far as I know neither they nor the missing money ever returned to Chiangmai.

The War on Drugs

The Chiangmai Consulate was a small, multi-purpose post, much like the Consulates in Hué and Danang where Tuy-Cam and I had previously worked. There were three American FSOs: Jim Montgomery, the principal officer; me as deputy, with primary responsibility for political and economic reporting; and Jim Henderson (later replaced by Terry Owens), a junior officer responsible for administration and consular work. There were also four professional-level Thai Foreign Service National employees. Sharing the large Consulate compound were several representatives of other U.S. government agencies. USIA had a separate facility housing an American cultural center and library.

U.S.-Thai relations were cordial and extensive. Thailand was an American ally in the Vietnam War as well as a recipient of U.S. military and economic assistance. Moreover, it was then in the early stages of economic development that would soon earn it a place among the prosperous "Asian tigers" such as Taiwan and South Korea, so there was a growing focus on bilateral trade and investment. We had many official visitors from Washington and Bangkok to host. My political and economic reporting work was interesting, though not nearly so intense and high-profile as it had been in Vietnam.

In the United States, the epidemic of illicit drug use that developed along with the rise of the hippie counter-culture in the 1960s had become a major political concern by the early 1970s, and the Nixon Administration was eager to find ways to combat it. Since most of the drugs were imported, programs were developed to attack them at their source, where they were grown, processed, and introduced into global trafficking networks that eventually brought them to the streets of American cities. The most feared of these drugs at the time was heroin, a derivative of opium; and the largest global source of opium was the "Golden Triangle," the mountainous region of northern Burma, northern Thailand, and Laos, where opium poppies thrived. Chiangmai is at the heart of this region, and it served as an important point of origin for global heroin shipments.

In 1972, the Chiangmai Consulate became an outpost of the Administration's "War on Drugs," as the U.S. Drug Enforcement Agency opened its first overseas office in the Consulate compound. By the time my assignment ended in 1973, half of our work was related to narcotics. I reported on conditions in hilltribe villages where the poppies were grown, visited small towns on the Thai-Burma border through which the principal trafficking routes passed, and assessed a U.S.-financed project to persuade hilltribe farmers to substitute beans and other crops for poppies.

In spite of my personal involvement in it, I was skeptical that our anti-narcotics war could achieve victory as long as demand for drugs was high and the profits from trafficking them were so enormous. I came to regard most of our international narcotics work as well-intentioned but wasted effort, at best an expensive whack-a-mole game that might eventually produce some success in one place or with one drug, only to have another region or another drug emerge to meet the market's demand. The Southeast Asia Golden Triangle eventually faded as the world's leading opium producer, only to be replaced by other areas (currently, Afghanistan) and other drugs, such as cocaine.

Ham Radio, Blessed by Buddhist Monks

Even though I had sufficient work to keep me occupied, with both narcotics matters and traditional political and economic reporting, I had enough leisure time to resume the amateur radio hobby[14] I had begun in high school but had been unable to practice since my early years at Auburn. Now, we had a house with plenty of room for a radio station plus a large yard for antennas. Moreover, the recently-departed USIA officer, Fred Laun, was a serious ham, and he had left me some of his equipment as well as contacts with Thai hams and tips on how to get the necessary license from the Thai government.

Effective long distance short-wave radio communication requires an external antenna, the bigger and higher in the air the better. I built a huge one, called a "cubical quad," with a 30-foot long aluminum boom to which were attached sixteen 12-foot bamboo poles forming four big X-es that supported 180 meters of copper wire in concentric squares. This was mounted on a 40-foot tower, together with an electric motor operated from my "ham shack" inside the house, that rotated the antenna in the direction of the station with which I was communicating.

The antenna worked magnificently, making mine one of the strongest ham radio signals out of Southeast Asia and enabling me to talk to other hams throughout the world. It also gathered crowds of curious neighbors who watched its majestic rotations in awe, speculating on why the strange American would build such a contraption. My problem was not keeping it on the air, but in the air, as my skills at fabricating a tower proved to be considerably short of what was required for this monster.

---

[14] Amateur, or "ham" radio was a popular hobby in the 1950s and 1960s, and it was viewed as technologically cutting-edge, somewhat like computers in recent years. I took a radio technology correspondence course while in Chiangmai, and on return to the United States passed the Federal Communication Commission's highest level amateur exam, for my "Extra Class" license. For an account of my ham radio activities, see "N4HX: Amateur Radio Ambassador," *QST Magazine,* June 2009.

The third time the antenna blew down in one of the frequent thunderstorms that swept through Chiangmai, Khun Chat, one of the Thai employees at the Consulate, whom I had enlisted to help with erecting it, informed me that the problem was undoubtedly related to the fact that our house was on the site of an ancient battle between the forces of the Thai king and an invading army from Burma. The antenna was disturbing the ghosts of the soldiers buried there, he said. So, with Khun Chat's help, together with the support of Tuy-Cam, who is Buddhist, we engaged a group of monks from a nearby pagoda to come to the house and perform a ceremony to propitiate those unhappy spirits.

The monks, chanting and burning incense as they strung a white ribbon around the yard, must have done their work well, since the next antenna erection survived until the end of my tour in 1973. Or, perhaps it survived because I had hired an instructor at the local technical school to build a new, professionally engineered tower. One never knows.

Chiangmai was the first of five posts at which I was able to pursue ham radio. It provided me with endless hours of relaxation, and once, in Benin, it provided a way to contact Washington and call for help in a serious emergency. It also served on several occasions as unusual after-dinner entertainment for official guests.

An Enduring Friendship

Another benefit of ham radio was the development of enduring friendships. One was with a young physics student at the University of Chiangmai, Apichart Sajchwong. He was interested in ham radio and volunteered to help with some of my antenna projects. I invited him to my "ham shack" in the house, gave him some of my ham magazines, and ordered a Heathkit ham radio transceiver kit for him. Through me, he also met some other American hams in Thailand.

I had not thought of this relationship with Apichart as particularly important or in any way unusual. He was just a nice young man with whom I shared a hobby interest for a couple of years, but there were no really close connections. When I left Chiangmai, I never expected to see him again. However, many years later, when I was in Africa, Apichart contacted me via ham radio. We exchanged correspondence, and after I had retired from the Foreign Service, we exchanged several visits, Apichart and his wife Tippawan to Norfolk and Williamsburg, and Tuy-Cam and I to Chiangmai and Bangkok.

Apichart became a very successful businessman, as founder and CEO of Cheval Group, a large manufacturer of enclosures for electronic equipment with customers throughout the world, including some American electronics companies. To my surprise, he credits me with opening the pathway to his career. He explained that he was from a poor family, and until we met he had no exposure to Western culture and had never known a foreigner. He said that I helped reveal a new world to him, in which he overcame his shyness and developed goals for a better future as well as some tools to achieve it.

I've reflected that most of us rarely realize the impact we sometimes have on others, particularly younger people. As I've gotten older, I've tried to be a mentor more consciously, and perhaps I've met with some success. I wonder if Ambassador Timberlake, the FSO who introduced me to the Foreign Service and recommended me in the examination process, realized how important he was in determining the trajectory of my life. Although I looked him up in Washington when I was there as a junior officer, I didn't really thank him enough.

A Growing Family

Our second daughter, Eva, was born in Chiangmai in 1972. Tuy-Cam's obstetrician, a Thai doctor who had been trained at the University of Edinburgh, was outstanding, as were the facilities at the local hospital.

Overall, the medical care she received during the pregnancy and birth was better than she experienced in Arlington when Kim was born. It was no surprise to us to learn that Thailand has now developed a thriving "medical tourism" industry, in which many Americans have found that they can travel to Thailand, enjoy a vacation, and have major medical procedures done safely and effectively for less than the procedures alone would cost in the United States.

Both Eva and Kim were raised as Foreign Service kids, accompanying us on our subsequent assignments in Burma, Benin, and Burundi. They attended the American International School in Rangoon, and schools sponsored by the French government in Cotonou and Bujumbura, where there were no English-language schools.

A Career Restored

We enjoyed living in Chiangmai and looked forward to a long Foreign Service career, but by 1972 it seemed my career aspirations might prove unrealistic. The Foreign Service is highly competitive, with a personnel system similar to the military. Unlike the Civil Service, in which personal ranks are determined by the position being filled and promotion normally requires movement to a position with greater responsibilities, the Foreign Service, like the military, is based on the concept of rank-in-person. That is, just as an Army Colonel retains that rank no matter what job he or she currently fills, an FSO has a personal rank that is not tied to his or her current assignment.

Moreover, as in the military, promotions depend on annual performance evaluations prepared by the officer's boss. Based on these evaluations, a review board of higher ranking officers develops rank-order lists of all officers in each grade; State Department management determines the number of openings available that year at the next higher grade; and a line is drawn accordingly on the rank-order list. Those officers above the line are promoted; those below it are not. And again like the military and unlike the Civil Service, the Foreign Service is an up-or-out system: Officers have a limited number of years to remain in one grade. If they are not promoted within that time limit (which differs in different grades), they are what is euphemistically called "selected out."

I was promoted rapidly from the lowest rank (at that time, FSO-8) to FSO-5, which corresponded to Major in the Army. That promotion came in 1967. The average time for promotion from FSO-5 to FSO-4 was between three and four years, so when I was not promoted in 1971 I became concerned; and when I was again not promoted in 1972, my career prospects were looking grim. The time-in-grade limit for FSO-5 was seven years, so for me that limit was only two years away.

On consulting with my personnel officer in Washington, I confirmed that the reason for my low ranking was the highly negative performance evaluation by my former boss in INR. I had expected that this report would delay my next promotion, but I had not realized that one negative report could be enough to end my career. My personnel officer and FSO friends who were more familiar with the system than I was, all suggested that my only recourse was to file a formal grievance, seeking to have that report declared "falsely prejudicial" and removed from my file.

I submitted a detailed rebuttal of the INR performance report, solicited supporting letters from my INR colleagues who had also been treated badly and evaluated unfairly by my former boss, and asked the NSC staff member who was my *de facto* supervisor during most of the time I was officially assigned to INR, Larry Lynn, to provide an evaluation of my work on the VSSG project. Larry prepared a glowing report on my performance in the form of a personal letter of commendation from Henry Kissinger. I doubt that Kissinger personally did anything more than sign it, but that was enough.

I also sought support from the American Foreign Service Association, the professional organization that serves as a union for FSOs, and they assigned a staff member to be my counsel in the grievance proceeding.

The process took five months, but in January 1973 I received the following notification from the Foreign Service Director of Personnel:

> I have concluded that the efficiency report at issue contains erroneous and falsely prejudicial comments and that it constitutes an injustice which should be removed from your performance file.

There was nothing positive about the experience of being passed over for promotion and nearly selected out of the Foreign Service. It did teach me, however, that there were a few things in life that I couldn't handle alone, and that -- as difficult as it was for me to do -- sometimes it might be necessary to ask for help. But requesting help still does not come easily for me.

In 1973, I was promoted to FSO-4 (equivalent to Lieutenant Colonel), and thereafter I continued to advance through the ranks at an above-average pace. At retirement, I was a Minister-Counselor in the Senior Foreign Service, which corresponds to Major General.

***

Departure for Chiangmai, with baby Kim and family dog, Ti-ti.

Visiting Tuy-Cam's family in Hué, en route to Chiangmai.

***

Our house in Chiangmai.

My ham radio station in Chiangmai.

Entrance to the U.S. Consulate in 1972. In recent years, a fortress-like wall, gate, and guard station have been added.

Tuy-Cam with Kim and Eva, at our new house in Arlington, after leaving Chiangmai.

****

5.

Vietnam: The Bitter End, 1973-75

After completion of my two-year tour of duty in Chiangmai in March, 1973, I was slated to be transferred to Bangkok for a job in the Embassy political section. However, this changed after the Paris Agreement of January, 1973, which was supposed to end the Vietnam War. With the ensuing withdrawal of U.S. military advisors, the State Department needed to augment its staff at the Embassy and some newly-created consular posts in Vietnam, as well as its Vietnam office in Washington. The purpose of this build-up was to monitor evolution of the situation under the peace agreement, as well as to demonstrate continuing political and economic support for South Vietnam. Officers with prior Vietnam experience were needed for these jobs, and I was among the group selected.

Although I would have preferred one of the positions in Vietnam, I was assigned to the Vietnam Working Group in the State Department's East Asian and Pacific Affairs Bureau. There were nine people in this office, which is large for a State Department "country desk," as such offices are normally identified. I was to be the political officer.

Since I had not been involved in Vietnam affairs for the past three years, I received permission to visit Vietnam on the way back from Chiangmai, for two weeks of orientation and consultations. This was also a good opportunity for Tuy-Cam to visit her family in Hué and introduce them to Kim and Eva.

Over the past decade in the Foreign Service, I had managed to pay off my student loans and accumulate enough savings for a down payment, so we bought our first house, a small brick cottage in Arlington. We also bought our first new car as well as a small Honda motorcycle for my commute to the State Department.

Work on the Vietnam Desk

The ceasefire called for by the Paris Agreement never took effect for the Vietnamese combatants, as each side tried to consolidate its hold over disputed areas, so the evolving security situation required constant monitoring and analysis. There were lots of associated diplomatic protests to be made, though none produced results. The passionate domestic conflict over U.S. participation in the war also continued unabated, and much of our time on the Vietnam desk was spent preparing background papers and Congressional testimony for senior officials and responding to Congressional and press inquiries. I wrote speeches and provided staff support for Ellsworth Bunker, who replaced Henry Cabot Lodge as Ambassador in Saigon, and for Graham Martin, who replaced Bunker in late 1973, on their frequent visits to Washington. (I came to admire and respect Bunker; I found Martin difficult to work with.) We also supported the U.S. delegation that was continuing negotiations with the North Vietnamese in Paris.

Most of our assessments were related to whether South Vietnam was going to be able to survive in the situation brought about by the Paris Agreement. My outlook on that subject was influenced by my previous work on the Vietnam Special Studies Group. I followed up on its findings, using data and reporting from the Embassy, the Pentagon, and the CIA, plus another extended visit to Vietnam in late 1973. After that visit, I reported the following conclusions:

- From 1970 until 1973, pacification progress had continued, but more slowly than previously. After the Paris Agreement, the struggle for control of the countryside was essentially stalemated.
- At the time of the Agreement, the South Vietnamese government controlled 80% of the rural population plus all the urban population, or about 90% of the total. Enemy control was about 5%, with the rest contested.

121

- The South Vietnamese Army (ARVN) and territorial forces had continued to improve under the "Vietnamization" program as U.S. forces were withdrawn. This was demonstrated when they successfully turned back the all-out enemy offensive of 1972 without the assistance of U.S. ground combat forces (albeit with massive U.S. air and logistic support).

- The Viet Cong insurgents had been weakened to the point that they were no longer a major factor in the war, which by 1972 had lost almost all the characteristics of an insurgency. It had become overwhelmingly a conventional war fought by conventional forces.

- After the Paris Agreement and the drastic, Congressionally-mandated reduction of U.S. military and economic assistance that shortly followed, the effectiveness of the South Vietnamese forces had begun to decline. [This decline accelerated in 1974 and 1975.] In contrast, the North Vietnamese forces, which the Paris Agreement had permitted to remain in their bases along South Vietnam's mountainous western border and nearby areas of Laos and Cambodia, were rapidly recovering from their 1972 losses. Thanks to abundant Soviet and Chinese support, they were becoming stronger than ever before. The Ho Chi Minh trail was now a highway, bringing more and more North Vietnamese Army divisions into these base areas, where they were preparing another all-out offensive.

Final Visit

On my last visit to Vietnam, in late 1974, I spent three weeks traveling in Quang Tri, Hué, and Danang, as well as consulting with Americans in the U.S. Embassy and meeting with Vietnamese friends. Even though the government was still in control of an overwhelming majority of the population, it was clear that the situation was becoming desperate. While NVA attacks were increasing, and rapidly growing North

Vietnamese forces were almost certainly about to launch another massive general offensive, supply shortages were forcing the South Vietnamese to reduce military operations and curtail training; lack of fuel and spare parts had grounded most of the Air Force; some units at the end of long supply lines were running out of ammunition; and – not surprisingly in such circumstances – morale was declining.

Combining these findings with data available in Washington, I wrote a report that drew high-level attention in the State Department, including from Secretary Kissinger. Contrary to the still-optimistic reports coming from Ambassador Martin and the U.S. Embassy, I concluded that in the absence of immediately and massively renewed American support (which had become politically impossible because of Congressional opposition) South Vietnam would fall and the war would be lost not later than the summer of 1975.

In his memoirs, Kissinger discussed my report and quoted from it:

> On December 20, 1974, the State Department's Vietnam desk officer, James R. Bullington, wrote a moving and extraordinarily prescient report after a visit to [Vietnam]....Interspersing his report with human interest vignettes of the growing despair among South Vietnamese, Bullington concluded that, without the supplemental [appropriation from Congress], South Vietnam's position was hopeless. We had reached the point where, if the supplemental failed to materialize, only one option would be left to mitigate our country's dishonor:
>
> *"If the supplemental fails, we should also consider ways and means of saving as many anti-Communist South Vietnamese as possible. For example, do we not have a certain obligation to those many thousands of Vietnamese and their families who are present or former employees of the*

USG? To fail to help such people escape would, I believe, add considerable dishonor to our defeat in South Vietnam.[15]

Conclusions and What-Ifs

The counterinsurgency war we waged in Vietnam was failing prior to 1968, but thereafter the new population-centric strategy, increased support for South Vietnamese forces, heightened focus on pacification, and improved effectiveness achieved with the CORDS reorganization, all combined to bring success during the 1968-72 period. By the time of the Paris Agreement, the Viet Cong insurgents were no longer capable of playing a major role in determining the outcome of the war. In 1975, it was not insurgents, but 500,000 troops of the regular army of North Vietnam, operating in division-size formations and supported by armor and heavy artillery, that defeated the armed forces of South Vietnam, which had been crippled by drastic cuts in U.S. funding and supplies.

The North Vietnamese were forced to adopt this conventional war strategy, a massive cross-border invasion, because of the failure of the insurgency they had sponsored in the South.

Whether or not South Vietnam could have prevailed in the conventional war with North Vietnam that followed the insurgency, had we continued to provide air support plus sufficient military and economic assistance after the Paris Agreement, is a question of counter-factual history that can never be answered.

Trying to Rescue our Friends

When the NVA launched their massive offensive in March, 1975, and quickly overran the Central Highlands and I Corps, including Hué and Danang, it became clear to me and most other experienced Vietnam

---

[15] Kissinger, Henry, *Years of Renewal*, Simon & Schuster, 1999, p. 483

hands in Washington that the war was lost and South Vietnam could not continue to resist for more than a few weeks. It seemed self-evident that the highest U.S. priority should no longer be sustaining the independence of South Vietnam, which had become impossible, but the evacuation of the remaining Americans plus those South Vietnamese who were closely associated with us and would be gravely at risk of death or imprisonment under Communist rule. However, this perception was not shared by Ambassador Martin or by my high-level superiors in the State Department, who understandably tended to rely most heavily on the reporting and recommendations of the senior U.S. representative in South Vietnam.

For reasons I still cannot understand, Ambassador Martin did not agree that South Vietnam was about to fall, and Embassy reporting reflected this position. Consequently, he refused until the final week to begin large-scale evacuations or even to develop realistic evacuation plans, on grounds that such moves might trigger panic. (This concern might have been reasonable but for the fact that panic had already been provoked by the NVA's rapid advance on Saigon and collapsing South Vietnamese defenses.) Moreover, Ambassador Martin, at least in the Embassy's reporting, evidenced no sense of moral obligation to our South Vietnamese employees and allies.

Five of my mid-level FSO friends and I began to meet daily to consider this situation and how we might be able to influence it. They were on the personal staffs of Secretary Kissinger and other top Department leaders and could at least gain their attention. We decided that Ambassador Martin, for whatever reason, had lost touch with reality, and that action had to be taken to overcome or bypass his opposition and begin saving as many South Vietnamese as possible. We saw this as a moral imperative, both personally and as national policy. We prepared out-of-channel briefings and recommendations for the Secretary and other senior leaders, developed estimates of the

125

numbers involved (between 100,000 and a million South Vietnamese), lobbied for more evacuation flights, and pressed (eventually with success) for creation of an inter-agency task force to begin planning to receive in America the tens of thousands of refugees we expected to flee Vietnam after the Communist takeover.

Two of our number, Lionel Rosenblatt and Craig Johnstone, decided to take direct action. Using personal resources and without any authorization from the Department, they flew to Saigon on April 19 to implement their own evacuation plan. They managed to save some 200 Vietnamese before they were also forced to leave, just before the fall of Saigon on April 30. Ambassador Martin was furious and wanted them fired for insubordination, but eventually Secretary Kissinger declined to discipline them.[16]

Although we were unable to overcome Ambassador Martin's resistance and change U.S. policy on evacuations until it was too late, and many thousands of Vietnamese who should have been evacuated were left behind to face harsh "re-education camps" or worse, we did what we could, and were able to save hundreds more than would have escaped had we not acted. Among them was Tuy-Cam's uncle Thuan, who had been a senior government official, and his family.

The fall of Saigon was devastating for Tuy-Cam and me, and the experience was exacerbated by concern for those left behind, including Tuy-Cam's mother, five sisters, and a brother as well as many friends and colleagues. In the next few months, we busied ourselves trying to help the thousands of Vietnamese refugees (ultimately, about a million) who began arriving in the United States. I was working on the inter-agency refugee task force, and Tuy-Cam took a leading

[16] For a detailed account of the activities of our small mid-level FSO cabal and our work outside the normal State Department command structure, see an article by one of the members, Parker Borg, in the April 2015 *Foreign Service Journal*, "Mobilizing for South Vietnam's Last Days."

role in a group of Vietnamese and American volunteers (mostly military wives) who collected and distributed clothes and other supplies for the refugees.

My tour of duty in the State Department ended in June, and we prepared to start down another less-traveled road, this time to Mandalay, Burma, where I was to be principal officer at the U.S. Consulate.

Refugees fleeing the advancing North Vietnamese forces in 1975.

***

127

NVA tank entering the presidential palace in Saigon,
April 30, 1975.

Ambassador Graham Martin, aboard the *USS Blue Ridge*,
after his evacuation by helicopter from Saigon.

****

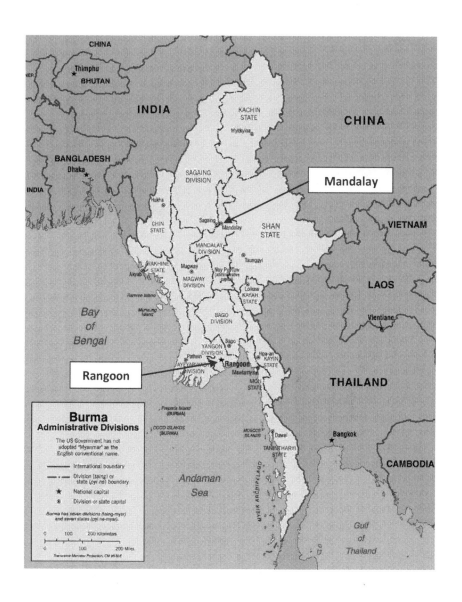

6.

The Best Bluegrass Band in Burma:

Mandalay and Rangoon, 1975-78

Having asked to return to Southeast Asia after the Vietnam Working Group job, I was assigned to Burma[17], beginning with a year as principal officer at the Consulate in Mandalay, followed by two years as chief of the Political/Economic Section at the Embassy in Rangoon. This offered the Foreign Service romance and adventure that I sought as well as the increased management responsibility that was necessary for promotion in the competitive, up-or-out Foreign Service system. We sold our Arlington house, wrapped up our Vietnam refugee-related work, and readied ourselves for the long journey. I was able to arrange only four weeks of language training, since English was so widely spoken in Burma that the Department did not consider Burmese necessary for the positions I was to occupy.

Introduction to a Marxist Police State

Burma was conquered by the British in three wars beginning in 1824 and culminating with the fall of the royal capital, Mandalay, in 1885. The country was annexed as a British colony and administered as part of British India. Burma was attacked and mostly occupied by the Japanese in World War II. There was intense fighting and substantial destruction as British and U.S. forces, coming in from India, together with Nationalist Chinese units coming from southern China, retook the

---

[17] In 1989, the military government officially changed the English translation of many geographic names, including the name of the country. Burma became Myanmar, Rangoon became Yangon, Pagan became Bagan, etc. The purpose was to erase what the regime considered relics of colonialism. However, the older names remain in use by the U.S. government and will be more familiar to most readers, so I have retained them here.

country in 1944-45. In 1948, the British granted independence to Burma, along with the rest of their Indian empire.

More than 80% of the Burmese people are Buddhist, with a Christian minority of about 7%. The largest ethnic group, called Burman, constitutes over two-thirds of the population and is concentrated along the Irrawaddy River valley, running the length of the country from north to south. The Shan, about 10%, live along the border with Thailand, and are closely related to the Thai people. There are several other ethnic groups, the largest of which are the Karen and the Kachin, living in the mountainous regions along the Thai, Chinese, and Indian borders. The official language is Burmese, which is related to Tibetan. Burma's current population is about 51 million, with about five million in Rangoon, and a million in the second largest city, Mandalay.

At the time of independence, Burma was considered the most prosperous and promising of the colonial territories in Southeast Asia. Under the British, it had been the world's leading exporter of rice, and it was the source of 75% of the world's teak. It also exported petroleum, tungsten, and gemstones (rubies, sapphires, pearls, and jade). Moreover, it had a large number of literate, English-speaking people, a fairly good road and rail infrastructure, and a well-developed government administration. It was a democratic republic, with free elections, between 1948 and 1962.

Burma's situation changed drastically when General Ne Win took power in a 1962 military coup, imposing one-party dictatorship, a Marxist economy, and a Stalinist political system. Almost all aspects of society were nationalized or otherwise brought under government control in what was called "The Burmese Way to Socialism." The regime was also nationalistic and xenophobic, discouraging contact with foreigners to the point of preventing even tourism. Internationally, while it called itself non-aligned, Burma was a reliable supporter of the Soviet Union and its allies, with which it developed close ties. Its relations with the United States and other Western countries were at best distant and often hostile.

Under this regime, the economy deteriorated, and from its initial position as one of the most economically advanced of the countries emerging from colonialism, by the mid-1970s it ranked among the world's 10 poorest countries. It was no longer even self-sufficient in rice production. Exports of other raw materials had dropped drastically as well; industrial production had largely ceased; and the currency lost most of its value. There was no foreign investment, and Western countries reduced and finally ended their economic aid. The jails were full of political prisoners, and the hilltribe people (Shan, Karen, Kachin, etc.) were in various stages of rebellion.

To resident foreigners, Burma seemed to be frozen in the 1940s, a hermit country with few connections to the modern world. Most of the vehicles on the crumbling roads were either of pre-World War II vintage or surplus trucks and jeeps left behind by Allied forces after the war. The grand colonial-era buildings, except for those few still occupied by foreigners, were decayed reminders of former prosperity. We quipped that the "Burmese Way to Socialism" should also be known as the "Road to Ruin." I recall a dinner conversation in Rangoon with the Soviet Ambassador in which he commented, shaking his head sadly, "You know, the Burmese give socialism a bad name!"

This was the situation throughout my three years in Burma, 1975-78. General Ne Win was still the dictator and would remain so until 1988. His successors, also military officers, maintained the regime he created and its policies without significant change until 2011, when gradual political and economic liberalization began.

Mandalay

When we arrived in 1975, Mandalay, the former royal capital, was a faded but still important political, cultural, and commercial center. It was also poor, isolated, and extremely hot, bearing little relationship beyond its name to Rudyard Kipling's well-known poem, "On the Road to Mandalay."

The Consulate had been established as a political and economic reporting post to keep tabs on developments in central and northern Burma. Its staff consisted of me, a Vice Consul, Jim Marx, and three locally hired Burmese professional-level staff. I soon discovered, however, that that the police-state nature of the government and the collapsed economy left few possibilities for political and economic reporting. During my year there, the provincial governor refused even to receive me for a courtesy call, and my contacts with other officials were infrequent and non-substantive.

The principal American interest in Burma had become its status as the world's leading producer of opium, which was transformed into heroin and trafficked through Thailand to the United States. However, the poppy fields and heroin labs were all in the mountainous border areas inhabited by hilltribes and not under government control. These areas were off limits for foreigners, and we could learn little about them.

We at the Consulate were the sole resident Americans in Mandalay. The only other diplomatic post was an Indian Consulate, with one officer and his family. It was there to look after the numerous Indian community, mostly merchants who had moved to Burma during the British administration. The European community consisted of three German technicians and their families, who were finishing up a German agricultural aid project that began a few years previously.

I tried to find useful reporting to do, but with little success. My access to local government officials was nil; independent civil society organizations did not exist; and private citizens were afraid to meet with foreigners, especially Americans. There were no functioning private businesses of any consequence. Foreigners were not permitted to travel outside of Mandalay except to Taunggyi, the capital of the Shan State, to Pagan and its ancient ruins, and to Maymyo, a decaying British-era "hill station" a couple of hours drive from Mandalay where colonial officials had gone to escape the oppressive summer heat. It was impossible to gather any information on our primary interest in the region: narcotics production and trafficking.

With such limited possibilities for productive diplomatic work, I struggled to find things to do. I studied Burmese (with mediocre results -- it's a more difficult language to learn than Vietnamese or Thai); I took tennis and golf lessons; and I did lots of reading. The government would not permit ham radio operations, so I revived a childhood interest in philately and acquired some interesting Burmese stamps from the Japanese occupation period.

One of the few good things about our Mandalay experience was the Consul's residence (see picture at the end of this chapter), which included the attached Consulate office. The building dated from the early years of the 20th Century, when it was a "chummery," a bachelor officers quarters, for the Bombay-Burmah Trading Company, which dominated the harvesting and export of teak from the region during the colonial era. The house was built of teak, and it was a spacious, attractive place to live. The compound enclosed about five acres, with lots of bougainvillea and other flowers, maintained by a full-time gardener. We also employed a cook, a "houseboy" for cleaning, and a nanny to help care for Kim and Eva.

Tuy-Cam managed the household and mothered the children, but like me she sometimes struggled to find enough to do. One of her projects was to build a smoker for curing meat, with the help of one of the German technicians. There were few people with whom we could socialize, so we entertained infrequently. We made several family trips to Taunggyi and Maymyo and visited some of the Buddhist temples and other cultural sites near Mandalay.

We hosted several visitors from the Embassy, including our close friends from Vietnam, Joe and Trinh Murphy, who were now stationed in Rangoon. During their visit, we arranged an excursion down the Irrawaddy, the great river that flows from the Himalayas south through the length of Burma to the Bay of Bengal. Early in the morning we boarded a steamer that dated from the days of the British Irrawaddy Flotilla and set off for Pagan. The ship was crowded with people, farm animals, and agricultural cargo, and it stopped at several small towns along the way. We had booked the first class cabin, but we were required to share it with several Buddhist monks who came aboard. It was not a comfortable trip, but it was certainly colorful.

Near sundown, still an hour from Pagan, the boat ran aground on a sandbar in the middle of the river, which was about a mile wide at that point. The captain assured us that there was no cause for alarm, and a sister ship would be along early the next morning to assist. Tuy-Cam and Trinh had packed plenty of food for the trip, and Joe and I had brought along a large cooler full of beer and soft drinks, so we enjoyed a good dinner and impromptu party as we sweated and swatted insects through a long, hot night. The sister ship came as promised and pulled us off the sandbar, so we arrived in Pagan about 8 a.m.

Pagan (now officially spelled "Bagan") was the capital of the first kingdom to govern the territory constituting modern Burma. It flourished between the 11th and 13th Centuries, and was comparable to the contemporary but now better known Cambodian kingdom of Angkor Wat. Some 10,000 Buddhist temples, pagodas, and monasteries were constructed in Pagan, and the remains of more than 2,200 still survive. It's an impressive archeological site, but for me the river voyage and night on the sandbar were more memorable.

Mandalay was our least interesting assignment in the Foreign Service, and we were happy to move to Rangoon in the summer of 1976. My final official report was an assessment of the post's utility, concluding with a recommendation that it be closed. It was, though not for another five years. Bureaucracies move slowly.

Rangoon: Political/Economic Counselor and DCM

The Embassy in Rangoon was staffed by about 30 Americans, including military attachés, U.S. Information Agency public affairs and cultural officers, a Drug Enforcement Agency representative, intelligence personnel, and Marine security guards, as well as the normal contingent of State Department diplomats. A USAID office had been closed in 1972. Despite limited U.S. interests in Burma and strained relations with its government, there was ample work to be done.

My job was Counselor of Embassy for Political and Economic Affairs, supervising three American officers, an American secretary, and five Burmese Foreign Service National employees. I served concurrently as the Mission's Narcotics Coordinator, responsible for coordinating activities of the agencies involved in our "war on drugs," as well as liaison with Burmese officials and oversight of the U.S. Narcotics Control Assistance Program for Burma. My narcotics duties took more of my time than traditional political and economic reporting.

Most of our narcotics assistance, amounting to $6 million per year, was in the form of helicopters for the Burmese Army. This was a case of two mutually suspicious, often hostile countries finding common ground for cooperation. We wanted to stop the flow of heroin into the United States and recognized the need to attack it close to its source. The Burmese were not concerned about our heroin addiction problems, but they recognized that the hilltribe rebels, the principal producers and traffickers of heroin, were dependent on profits from it to finance their rebellion. Thus, we and the Burmese shared an important objective, though for different reasons.

A few months after my transfer to Rangoon, the wife of the DCM (Deputy Chief of Mission) became gravely ill, and he had to curtail his tour of duty to return to Washington. As the next-ranking officer, I became Acting DCM, and I remained so for four months, until the arrival of the new DCM, Ammon Bartley. Ammon had been my boss as Deputy Director of the Vietnam Working Group, and he was a friend as well as mentor. That relationship continued and deepened for the next year, until Ammon developed a brain tumor. Following his evacuation, I again became Acting DCM and remained so for the next seven months, until the end of my assignment in July 1978. Thus, for half of my time in Rangoon, I was Acting DCM as well as Political and Economic Counselor and Narcotics Coordinator. The professional boredom I had suffered in Mandalay was no longer a problem.

The Leadership Role of Ambassadors and DCMs

Readers not familiar with the Foreign Service and American Embassies may need some explanation of the leadership role of Ambassadors and their deputies, since it differs in important ways from their counterparts in business, the military, and elsewhere in government.

Until the middle of the 20th Century, almost all American civilians working for the U.S. government abroad were State Department employees. Beginning in the years after World War II, with America's rise to super-power status and the accelerating process of globalization, more and more government departments and agencies needed to station representatives in foreign countries. Today, State Department personnel constitute only a third of the total American staff at our Embassies and Consulates. At large posts, there may be 25 or more different elements of the U.S. government represented, including the Defense Department, CIA, Commerce, Agriculture, the FBI, Treasury, the Center for Disease Control, the Federal Aviation Administration, the Internal Revenue Service, etc., etc. For State Department staff, the chain of command is clear, from the President through the Secretary of State, the Ambassador, and DCM to the State elements of the Embassy, typically political, economic, management (administration), public diplomacy, and consular affairs sections. But what is the Ambassador's authority over the other sections, the people in the Embassy who don't work for the State Department?

The Ambassador's authority over non-State personnel comes from the Foreign Service Act of 1980, plus a personal letter to each newly-appointed Ambassador from the President. In this letter, the Ambassador is specifically mandated to:

- Be the President's personal representative (NOT the representative of the Secretary of State);
- Represent the whole of the U.S. government and the American people;
- Develop a cohesive, unified U.S. policy toward the host country; and
- Have full authority over all U.S. government agencies, activities, and personnel in the country, along with the right to all information relevant to implementing this mandate.

In theory, the Ambassador's authority is clear; in practice, it is often ambiguous. With email and other modern communication systems, it's easy for the representative of, say, the Treasury Department, to bypass the Ambassador and communicate directly with Treasury Department staff in Washington. For routine matters and in most circumstances, this is of no consequence, and most people understand and comply with the President's mandate. But in situations that are high profile and divisive in Washington, problems can and do arise.

Moreover, Ambassadors have no control over the budgets of non-State agencies at the Embassy, and no control over the careers of their representatives (although a determined and bureaucratically skilled Ambassador can influence both).

The DCM's authority over non-State personnel derives from that of the Ambassador, but since the DCM has lower rank and status, even greater tact and leadership skills are required to exercise it effectively.

As only the Acting DCM in Rangoon, this was a particularly big challenge for me.

Nonetheless, I found my experience as Acting DCM enjoyable and career-enhancing. During my second year in Rangoon, I was promoted to FSO-3, which was equivalent to a full colonel in the Army or a captain in the Navy.

A Failed Coup, and Asylum Request Denied

My most memorable professional adventure in Rangoon came during my second stint as Acting DCM. Tuy-Cam and I were at a dinner party at the home of a French diplomat when I received a telephone call about 9 p.m. from the Embassy duty officer, who happened to be my good friend Joe Murphy of CIA. Joe told me the Marine guard at the Ambassador's residence had reported that a man entered the compound to ask for political asylum and was currently hiding in some bushes near the gate.

Joe picked me up from the dinner and we went to investigate. We induced the man to come out of the bushes and talk. He turned out to be a young Burmese Army captain who had led a plot to assassinate President Ne Win and overthrow the government. The plot had gone awry, and he had come to the Ambassador's house to seek political asylum and our help in getting out of the country.

Joe and I recognized there was nothing the U.S. government could do. We couldn't provide asylum to someone who had just tried to kill the President and carry out a *coup d'état*. On the other hand, the United States had no obligation to help protect the Burmese government, which held hundreds of political prisoners and was unlikely to provide a fair trial to its opponents. Moreover, we thought the captain was probably carrying a pistol, and we didn't want to try to disarm him.

In this case, our best course of action was inaction.

We persuaded the captain to join us in the car, in order to get him away from the Ambassador's residence, and drove around for a few minutes while getting details of his story. Finally, we told him that we couldn't provide any help, and certainly not political asylum. At his request, we let him out of the car near the train station.

The captain was captured the next day and was soon executed. The government newspaper printed a lengthy article about the failed plot and the captain's capture and execution. It described his attempt to get asylum at the Ambassador's residence, and named Joe and me, criticizing us for not turning him over to the police. However, the article did not claim the U.S. was in any way involved in the plot, nor did the government make a formal protest, so the incident had no impact on U.S.-Burmese relations.

Life in Rangoon

With its repressive police state controls, international isolation, pervasive poverty, crumbling infrastructure, and unreliable public utilities and communications services, many foreigners found Rangoon a difficult place to live. However, for Tuy-Cam and me, it was enjoyable. We had an attractive, comfortable house on the shore of a small lake, with four servants to help Tuy-Cam manage it. There was a good American school for Kim and Eva. Food was excellent and cheap.

While there were only a few Burmese who were willing to take the political risk of associating with Americans, Rangoon's large diplomatic community provided an active social life, with several dinners, receptions, and parties every week. We entertained frequently in our house, sometimes with dinners for as many as 60 people. On weekends there were tennis tournaments and parties at the house of Joe and Trinh Murphy, swimming and movies at the Embassy's American club, and occasional excursions to a guest house the Embassy maintained on the remote Arakan coast of the Bay of Bengal, near the frontier with Bangladesh. It offered excellent fishing and a beautiful beach.

I discovered that one of the CIA officers, Floyd Paseman, was a skilled banjo player who shared my love of bluegrass. I honed my meager guitar capability with a Burmese teacher, and Floyd and I joined together with an American who worked for the UN and played lead guitar, and a British Embassy communications technician who played bass and enjoyed American country music, to form what we called the "Lower Irrawaddy People's Bluegrass Music Corporation Number 46." (The name satirized the Soviet-style names the Burmese gave to all their state-owned enterprises.) We had great fun performing at the American club and at a dinner concert Tuy-Cam and I hosted. Our claim to be "The Best Bluegrass Band in Burma" was irrefutable, since we were the only bluegrass band in Burma .

The value of the Burmese currency, the kyat, was very low, and those of us paid in dollars found prices extraordinarily cheap. We were able to purchase hand-carved teak furniture, lacquer and gold-leaf panels, and several antiques including a life-size Buddha statue, all of which are still in our home. Tuy-Cam was also able to acquire some high-quality jewelry -- pearls, jade, sapphires, and rubies -- for a small fraction of what it would have cost in America. These gemstones, one of Burma's few remaining exports, were sold at an annual trade show attended by wholesale buyers from all over the world. The day before the show's opening, the government had a special showing and sale exclusively for foreign diplomats. This was a much-anticipated occasion for the ladies of the diplomatic community. Their husbands were less enthusiastic.

***

The Consul's residence in Mandalay, where we lived in 1975-76. The Consulate office is the small, one-story structure attached on the right.

Tuy-Cam and I, along with Kim and Eva and two of our locally hired Burmese staff members, welcome American folk singer Greg Hildebrandt and his wife to Mandalay. He was on a U.S. Information Agency-sponsored tour to promote American culture.

Attempting (unsuccessfully) to learn to play golf in Mandalay.

Tuy-Cam, with Kim and Eva, visiting Mandalay temple.

Our house in Rangoon. Built of teak, it is on the shore of a small lake in a U.S.-owned residential compound for Embassy staff.

The Lower Irrawaddy People's Bluegrass Music Corporation Number 46, in a June 1978 concert for 60 dinner guests in our house.

****

7.

Fitness, Leadership, and Selection as DCM:

The Army War College, 1978-79

My next assignment was to a year of training at the U.S. Army War College, Carlisle Barracks, Pennsylvania. The State Department sends one or more FSOs to each of the military service war colleges as well as to the National War College and the Industrial College of the Armed Forces. This training is designed to prepare military officers for potential command as generals and admirals, and about one fourth of the graduates achieve flag rank. It's also good preparation for FSOs aspiring to ambassadorial positions. I was delighted to have the opportunity to attend. I recognized that I needed the training, and based on my Vietnam experience I knew I would be comfortable in a military setting. We were provided a small house on the base, which proved to be an ideal environment for us, especially the children.

Carlisle Barracks is the Army's second oldest post (after West Point), and it was used to hold Hessian prisoners during the Revolutionary War. It's near Gettysburg, and the town of Carlisle was occupied briefly by Jeb Stuart's Confederate cavalry on the way to that battle. Today, Carlisle Barracks is a blend of military installation and college campus, with a family-oriented culture. Of all the places we lived during my career, this was among our favorites.

My 233 classmates were mostly Army colonels and senior lieutenant colonels, with a substantial number of comparably ranked officers from the other military services and a few civilians. Almost all of the Army officers had served multiple tours in Vietnam. They recognized that the Army, which by that time (1978-79) was being called "hollow" because of post-Vietnam cutbacks, was in deep trouble, with recruitment difficulties, narcotics problems, and inadequate training.

145

But this was the generation of Colin Powell and others who provided leadership to turn the Army and the other military services around and make them into the outstanding all-volunteer armed forces they became by the 1990s. I learned a lot from my classmates and enjoyed living and working with them.

The War College curriculum was focused on the development and implementation of national security strategy, but the two elements of the program that I found to be of most benefit were physical fitness and leadership.

Physical Fitness

Throughout my youth, I had always been fat -- not quite obese, but substantially overweight. This was partly genetic (many family members have been similarly afflicted); partly caused by growing up on high-calorie Southern comfort food; and partly due to a lack of athletic ability, exacerbated by a polio-weakened leg, that disinclined me to sports and exercise. I had often lost weight by dieting, but always gained back more than I lost, and by the time we were in Burma I was up to 240 pounds. At six feet two, this would have been OK had I been an NFL linebacker; but as a non-exercising diplomat, I was just fat.

Thanks to the warning I received at my annual State Department physical exam in 1978, plus the War College's excellent exercise facilities, the health and fitness elements in the curriculum, and the good example set by my classmates, during my year at Carlisle Barracks I was able to lose weight and keep it off with regular exercise. I've maintained a daily exercise program ever since. In retirement, I intensified it, and I've kept a healthy weight of about 170 for the past several years. Readers who have struggled with weight control will understand my gratitude for this War College experience that changed my life for the better, and probably prolonged it.

Leadership

The other enduring impact of my training at Carlisle was to enhance my leadership skills in preparation for the more senior roles that were soon to come.

Beginning with my election as editor of the Auburn *Plainsman*, I held several positions in which I had executive responsibilities and supervised other people. However, until the War College training, I had never thought of leadership as a discipline, something that could be studied and analyzed and learned, a professional skill that required practice and development. Leadership was not a course that could be taken at Auburn or at Harvard, nor was it part of the training offered by the State Department until the late 1980s. For military officers, however, it has always been a vital part of their training and career development.

The concept of leadership presented at the War College resonated with me, and it was the subject of one of the papers I wrote while there. In the paper, I developed a personal "philosophy of leadership" in which I concluded that leadership's central ingredient, its most important and fundamental element, is the capacity to generate and sustain <u>trust</u>.

Following this foundational leadership training, I continued to study the subject on my own and at the Federal Executive Institute in Charlottesville, and I put what I learned into practice in all my subsequent jobs. As Dean of the Senior Seminar, the State Department's analog to the war colleges, I made leadership a principal element in the curriculum. This was the first time it had been taught at the Foreign Service Institute.[18]

---

[18] For a discussion of my philosophy of leadership, see Annex 3, a much-revised and evolved rendering of the paper I wrote at Carlisle.

Selection as DCM in Chad

In the early spring of 1979, my friend, mentor, and former boss, Ammon Bartley, died from the brain tumor that had developed while he was in Rangoon. His wife, Carmen, asked me to deliver the eulogy at his funeral, and I felt honored to do so. Because of my respect and affection for Ammon, I put my best effort into the speech.

Although I didn't know this until after the service, among the many FSOs present at the funeral was Ron Palmer, who was then the Director of Foreign Service Career Development and Assignments. He had also been a friend of Ammon. Ron chaired a committee that, during the week of the funeral, was in the process of selecting officers to fill DCM positions open that summer. Ron approached me after the service (I had not previously met him), and spoke of his regard for Ammon and his appreciation for my eulogy. He told me I was high on the list of candidates the committee was considering for DCM jobs and implied that I could expect to be selected.

In the Foreign Service, selection for DCM is analogous to selection for battalion or brigade command in the Army: It's a career hurdle that only a minority of officers cross, and successful service as DCM is required for those who aspire to ambassadorial rank. It is impossible to know if I would have gotten my next assignment, as DCM in Chad, in the absence of this chance encounter with Ron Palmer at Ammon's funeral, but odds are good that it played a role. If I were of a more spiritual inclination, I might be tempted to think that Ammon was continuing to mentor me from beyond the grave. But as a secular realist, I expect that it's just another example of the important role of luck in determining the course of my career.

**

Our house on the post at Carlisle Barracks, complete with my ham radio antenna. It was considerably smaller and less elegant than our houses in Burma, but it was the same as provided for all of my military student colleagues and was fully adequate for our needs.

****

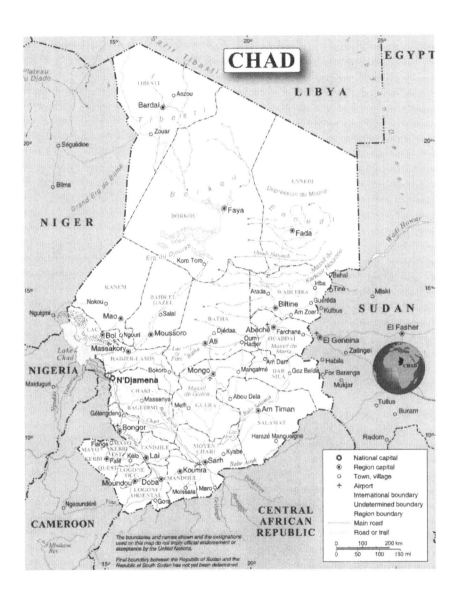

8.

Exciting Introduction to Africa:

Civil War in Chad, 1979-80

During our final weeks at Carlisle Barracks, as I learned more about Chad and my assignment there as DCM, I began to realize some of the challenges that lay ahead. The most immediate was making arrangements for the family.

Family Separation

In February, just two months before my assignment was made, Chad's longstanding civil war between the Muslim north and the largely Christian south had erupted in the capital, N'Djamena. The northern rebel coalition was victorious, and the southern-dominated government disintegrated. The city was extensively damaged in heavy fighting, and all the Christians, nearly half the population, abandoned their homes and fled to the south. Foreigners were not targeted, but living conditions became difficult, and security was precarious. Consequently, the U.S. Embassy (like most others) had evacuated dependents and non-essential staff, though it remained open. The State Department told me that dependents would be allowed to return as soon as possible, but no one knew when that might be.

This meant we would have to get Tuy-Cam and the children a place to live before my departure for what could be a prolonged separation. We bought a small townhouse in Falls Church, a Virginia suburb of Washington, and we moved in right after my graduation.

Challenges of Chad

Chad is a former French colony, south of Libya and west of Sudan. It's twice the size of Texas, but in 1979 it had fewer than 10 million people (14 million in 2015). The northern half of the country falls within the

151

Sahara desert and is populated mostly by nomadic herders. The semi-arid Sahel belt south of the desert stretches across the country from N'Djamena to Sudan and supports patches of dry-land farming as well as herding. Further south is the more densely populated savannah.

The people of the Sahara and Sahel regions are Muslims, of Arab and Berber descent. They constitute slightly more than half of Chad's population. The Bantu people of the south are mostly Christian, both Catholic and Protestant, along with a substantial number of animists. Northerners and southerners are further divided into more than 100 ethnic groups, each with its own language, so French is the *lingua franca* spoken by all educated people. Chad still ranks near the bottom on the UN's Human Development Index in spite of oil exports beginning in 2003. More than 80% of the people are below the poverty line.

Like most other French African colonies, Chad gained independence in 1960. Southern Christians, who were better educated and favored by the French, dominated the new government and its army, but by 1965 a civil war had begun between the government and northern rebels who demanded a greater share of power. This conflict was to persist, in different forms and with varying degrees of intensity, for the next quarter century. The February 1979 fighting that drove the southerners out of N'Djamena brought to power a loose, mutually hostile coalition of northern factions. A provisional government was proclaimed, but it never even began to function. The professional civil servants, almost all Christian, had fled to the south, and the desert warriors now in power were mostly illiterate and had no experience in governance. Political power remained with the leaders of the factions, essentially power-hungry warlords backed by ill-disciplined

152

"*combattants*,"[19] many of them teenagers, brandishing AK-47 assault rifles.

The two largest factions were the FAP (*Forces Armées Populaires*), led by Goukouni Oueddai, and the FAN (*Forces Armées du Nord*), led by Hissene Habré. They were bitter rivals. There were nine other factions, including one that nominally represented southerners, included in the interim coalition government; but none had more than a few dozen armed *combattants* in N'Djamena. FAP and FAN, each with several hundred *combattants*, exercised police power and political control in separate parts of the city. Government offices were occupied by *combattants* and their commanders, some of the latter with ministerial titles, but normal civil government operations such as trash collection, public health, the postal system, etc. ceased to function.

Arrival in N'Djamena

This was the situation when I arrived in N'Djamena on July 25. "Welcome to the civil war," said my predecessor, Tony Dalsimer, on greeting me at the airport. The Ambassador had completed his tour of duty and departed in early July, so Tony was the *Chargé d'affaires ad interim*[20]. I was to have five days of overlap with Tony before he departed and I assumed that role.

On the way to N'Djamena, I had stopped in Paris for a couple of days of consultations at the French Foreign Ministry. The French were by far the most important foreign presence in Chad. They maintained an

---

[19] I'm reluctant to use an English term such as "combatants" or "soldiers," since this might imply a degree of organization, training, and discipline that they totally lacked. They were more akin to an armed mob than to a military force as we normally think of it. So, I will use the French word by which they were known.

[20] This is the diplomatic title of the head of an Embassy during the temporary absence of an Ambassador, and is usually abbreviated in English to just "Chargé."

airbase just north of N'Djamena, which was secured by a battalion of Foreign Legion troops; they financed and operated vital public utilities including electricity, the telephone system, and the water supply; and they dominated trade and commerce. Moreover, there were several hundred French citizens, mostly holdovers from the colonial era, still resident in the country. However, as I learned in Paris and later from their ambassador in N'Djamena, the French had little influence over the Chadian warlords now in control, nor did they have any inclination to take sides in the civil war or to become otherwise engaged militarily except in self-defense. They shared our objectives of a negotiated end to the conflict, a return to political stability, and provision of humanitarian assistance, as well as our frustrations in trying to advance those objectives.

The American Embassy I took over was staffed by 24 Americans -- a third of them from State and CIA, a military attaché and his assistant from Defense, and the rest from USAID. There were more than 100 locally hired staff, all of them Chadian except for four Canadians, who were Baha'i missionaries and long-time Chad residents. A CARE office with three Americans was closely associated with the Embassy because it administered a U.S. food distribution program. Our annual budget was $1.5 million for Embassy operations plus $2.5 million for foreign aid programs.

Like most other small U.S. embassies during this period, N'Djamena had no U.S. Marine guards. For our security, we were dependent on the local government, which is required by the Vienna Convention and centuries of diplomatic tradition to protect foreign diplomats and their property. In view of the current situation in Chad, protection by the government meant that we had no protection at all. This did not seem to create a great deal of concern in Washington, and most of us in N'Djamena saw it as a risk that was our duty to accept as part of our Foreign Service careers, just as military personnel accept the risks associated with their jobs. Today, the State Department is much more sensitive to security threats and provides greater protection for its staff, including posting Marine guards and security officers at almost all Embassies, but the risks can never be fully eliminated.

Conducting Diplomacy with a Non-Functioning Government

The ambassadorial assignment process is lengthy, and the new Ambassador was not to arrive until November. Therefore, I was Chargé for four months. This was a challenge, particularly since I had no previous experience in Africa. I did have experience in armed conflict, however, as well as recent leadership training, and I welcomed this prolonged time as Chargé. It was the sort of job I had been aiming for, and it provided an opportunity to demonstrate that I could handle higher levels of responsibility.

I had meetings with FAP chief Goukouni, who was the interim Prime Minister (later President), FAN chief Habré, who was Minister of Defense, and other government and faction leaders. The Foreign Minister, who would normally have been my principal point of contact, was chief of one of the minor factions and had no real power, so my meeting with him was only a courtesy call. I also had conversations with other diplomats, especially French Ambassador Marcel Beaux, a senior French diplomat with extensive Africa experience including several years in Chad. He provided a memorable caution: "You will find it very difficult to conduct diplomacy with a non-functioning government."

With the information I gathered, together with that collected by my Embassy colleagues, I was able to meet Washington's need for frequent situation reports and analysis, and after a few weeks I recommended some policy updates. My proposals for further cutbacks in USAID programs and staffing, to reduce our exposure and because the government was not sufficiently functional to utilize development assistance, were met with strong opposition by USAID and were not implemented. Also, had my opinion been asked, I would have advised against Washington's decision to permit adult dependents, who had been evacuated in February, to return to N'Djamena. I judged the security situation to be too fragile to have any more Americans at post than absolutely necessary. However, the USAID Director and State Department Africa Bureau officers with extensive Africa experience thought otherwise, so I didn't press my objections.

The new government leaders had all expressed their desire for continued American aid and good relations with the United States. Moreover, the people of N'Djamena and the occupying *combattants* seemed friendly, and there were no signs of anti-American attitudes. Foreigners had never been targeted during the civil war, and the French, the most numerous members of the international community, had not evacuated their citizens. So, a reasonable argument could be made that the threat to foreigners was not high.

On the other hand, there was no police force, the factions (especially FAP and FAN), were mutually hostile and had fought each other in the past, and the city was filled with hundreds of armed, undisciplined *combattants*. The danger, it seemed to me, was not from planned action against us but from random violence, banditry, and becoming "collateral damage" should fighting break out in the city. My experience in Hué had given me a lively appreciation of the impact of urban combat on a civilian population.

The first crisis came when a young Embassy staff member was stopped on his way home by three armed *combattants* who got in his vehicle and forced him to drive to their headquarters. Their objective was probably to requisition a car for their commander. However, the American was deemed uncooperative and was bound and detained at the headquarters.

We learned of this incident about 9 p.m. from one of our local employees who lived near the headquarters. It was in a part of town known to be controlled by FAN, so together with the Embassy driver I set out to find the FAN leader, Defense Minister Habré. We eventually located his house about 11 p.m. and with some difficulty persuaded his security guards to let us in. After contacting some subordinates, Habré acknowledged that an American was indeed being held. I explained the grave potential implications if our man, who had a diplomatic passport, were not promptly released. The best educated of the northern leaders, Habré indicated that he understood and would resolve the problem. We departed his house, and the captive and his vehicle were released as promised.

I saw this armed detention of an American diplomat as an indicator of the danger we faced and a portent of worse to come. Washington seemed to view his prompt release, unharmed, as an indicator that the danger level was not high and could be managed.

Two weeks later, a USAID American lost his vehicle in an armed hijacking. Also, the *combattants* began to requisition (*i.e.*, steal) food from the CARE warehouse, effectively ending our program to feed refugees and war victims. Other embassies experienced similar problems. Gunfire could be heard in the streets almost every night. I imposed a 6 p.m. curfew on non-essential travel. In mid-October, the government, with French assistance, established a mobile police unit designed to protect the diplomatic community, and I lifted the curfew.

Life in N'Djamena

Although I enjoyed my job, N'Djamena was not a pleasant place to live. The biggest problem was separation from Tuy-Cam and the children; but difficult living conditions as well as the security threat made me realize that I did not want to bring my family, even if the State Department authorized them to come.

Since it's on the edge of the Sahara, N'Djamena is hot, well above 100 degrees Fahrenheit on most days, cooling to the mid-80s only for a couple of hours just before dawn. The DCM residence, a spacious villa immediately adjacent to the Ambassador's residence, was air-conditioned, but during the time I was there electricity was available only from 10 a.m. to 1 p.m. and again from 6 p.m. to 2 a.m. With no air conditioning or fans, the house quickly became insufferably hot. I had a cook and a housekeeper, and there was a swimming pool in the yard, so I sometimes had guests for lunches and pool parties on weekends and holidays. There was only one restaurant in town where the food was safe to eat. I usually had dinner at home alone, listened to the news on *Radio France Internationale*, VOA, and BBC, read for an hour or so, and went to bed early.

I also got up early, to continue the regular exercise routine I had begun at Carlisle Barracks. I took advantage of the cooler morning air to jog along the street in front of the house, which was lined with the homes of diplomats, expatriate businessmen, and a few wealthy Chadians. Once, as I was returning from one of these runs, I heard the sound of gunfire behind me and saw puffs of dust from bullets hitting the road ahead. I set a personal speed record for the rest of the run.

Life outside of work became less boring with the arrival of my air freight in September. In addition to some food supplies, it contained my hi-fi equipment and collection of bluegrass records, as well as my ham radio gear.

Ham operation required a license from the Chadian government. When I located the relevant office, I found it closed and without any staff, so I sought out the Minister of Communications. The leader of one of the minor factions in the coalition, he spoke little French and had no experience in telecommunications or knowledge of ham radio. I explained it as best I could and asked permission to operate. He nodded in seeming assent, but I doubt that he understood much of what I was saying. Nonetheless, I decided that a "memo to the files" recording this conversation would serve as my official ham license for Chad, and I proceeded to assemble my station in an unoccupied office of the Embassy. While this was highly irregular, and would likely not have been approved had I requested permission from Washington, I reasoned that the Embassy was sovereign U.S. territory, I had a valid U.S. ham license, and I was in charge of the Embassy...so why not? I was able to enjoy my hobby for the rest of my time in Chad.

Arrival of Ambassador and Home Leave

Ambassador Don Norland and his wife, Pat, arrived in November, 1979. He was previously Ambassador in Lesotho, and he was an experienced, capable professional diplomat. We quickly established a close working relationship, and both Pat and Don became good friends. As much as I had enjoyed my time as Chargé, I needed a break from the stress of the past four months. After Don completed his introductory calls and was settled in, I left on December 12 for a month of consultations and home leave in Washington.

Tuy-Cam, the children and I enjoyed the holiday season with friends and family. I briefed officials responsible for Chad in State, Defense, CIA, and USAID, and tried, with some success, to give them a deeper appreciation of the non-functional nature of the Chadian government and the chaotic situation that prevailed in N'Djamena.

The State Department's Africa Bureau agreed that the security threat and lack of a school made the return of minor dependents unlikely in the foreseeable future. Since the normal length of an unaccompanied assignment was one year, they accepted my request to end my tour in Chad the following summer. We identified some potential DCM jobs elsewhere in Africa, and they began the reassignment process.

I returned to N'Djamena on January 15 to find the situation little changed. The newly-created police unit, even though supported by the

French, was crippled by internal conflict and had proved incapable of controlling the mounting lawlessness. Security was again deteriorating, with looting and banditry extending to private homes and foreign-owned businesses as well as public property. Moreover, political tension was rising among the government factions, and additional *combattants* were moving into the city. At the Embassy, we burned most of our classified files, updated and exercised our emergency evacuation plan, and prepared to further reduce our staff. CARE closed down its operations, and some of the remaining French citizens began to leave.

Combat and Evacuation

In the pre-dawn hours of March 21, we awoke to the sound of gunfire just outside the Ambassador's and DCM's residences. Such sounds in the night were no longer unusual in N'Djamena, but this was more intense, widespread, and prolonged than before. The Ambassador and I consulted, and he began calling French contacts while I conducted our regular 7 a.m. staff radio check, telling everyone to remain in their homes and not go to the Embassy. The gunfire continued all morning, and by noon we were able to determine that there was combat throughout the city between the forces of FAP and FAN. The Embassy was located downtown in an area of particularly heavy fighting, and there was no way we could reach it without grave danger of being shot, so we instructed the staff to "stand fast" in their homes until further notice.

Without access to the Embassy, our only means of communicating with Washington was a short-wave radio installed in the Ambassador's residence for just such contingencies. Our communications technician lived in another part of town, so as the only person present with the technical skills to operate this radio, I became our communicator. Through this link, we were able to provide situation reports to the State Department.

As the day wore on, the chatter of rifles and machine guns was supplemented by the boom of mortar, rocket, and recoilless rifle fire. I drew on my Vietnam experience to tell our staff members, none of whom had ever been under fire in a combat zone, to resist the impulse to flee, and to make a shelter in an interior part of the house, where they would be much safer than anywhere outside.

Our plan, which had been coordinated with the French, was that in the event of the outbreak of hostilities, Americans and other foreigners would drive to the French military base in convoys, escorted by French military vehicles. However, at least a brief ceasefire was an essential part of this plan. The local telephone system continued to function (even though electricity and water had been cut), so it was possible for Don Norland and Ambassador Beaux to contact the FAP and FAN leaders to try to arrange a ceasefire. Nonetheless, combat continued into the evening. After a few hours of respite after midnight, it resumed the morning of March 22 and continued throughout the day. Several American homes, including the Ambassador's residence, were hit by errant small arms and mortar fire, but everyone remained in their improvised shelters when the fighting became heavy, and there were no injuries. There were a few close calls, however.

The night passed in relative quiet, but heavy firing again resumed the morning of March 23. A one-hour ceasefire had finally been accepted by the faction leaders, to begin at 10 a.m., but continued gunfire indicated that it was not implemented. By mid-afternoon, the firing had diminished, and we determined, together with the French, that the best course of action was for foreign residents to form small convoys and make their way to the French base as best they could without the planned military escorts. This process began about 4 p.m.

The nine of us who were in the Ambassador's and DCM's residences set off in three cars, each displaying a white flag. We were joined by a couple of French neighbors as we drove though the devastated city, and we reached the safety of the French base in less than half an hour. By nightfall, all of the American staff, plus our Canadian local employees, were on the base.

The French offered us a choice of evacuation by air to Douala, Cameroon, or by land via an escorted convoy to a ferry that would take people and vehicles across the Chari River to Cameroon. Since we did not have our private vehicles or, as did several staff members, dogs to take along, the Norlands and I chose the aerial alternative. After dinner in the French mess hall and a hot night on cots set up in an empty warehouse, we boarded a French cargo plane the next afternoon, March 24. There was a U.S. Consulate in Douala, and the staff helped us arrange onward commercial flights to Washington.

Reflections

The Embassy staff had responded to the crisis with patience and courage, and thanks to the French military presence, everyone was evacuated safely. We were fortunate, in view of the intense combat and chaos in N'Djamena, to have avoided any injuries or losses beyond our possessions that had to be left behind. (The French told us to bring no more than one suitcase to the base.)

In retrospect, it is clear that we should have closed the Embassy, or at least drawn down to a skeleton staff of no more than half a dozen, well before the situation forced a hazardous evacuation under combat conditions. Neither our interests in Chad nor our ability to affect the situation was sufficiently great to justify the risks.

After our departure, the conflict persisted until the FAN forces prevailed and Habré established himself as President in 1982. His dictatorial, corrupt, and brutal rule continued until he was overthrown in a 1990 coup. He fled the county and lived unmolested in Senegal for 25 years, until a campaign by some of his victims resulted in a lengthy trial by an international tribunal. In 2016, he was convicted of "crimes against humanity" and sentenced to life imprisonment.

Today, Chad remains one of the poorest and most conflict-prone countries in the world.[21]

Safely back in Washington, I wrote some after-action reports for the Department, filed a reimbursement claim for my abandoned possessions, enjoyed the reunion with Tuy-Cam and the children, took some vacation time, and prepared for my next assignment, as Permanent Chargé in Benin.

Left: Serving drinks at a party in my house. Because of the security situation, the household staff went home before dark, so we had no servants in the evening.
Right: Greeting the Nigerian Chargé at their national day reception.

***

---

[21] For a more detailed account of the Embassy's ordeal in Chad, see Patricia Norland's article, "Evacuation from N'Djamena," *Foreign Service Journal*, July/August, 1980.

At the Chinese national day reception. To my right: East German Ambassador, an interpreter, Mayor of Ndjamena, Chinese Ambassador.

Ndjamena and the Chari River, which was reduced to a trickle of water except during the brief rainy season.

****

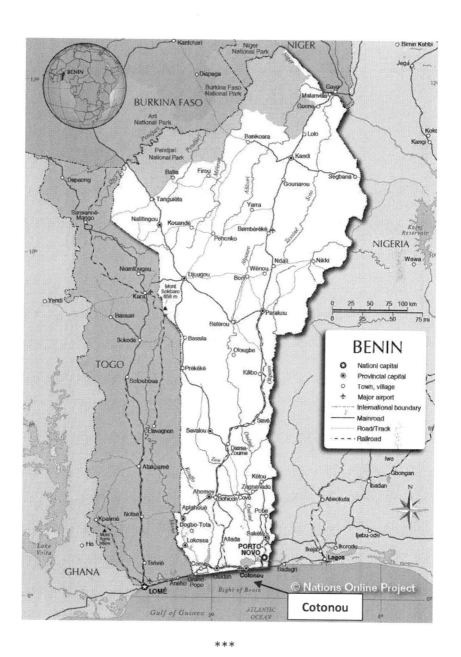

***

9.

A Police State Poorly Policed:

Benin, 1980-82

n January, 1980, just a couple of weeks after I had returned to N'Djamena from home leave, I was offered an assignment beginning the following summer in Benin, as "Chief of Mission, with the rank of Permanent Chargé." This was the functional equivalent of an ambassadorship, and I was pleased to receive such a plum job early in my career, at age 39.

The Deputy Chief of Mission is designated as "Chargé d'affaires ad interim" when the Ambassador is temporarily out of the country, or to fill the gap between the Ambassador's departure and the arrival of a new Ambassador. A Permanent Chargé is appointed only in unusual circumstances: when an Ambassador has been withdrawn and we have decided, normally as an expression of strong political displeasure with the government concerned, to downgrade the level of our representation by not sending a replacement. This was the case with Benin, when the U.S. Ambassador was withdrawn in 1976 because of the government's harsh anti-American propaganda attacks and its nationalization of U.S. companies without compensation.

Benin Overview

A former African kingdom and French colony known as Dahomey, Benin is located on the Atlantic Ocean in what is sometimes called the "armpit of West Africa," formed by the Gulf of Guinea. It is only six degrees north of the equator, and the climate is hot and humid all year, with temperatures in the high 90s, rarely falling below 80 even at night. Its population was just over three million in 1980 (11 million in 2015), divided into 40 ethnic groups. French is the official language and serves as the *lingua franca*, enabling people to communicate with each other as well as with the outside world.

Beninese are divided by religion as well as ethnicity and language, with 43% Christians and 24% Muslims, the latter concentrated in the north. Vodun (Voodoo), of which Benin is the birthplace, is the professed religion of 17%, but its influence can be seen among Christians and Muslims as well. One of the country's most interesting tourist destinations is the town of Ouidah, the spiritual capital of Vodun as well as the site of one of Africa's historically most important slave-trading ports.

From the 17th to the 19th Century, the coastal area of modern Benin and Togo was called by Europeans the "Slave Coast." Dahomey and other constantly warring kingdoms of the region sold hundreds of thousands of their war captives to European slave traders for transport to the Americas. This trade declined in the 19th Century, and the French finally ended it when they made Dahomey part of French West Africa in the 1890s.

Dahomey was granted independence in 1960, changing its name to Benin in 1975. It was (and remains) poor, with per capita GDP currently at $745, literacy at less than 30%, high infant and child mortality rates, and few natural resources.

For reasons related to ethnic balancing, the nominal capital of Benin is Porto Novo, but Cotonou is the seat of government, the economic center, and the largest city as well as the site of all foreign embassies.

Rise of the Marxist-Leninist Police State

During its first 12 years of independence, Dahomey became a model of African political instability, with collapsing governments and frequent coups, until a group of young military officers led by Lt. Col. Mathieu Kerekou overthrew the feuding politicians in 1972. These officers managed to achieve stability, with Kerekou as President, but as former French Army sergeants with little education, they were ill-equipped to govern. Their purge of the French-era elite left a vacuum that was soon filled by Paris-trained Marxist radicals, who gained effective intellectual command of the regime.

In 1974, the government embraced Marxism-Leninism, and the "People's Republic of Benin" was proclaimed. Private companies were nationalized; military and security ties were developed with the Soviets, the Chinese, and other Communist countries; and a Leninist-model government was established. The regime's totalitarian ambitions were tempered, however, by its incompetence and corruption. We called it a police state poorly policed.

Under these conditions, relations with the West, especially the United States, deteriorated. My instructions from the State Department on taking charge of the Embassy were to monitor activities of the Soviets and other Communist bloc countries (this was during the height of the Cold War); look for opportunities to improve relations; protect the few remaining American interests in Benin; and maintain a low profile.

The size of the Embassy and its programs had been reduced since the mid-1970s, but our presence seemed to me to be still unduly large in view of our limited interests and the regime's extremely anti-American posture. There were 13 American and 26 Beninese direct-hire employees, plus six American and 30 Beninese contractors. Active AID projects totaled $10 million. There was a USIA library and cultural exchange program, and a Peace Corps program with 80 Volunteers.

Life in Cotonou -- A Big House and Ham Radio

We moved into the ambassadorial residence, which had been newly constructed in the mid 1970s. There were four big bedrooms, and the huge entertainment area downstairs had marble floors, which Kim and Eva sometimes used for roller skating. It was on the ocean, but separated from the beach by a street and about 300 yards of marsh that, we were warned, was infested by poisonous snakes. Nonetheless, we had a nice view of the ocean from the second floor balcony. We also benefitted from a sea breeze that ameliorated the tropical heat and humidity. We put the swimming pool to good use, especially for the children.

Labor was cheap in Benin, and as Chief of Mission I received an "official residence allowance," so we could afford an adequate staff for the house. There was a cook, a housekeeper, a laundry man, and a gardener. I had an official sedan and driver, and we imported a Peugeot for Tuy-Cam and to use on weekends.

The house and its seaside location were ideal for ham radio. Its large, flat, easily-accessible concrete roof served as a platform on which to erect 30-foot bamboo poles to support several wire antennas. I took advantage of my initial calls on the Foreign Minister and President Kerekou to request their help in expediting a Beninese ham license, and in less than a month it came.

I soon had my station on the air with one of the most powerful signals coming out of Africa. Since I was the only active ham in Benin, other hams throughout the world were eager to make contact and get my "QSL card" to earn awards and points in international contests. My "QSL manager," Ghis Penny, a Belgian ham I had met on the air while I was in Chad, took care of all the paperwork associated with filling out and mailing several thousand of these cards during my time in Chad, Benin, and subsequently in Burundi and Niger. Ghis also visited Cotonou and Bujumbura to operate my station, and he and I became good friends. Like my Thai ham friend Apichart, he credits me with being a mentor. His visits with us inspired him to seek an international career, and he became a telecommunications technician on the staff of the United Nations.

French Schools

There was no American or other English-language school in Cotonou, so arranging schooling for Kim and Eva was a challenge. They had completed third and second grade, respectively, in Falls Church during the year I was in Chad, and they spoke no French. At this age, however, learning a new language is not a major problem. We found that there was a large French school in Cotonou, sponsored by the French government, and we decided to enroll them there. We arrived in Cotonou in June, a couple of months before the fall term was to begin. We hired a French lady to give them lessons, and Tuy-Cam arranged for some francophone playmates. They recall that the first French word they learned was "*serpent*," because the instructor showed them one.

When we took them to the school office, however, we were shocked to be told that they couldn't be enrolled, because they didn't speak French. This was a big problem. A Beninese school was not a viable option because of health and security concerns, and it would be extremely difficult to do home schooling, as my time was fully occupied with work, and Tuy-Cam had no experience with the American education system.

My solution was to go immediately to the French Ambassador. I explained the problem, and pointed out that in Rangoon we had accepted many children of French Embassy staff members as students at the American school. I also noted that there are many other capitals around the world where there are American schools but no French schools, and we always accepted the children of French diplomats. I concluded with a suggestion that French failure to reciprocate would not be welcome news at the State Department, which sponsored and partially financed the American Embassy schools.

The Ambassador graciously and promptly intervened with the school authorities, who then agreed to accept Kim and Eva as students.

The first few weeks in the French school were stressful for the girls. There was no special help for non-francophone students -- it was total immersion, sink or swim. Also, the French practices of corporal punishment and humiliation were different from what the girls were used to, and would probably have been illegal in the United States. However, they learned rapidly, and by the end of three months they were fluent in French and able to keep up with the academic program.

Kim and Eva remained in French schools for the next six years, in Cotonou, in Bethesda at the Lycée Rochambeau (during the period I was in Washington awaiting confirmation as Ambassador to Burundi), and at the French Embassy school in Bujumbura. They received a sound education and became bilingual, a skill they retained as adults.

Social Life, Sickness, and a Parental Visit

In spite of strained U.S. relations with the Beninese government, we had an active social life in Cotonou, both official and personal. We were responsible for hosting three July 4 receptions. These were major events, with more than 300 guests, and they required much work by Tuy-Cam and the household staff as well as by all the employees at the Embassy; but they were an important means of introducing ourselves and making professional contacts. All of the 30-plus Embassies in Cotonou gave comparable receptions for their national days. I soon came to recognize these and similar events hosted by the government and international organizations as part of my work routine, not as social occasions to be enjoyed (although occasionally they were enjoyable).

There was also a lot of informal entertaining among the American Embassy staff and within the diplomatic community, with swim and tennis parties, casual dinners, holiday events, excursions to beaches and other points of interest such as the slave-trade fort at Ouidah and the pre-colonial capital of the Dahomey kingdom at Abomey. We developed several good friends, including the West German Ambassador and his Scottish wife, and the manager of a new Sheraton hotel that was under construction near our residence.

One memorable social event was a dinner in the presidential palace for all the chiefs of diplomatic missions, hosted by President Kerekou. Many dishes were served including some dark meat I didn't recognize. When I asked a government official seated beside me what it was, he replied that it was "agouti." Not wishing to display my ignorance, I accepted this as sufficient explanation, although I had never heard of this animal, and proceeded to eat a generous serving. It tasted OK. On the way home I asked my driver what an "agouti" might be, to which he responded, "*Oh, monsieur, c'est le rat!*" Unfortunately "*rat*" means the same thing in French as it does in English. I don't know if the violent sickness I suffered soon after I got home was due to the rat or something else I ate at the dinner, or if the cause was psychological as well as bacterial, but I was ill all night. I later learned that agouti is a large field rat, the size of a rabbit, which is a delicacy in West Africa.

In general, however, we all stayed healthy in Benin, in spite of the high risk of infectious disease. The only exception was a malaria attack that I suffered, even though I was religiously taking the prophylactic prescribed by the State Department Medical Bureau. I had never before felt so much pain and discomfort, and never experienced such sickness again until my second malaria attack many years later, when we were in Niger. I gained an appreciation of why malaria is such a terrible disease as well as why the discovery of quinine was so historically important in encouraging European exploration and settlement in Africa. Quinine injections ended both of my attacks within 24 hours of finding a doctor to diagnose the problem and provide them.

A highlight of our time in Benin was a two-week visit by my parents. They had never been out of the United States, and it was an exciting experience for them. During the ride from the airport to the residence, I asked my mother what she thought of Cotonou so far. Looking more than a little shocked, she stammered, "Well, I...I guess it's OK, but...but the people here, they...THEY'RE ALL BLACK!" It's hard to imagine what she was expecting Africans to look like. But she and my father were soon able to adjust to the shock of an environment far different from anything they had experienced, and they mostly enjoyed the visit, including an introduction to diplomatic social life and a three-day trip to a game park in northern Benin. By the time they left, Mother was wearing a *bubou*, a traditional African dress.

Aligning Policies, Projects, and Presence with U.S. Interests

Following are excerpts from my first annual performance evaluation in Benin, prepared by the Deputy Assistant Secretary of the State Department Africa Bureau, Lannon Walker, in April 1981:

> Benin is a small sliver of a country of minor strategic or economic importance to the U.S. In the rush of events, Washington policymakers tend to allocate little attention to the specifics of our bilateral relations. Programs initiated long ago and under different circumstances roll along with little evaluation or assessment of how they serve our national interests. Our Chief of Mission in Cotonou must provide the kind of reporting that Washington can use to formulate a rational policy. Jim has done just that.
>
> Within two months of his arrival, he completed an assessment of the situation in Benin and involved the entire country team in the development of revised goals and objectives flowing from it. As the situation evolved over the following months, and with the installation of the new U.S.

Administration [Reagan], Jim developed a revised U.S. policy which will involve a major reorientation of U.S. activities. His reports are incisive and have focused U.S. Government attention on what we should be doing in Benin given U.S. global and country-specific interests....

Bullington has brought the AID program into closer harmony with U.S. interests and policy. His recommendations...have resulted in savings of well over half a million dollars in canceled or revised AID projects. He has also taken the initiative in recommending cancellation of an inappropriate and wasteful $20 million World Bank project....

He exercised good judgment in persuading [the Department's Foreign Buildings Operations Bureau] that its plan to spend $5 million [about $13 million in 2016 currency] to build a new Embassy chancery in Cotonou was unjustified in a country where U.S. interests are so limited....He has been consistently right in his judgments about Benin's politics and appropriate U.S. actions. He has maintained an unusually balanced perspective in very tough circumstances.

Jim has an active leadership style, making things happen rather than merely reacting to developments.

I had the opportunity in Chad and Benin to practice the leadership principles I learned at the Army War College.

The performance evaluation form has a work requirements section, which I drafted and the Department approved. My specific objectives for the following year were to:

- Increase production of information and analysis about the presence and activities of the Soviets, Cubans, Libyans, and other hostile elements.

- Conduct an orderly phase-out of economic assistance activities except for limited Peace Corps and food distribution programs.
- Present our point of view on international issues to Beninese leaders, and make clear that continued Beninese alignment with the Soviets has an adverse impact on relations with us.
- Maintain a low U.S. profile in Benin and remain vigilant in terms of security.

The Thanksgiving Crisis

On Thanksgiving Day, 1981, our communications technician and a visiting regional technician who arrived from Monrovia that day to repair our generator, went to a dinner party at the Public Affairs Officer's home. On leaving the party about 9 p.m., they made a wrong turn on a road that led to a Beninese military camp. There was a small sign on the road saying no entry after 6 p.m., but it was not visible at night (!); and there was no barricade. The Beninese soldiers later claimed they had shouted and motioned for them to stop, but whatever the details, they shot into the vehicle. Our communicator was wounded in the foot and was taken to the hospital. The incident took place near the Embassy, and one of our Beninese guards, learning that Americans were involved, called the Administrative Officer at home. He arrived on the scene about 10 p.m. to find our communicator gone and the generator repairman under arrest. After an unsuccessful effort to escort the repairman away, he called me, and we assembled the staff at the Embassy.

The most immediate problem was the wounded communicator, so I sent the Consul to the hospital where he had been taken. He arrived just in time to dissuade the doctors from amputating the injured foot.

The next problem was to establish communications with Washington or a neighboring U.S. Embassy so we could report what had happened and call for help. This was not easy, since the wounded communicator was the only staff member who could operate our telecommunications system. We tried our "emergency and evacuation" radio, which was in the Embassy for such contingencies, but no one at the neighboring posts with which it was capable of communicating was listening at that time of night (although they should have been). When it became evident that we were not getting any response to our calls, I went home to my ham radio station. Within minutes I had established contact with a ham in New York. I had him call the State Department Operations Center to relay the basic facts of our situation and request them to contact Embassy Lagos with instructions to listen for us on the emergency radio.

When I returned to the Embassy -- by this time it was after midnight -- we were able to establish contact with Lagos. We reported what had happened and asked for the Regional Medical Officer, a replacement communicator, and the Regional Security Officer to come the next morning. (It's only a three-hour drive from Lagos to Cotonou.) With nothing further to be done, we all went home to get some rest.

In the morning our reinforcements from Lagos arrived. The first order of business was what to do about our communicator. Although they had arrested and jailed his companion, the Beninese had neglected to post any guards at the hospital. Perhaps they thought that in view of his condition he wasn't going anywhere, or perhaps they were just negligent. Thus it was no problem for the Consul and our doctor to remove him from the hospital, put him in the doctor's van, and take him to Lagos. He was flown to a U.S. military hospital in Germany that evening. After 18 months of reconstructive operations there and in the U.S., he regained fairly good use of the foot. The Beninese Foreign Minister criticized me severely for having him taken out of the country without permission of the Government. I did not apologize.

Our attention next turned to the jailed repairman. We managed to locate him, in the central jail, and to establish consular access. I first tried to deal with the military authorities at the camp, since they were the people who had arrested him, in hopes that the Beninese would realize they had no right to imprison an American official with a diplomatic passport, and that they might agree to settle the matter quietly, without raising it to the political level. The military officers made clear, however, that the affair was out of their hands and that his release could only be ordered by President Kerekou.

The following day I made the first of many attempts to see Kerekou or at least the Foreign Minister. However, I was never able to get beyond minor officials in the Foreign Ministry. I was cut off from the decision-making levels of the government. They simply refused to see me.

Next, I sent the first of several diplomatic notes, which grew stronger in tone as the days wore on. I also enlisted the assistance of my diplomatic colleagues, particularly the French, German, and Nigerian Ambassadors and the United Nations Resident Representative. Since I had no access to senior Beninese, I needed their help to find out what was going on within the government concerning the affair, and, most importantly, to make sure our message about potential consequences got through: In the wake of the recent taking of our diplomats as hostages in Tehran, and since the repairman had done nothing wrong other than taking a wrong turn on a poorly-marked road at night, the U.S. government would not tolerate the prolonged jailing of one of its diplomats by the People's Republic of Benin.

After a full week had gone by without any response whatsoever from the Beninese, I advised, and the Department agreed, that we inform the government of the "suspension" of our USAID program and withdraw the Embassy's USAID officer and the American technicians who were there to implement our major project. The Department also concurred with my proposal to begin preparations for evacuating all Americans except for myself, the Consul, and the communicator, as we could no longer count on the government to assure our safety.

Finally, I asked that we appeal to Benin's principal aid donors and its neighbors to intervene with Kerekou on our behalf. Such appeals accordingly went out to France, Germany, Nigeria, Niger, and Togo.

The second week of the affair was occupied with continued futile efforts to approach the government directly, diplomatic maneuvers in Cotonou and abroad, and evacuation preparations. We destroyed all our classified material and began packing. Tuy-Cam and the children went to stay with the German Ambassador and his wife, and I moved in with the Consul. Our relocations were because of an assassination threat, of presumed Libyan origin, which was relayed to me by the Egyptian Ambassador. It was probably not a serious threat, but we couldn't ignore it.

As the second week wore on with our man still in jail and the Beninese still stonewalling, we set December 13 as "D-Day" for the evacuation.

On December 10, however, the French Ambassador told me that President Mitterand had been in touch with Kerekou and that Kerekou had agreed to release our man. We later learned that Kerekou had also received messages on the affair from the Presidents of Nigeria and Togo and the West German Foreign Minister. This concerted high-level diplomatic offensive evidently made Kerekou realize that it would not be in his interest to continue heeding his Soviet advisers who, we had been informed, were calling for the repairman to be tried as a spy.

The following day, the Beninese released their prisoner into the "custody" of the Nigerian Ambassador, with the agreement that he would stay in the Ambassador's residence until the government had completed its "investigation" into the affair. This was nothing more than a face-saving way for the Beninese to back down, since it would be unthinkable for them to re-arrest the repairman and forcibly remove him from the Nigerian Ambassador's residence. Also, Kerekou and the Foreign Minister finally agreed to see me. The meeting was far from cordial, but both sides were obliged to be constrained: the Beninese because they realized they had made an error and were forced to back down, and me because we still didn't have our man out of the country, and there were other Americans they could jail if they wished. But we had won our point.

It was another week before the Beninese arranged a curious ceremony at the Nigerian Embassy, in which they pretended to transfer the repairman from the custody of the Nigerian Ambassador to my custody. I then drove him straight to the border and turned him over to our people from Lagos who met us there.

The evacuation was called off. The Department at first wanted to reinstitute our major USAID project, but I successfully argued that it should remain suspended. Otherwise, I said, the radical faction within the government, which had long been involved in a power struggle with a more moderate group, would be strengthened, having demonstrated that they could kick the Americans around with impunity.

Crisis Aftermath

While a gradual phasing down of our presence and projects in Benin was already underway before the Thanksgiving crisis, in a further policy review we decided to:

- Suspend indefinitely all remaining USAID development projects;
- Close USIA and the American cultural center; and
- Cut the number of Peace Corps Volunteers from 80 to 40; but to
- Keep the Embassy open, primarily because of its value in gathering intelligence on the Soviet bloc and Libya.

Our tough response during the crisis and in subsequently implementing more sanctions produced not redoubled hostility from the Beninese but rather a reduction of their anti-American propaganda, renewed respect, and even a few friendly overtures. In April, the internal power struggle was resolved with the replacement of several of the leading radicals by moderates. We were pleased that the radical Foreign Minister, our principal nemesis, was replaced by a former Ambassador to Washington and Bonn who began his tenure by calling for the turning of a new page in U.S.-Benin relations. He attended our July 4 reception and even sent a pair of Foreign Ministry officials to accompany the family and me to the Lagos airport when we departed for home.

Another positive development was the government's sudden agreement, after two years of unresponsiveness to our pressure, to pay a $4 million dollar debt to a U.S. construction company, on which it had defaulted. The company had insured the project with OPIC (Overseas Private Investment Corporation, a U.S. government agency that insures exports of American companies to protect them from such defaults). The U.S. taxpayer would have been responsible for the debt if the Beninese government didn't pay.

While the process took several years, this April 1982 government shake-up marked the beginning of Benin's abandonment of Marxism and movement to democracy. In 1990, a new constitution was adopted and the country's name was changed to the Republic of Benin, dropping "People's." Kerekou lost the presidency in a 1991 election, and several successful democratic elections have subsequently been held, most recently in March 2016. While still far from prosperous, the country has recovered from economic collapse, foreign donors (including the United States) and private sector investors have returned, and annual GDP growth has exceeded five percent for the past decade.

Although it's impossible to prove, I believe that our strong stance against the radicals in 1980-82 contributed to this positive outcome.

Other happy outcomes from our time in Benin were that the Embassy was given a Group Meritorious Honor Award, and I was given a performance pay bonus as well as promotion into the Senior Foreign Service with the rank of Counselor (equivalent to Brigadier General). Although I had been under consideration for an ambassadorship even before the Thanksgiving affair, my performance under pressure and success in resolving the crisis assured that I would get one.

Bullington family at home in Cotonou, October 1980.

The Ambassadorial residence and pool, Cotonou.

***

Inaugurating a Peace Corps school project, 1981.

My ham radio QSL card from Benin, picturing a front view of the
residence and my visiting Belgian QSL manager, Ghis Penny.

***

Installing my ham antenna on the residence roof, with help from Embassy communications technician Larry Edwards.

Demonstrating ham radio to (left to right) the German Ambassador, the Beninese Communications Minister, and my administrative assistant, Pat Dorsey, during a dinner party at the residence.

***

Greeting the Foreign Ministry Director of American
Affairs and his deputy at July 4 reception, 1982.

With Foreign Minister, left, during Beninese and
U.S. national anthems at July 4 reception, 1982.

****

10.

Ambassador to Burundi, 1983-86

After our return from Cotonou in August 1982, we moved into an apartment in Bethesda. The reason for choosing suburban Maryland rather than northern Virginia, where we had previously lived, was to be near the Lycée Rochambeau, a French government-sponsored school for the Washington area. I expected another assignment in Francophone Africa, and we wanted to keep Kim and Eva in the French education system.

When I reported for duty, I learned that the Department had proposed me to the White House as its top candidate to be Ambassador to Burundi. I also learned that nothing was final until the White House had made its decision, at which time I would receive a call from the President. The decision normally took a few months, I was told; and after the President's call it would still be necessary to have a Senate Foreign Relations Committee hearing, followed by Senate confirmation, as well as to obtain *agrément* to my appointment from the Burundi government. The whole process was likely to last at least six months, even if there were no problems.

New York Interlude

I needed something to do while the nomination moved forward, so I was assigned to the U.S. Mission to the United Nations in New York as a Senior Advisor during the annual General Assembly meeting, which lasted from mid-September to mid-December. I had never spent time in New York, nor had I ever worked with the UN, so I thought this would be a good learning experience. My job was to be the Mission's Africa expert, report on Africa-related issues, and lobby African delegations on votes of interest to us. Also, I sometimes served as the American representative on UN committees, and I drafted speeches and statements for the U.S. Ambassador to the UN, Jeanne Kirkpatrick.

185

It was, as I expected, a good learning experience, but I didn't find it pleasant. My opinion of the effectiveness of the UN in dealing with the world's problems, never high, fell even further as I listened to rambling speeches and read mountains of paper that were destined to have no impact on reality. An example was the endless, bitter wrangling over commemorating the upcoming (in 10 years) 500th anniversary of Columbus' discovery of America. The Italians and Spanish wanted to honor it; most of the Latin Americans wanted to condemn it as the beginning of colonialism; and the Scandinavians wanted to unmask it as a fraud, since Leif Erikson got there first.

While there were occasional substantive discussions and constructive initiatives, I considered most of what went on at the General Assembly to be a waste of time and resources.

My living conditions in New York were also unpleasant. My government per diem allowance was insufficient to cover expenses, even though I was staying at a third-rate Manhattan hotel in a closet-like room with a bed that pulled down from the wall, and eating mostly hot dogs, bagels, and Chinese take-out food. I was too busy at work to have time to enjoy the city's cultural attractions, even those few I might have been able to afford. My favorite times in New York were Friday evenings when I made my way to Penn Station to board the Amtrak train for Washington and weekends with the family.

This redneck hillbilly was definitely not suited for life in New York.

The President's Call[22]

The call could not have come at a better time or place. Along with 65 other senior Federal Government executives, on January 19, 1983, I was midway through a three-week "Executive Leadership and

---

[22] The material in this section, and in the following sections on Burundi, comes largely from a journal I kept beginning in January 1983 and continued throughout my assignment as Ambassador, until July 1986.

Management Program" at the Federal Executive Institute (FEI) in Charlottesville, Virginia. It was 11 a.m., and I was with a couple of dozen classmates in a foreign policy seminar, one of several electives in the program. As an exercise, we were pretending to be a committee of the National Security Council, convened to recommend to the President a course of action in response to a hypothetical request by a newly-elected West German government that we remove all nuclear weapons from its territory.

As we were deep in debate, one of the FEI front office secretaries came in and asked if I were there. The White House was calling, she said. As I was leaving, a seminar member wisecracked that it must be the President calling to ask for our recommendations on German policy.

The secretary led me down the hall to a vacant office and pushed the proper button on the telephone. When I picked it up, the White House operator confirmed my identity and said, "The President wants to speak to you." She passed me to the President's private secretary, who asked me to hold. During the 10-15 second wait that followed, I tried to think of what I was going to say. Then the familiar voice of President Reagan came on. "Mr. Bullington, I would like you to be my Ambassador to Burundi," he said. "Mr. President, I am delighted to accept," I replied; and he said something like, "Well, that's very good." There was a brief pause, as I waited for him to continue. He didn't, so I expressed appreciation for his confidence and said something like, "I want you to know, Mr. President, that I support you and your program, and I'll do my best to help you carry it out." "I'm gratified to hear that," he responded, with sincerity in his voice. After another brief pause, I thanked him again, and we exchanged goodbyes.

When I returned to the seminar room, a little dazed, there was a pause as I took my seat. Everyone looked at me quizzically. "It really was the President," I announced. There was silence, and I noted expressions of bemused expectation on the faces of my colleagues. They were awaiting the punch line of what seemed to be an obvious joke. After a few moments the professor volunteered to play straight man: "What did the President want?" "He asked me to be his Ambassador to Burundi," I replied. There was another pause, as the realization sunk in that this was no joke. Then the room came alive with cheers and applause.

The seminar topic suddenly became Burundi rather than nuclear weapons in Germany. The discussion began with my going to a wall map to point out where Burundi is located.

Classes continued that day, but it was difficult to concentrate. At lunch and dinner, the talk was all about the President's call. FEI Dean Bob Matson offered congratulations, and all the course participants and faculty members were interested. I called Tuy-Cam at the dinner break to give her the news. After the evening seminar session I had three or four beers with a few classmates and went to bed early. It wasn't easy to fall asleep.

Consultations, Swearing-In, and Meeting the President

Following conclusion of the FEI course, I concentrated on preparations for Burundi. My appointment was officially announced by the White House on February 9, and this initiated a series of meetings, mostly with offices in the State Department but also at CIA, the Pentagon, and on Capitol Hill. My Senate Foreign Relations Committee hearing on March 9 was *pro forma* -- there was no public or political interest in Burundi -- and I was confirmed by the Senate, along with half a dozen other new Ambassadors, on March 17.

Joan Clark, the Director General of the Foreign Service, presided at my swearing-in ceremony on March 31. It was in the Department's elegant diplomatic reception area on the 8th floor. My parents came from Chattanooga, and Tuy-Cam held the bible for the oath-taking. I invited 90 guests, including the Africa Bureau leadership, old friends from Vietnam and Auburn, Tuy-Cam's relatives, Foreign Service colleagues, and the Ambassador and senior staff from the Burundi Embassy.

Tom Corcoran, my boss in Hué in 1966 (and Tuy-Cam's boss as well, both there and in Danang), gave a reception for us at his club in Georgetown. It was a grand affair, with about 50 people. The surprise guest was Phil Habib, who had just flown in that day from the Middle East where he was our chief negotiator in the then-current peace effort. I first knew him when I was Ambassador Lodge's staff aide in Saigon and Phil was Minister-Counselor for Political Affairs, in the adjacent office. Also, he was Assistant Secretary for East Asia when I was on the Viet-Nam desk in 1973-75. Subsequently, he was Under Secretary for Political Affairs, the third-ranking job in the Department, and he was generally regarded as the "Mr. Foreign Service" of his generation. I was honored that he took the time to come.

My call on President Reagan was on April 4. Tuy-Cam and the children were included. Precisely at 4:45 p.m., a Marine major on the President's staff ushered Tuy-Cam, the children and me into the Oval Office. The President welcomed us. Eva asked him for his autograph, and he wrote her a note. Then, he took first me, followed by the whole family, to the fireplace/mantle as photographers clicked away. He gave me cuff links, Tuy-Cam a pin, and the girls bookmarks, all with the Presidential seal. I thanked him for appointing me, and we said goodbye and left. The meeting took 10 minutes. It was all form and no substance, but a nice gesture, and one we will always remember.

I departed for Bujumbura April 6. Tuy-Cam stayed behind with Kim and Eva to complete the school term, and they joined me on June 24.

The family with President Reagan in the Oval Office.

***

Burundi

***

Burundi Overview

Burundi is a landlocked country in the heart of Africa, about the size of Maryland. Its 11 million people are among the world's poorest. The poverty rate is 80%, and food shortages are frequent. Most people are subsistence farmers and herders, and the only significant export is coffee.

Just south of the equator, high in elevation, and mountainous, Burundi enjoys near-perfect weather year-round, with temperatures rarely above 85 degrees or below 70, and ample rainfall. This helps explain why it's Africa's second most densely populated country (after neighboring Rwanda). It was a lovely place to live...except for the grinding poverty, repressive government, and continuing internal tension manifested from time to time in civil war and genocide.

Burundi was one of the last African countries to be colonized. Like its near twin, Rwanda, it became part of German East Africa in the 1890s. When the Germans were stripped of their colonies after World War I, it was handed over to Belgium as a League of Nations mandate territory. In practice, this status was no different from being a colony, and the Belgians governed both Burundi and Rwanda as part of their far more important Congo colony.

Many of the post-colonial problems of African countries have been attributed to their being artificial creations of European powers, which drew colonial boundaries to suit their own interests, grouping together many different, often hostile, ethnic groups while splitting other groups apart. After independence, the Africans have been unwilling to change these boundaries, making it difficult to develop any sense of national unity. Hence, it has been convenient and partly valid to blame Europeans for Africa's constant political instability.

Burundi and Rwanda, however, are exceptions. Both existed for 400 years as local kingdoms, essentially within their present boundaries, before Europeans arrived; and they were inhabited by two groups, the Hutu and the Tutsi, in roughly the same proportions as today -- 85% Hutu and 15% Tutsi.

Hutu-Tutsi conflict began in both countries at the time of independence in 1962. It culminated in Rwanda with the 1994 genocide of Tutsis by Hutus. In Burundi, there was a 1972 genocide of Hutus by Tutsis, as well as a decade of civil war beginning in 1993.

This raises questions of ethnic identity. Normally, we think of a tribe or ethnic group as people who occupy a distinct territory and share a common language, culture, religion, etc., plus an historical experience that differentiates them from others. But there are no Hutu or Tutsi areas in Burundi or Rwanda; both groups live mixed together in the same areas. They speak the same language and have the same religion (Christianity), and they share a common history. Moreover, there has been much intermarriage, and while they claim to be able to identify by sight who is Hutu and who is Tutsi, an outsider cannot do so by appearance, dress, or any other visible marker.

So these are not different "tribes" or "ethnic groups" as we normally understand those terms. Rather, their relationship is more like an Indian caste system or perhaps a Medieval European feudal order, with the mostly cattle-herding Tutsi in a superior position to the mostly dirt-farming Hutu.

This is the social order the Europeans found and perpetuated, governing through the Tutsi royalty and aristocracy. On independence, in Rwanda the majority Hutus wrested control from the Tutsis, while in Burundi the Tutsi minority maintained itself in power. In both countries, the ruling group began persecuting the subordinate group, and uprisings were violently suppressed. Thus, the Tutsis in Burundi could point to Rwanda and tell each other, "See what will happen to us if the Hutus ever get control here," and *vice versa* in Rwanda. Sadly, both predictions were right.

Presenting Credentials

The first formal act of a new Ambassador after arrival in the country of assignment is "presentation of credentials" to the chief of state (in my case a letter from President Reagan to the President of Burundi, Colonel Jean Baptiste Bagaza).[23] This is an ancient diplomatic ritual, usually with little substantive content, but it is important because the new Ambassador, by tradition, cannot personally conduct official business with the host government until it is accomplished. I presented my credentials to President Bagaza on April 14, the second day after my arrival. This was unusually quick timing.

---

[23] The text of President Reagan's letter is formulaic, but it remains a cherished souvenir:

Excellency:
I have appointed James R. Bullington, a distinguished citizen of the United States, to represent me before your Government as Ambassador Extraordinary and Plenipotentiary of the United States of America.

He is well aware of the mutual interests of our two countries and shares my sincere desire to preserve and enhance the long friendship between us.

My faith in his high character and ability gives me complete confidence that he will carry out his duties in a manner fully acceptable to you.

Accordingly, I entrust him to your confidence. I ask that you receive him favorably and give full credence to what he shall say on the part of the United States as well as to the assurances which he bears of my best wishes for the prosperity of Burundi.

Very truly yours,
Ronald Reagan

I was picked up at the Embassy by the Foreign Ministry Chief of Protocol and driven to the Presidential Palace in the government's finest black Mercedes. Deputy Chief of Mission Joe Wilson[24] and a couple of other Embassy officers followed in an Embassy Chevrolet. We were escorted by police on motorcycles. On arrival, I reviewed an honor guard before being taken in to meet President Bagaza and give him President Reagan's letter. When this was done, we proceeded to the President's office, together with the Foreign Minister, for about 10 minutes of polite, non-substantive conversation, and then went to a reception room for champagne and pastry with a dozen Burundi officials and the Embassy staff members who had accompanied me. After a quarter hour of toasts and small talk, my staff and I returned to the Embassy for a much less formal celebration.

This was a promising start to my tour of duty in Burundi, and the first few months felt like a honeymoon period. However, the nature of the regime -- a repressive military oligarchy controlled by a dominant faction of the 15% Tutsi minority -- meant that U.S.-Burundi relations were likely to be problematic.

***

---

[24] Joe was to gain fame after his retirement from the Foreign Service because of a *New York Times* op-ed he wrote refuting the claim that Saddam Hussein had bought uranium from Niger, and the subsequent "outing" of his glamorous wife, CIA officer Valerie Plame. Sean Penn played Joe in the movie made about this episode, *Fair Game*.

Presenting my credentials to President Bagaza.

The U.S. Embassy in Bujumbura in the 1980s. A new $133 million Embassy, much larger and more secure, was opened in 2013.

***

The U.S. Embassy -- Surprisingly Large

The American Embassy in Bujumbura was surprisingly large in view of Burundi's small size and lack of any great consequence in the global scheme of things. I expected a slightly enlarged version of the Embassy in Cotonou. Instead, it was comparable to the one in Rangoon.

In the Embassy, there were 13 American Foreign Service officers and staff, plus six locally hired Americans. Additionally, there were 20 Americans and third-country contractors with USAID; a USIA American cultural center with two Americans; two Fulbright professors at the University of Burundi; a new Peace Corps program; and 150 locally-hired Burundi employees.

In all there were about 200 people working for the American Embassy.

Budgets also struck me as large for such a small country. USAID's was by far the biggest, with $5 million per year in project money, another $5 million in food aid, and $1 million in operating/overhead expenses. The State Department budget for Embassy operations was $1.5 million per year, and the USIA budget was $0.5 million. Peace Corps, just getting started, would be spending $1 million annually by 1985. There was also an ongoing refugee project, administered by SAWS (Seventh-Day Adventist World Services), that would receive $2 million of State Department money over its three-year duration.

Overall, the U.S. Government was spending $15 million per year on its programs in Burundi. This would be $37 million in 2016 dollars.

Living in Bujumbura

Our house in Bujumbura was located on a hill overlooking the downtown area and Lake Tanganyika. The grounds included a swimming pool and tennis court (which we made available to Embassy staff and Peace Corps Volunteers) as well as a large garden for outdoor entertaining. An inspector for the State Department's Foreign Buildings Office (which is responsible for Government-owned real estate abroad) wrote the following report:

> This is truly an Ambassadorial residence in every sense. Along the entire front of the property there is a security fence that is both tasteful and functional. The grounds are delightful, well laid out with flowers and grassy areas, and just plain beautiful. I understand that Mrs. Bullington is responsible for the work on the grounds, and I compliment her on taking such good care of the property.

Tuy-Cam and our two Burundi gardeners invested a lot of time and effort in upgrading the grounds, which the comfortable weather made it possible for us to enjoy year-round and to use frequently for both official and personal entertaining.

Our Fragile Security

In the mid-1980s, security for American diplomatic posts and personnel was not yet the major concern it was soon to become. Small Embassies, such as Bujumbura, did not have Marine Security Guards, and there were only four RSOs (Regional Security Officers) posted in Africa to cover all 50 posts. Our security was the responsibility of the host country government, as mandated by the Vienna Convention, to which all countries adhered. We hired a few local, unarmed watchmen to stay at the Embassy compound and our residences at night, but they were at best a deterrent to thieves. Nonetheless, we did not perceive ourselves to be in any great danger, since the threat of violence was low.

I came to realize how fragile our security really was late one night in 1984. Tuy-Cam, the children, and I were asleep in the residence when we were awakened by our barking dog and shouts in the yard. I went to investigate and discovered that our two night watchmen had intercepted an intruder who had climbed over the fence. They were holding him down and asked me for rope to tie him up, which I provided.

I then telephoned the police emergency number. "This is the American Ambassador," I explained, "and an unknown intruder has come into my compound. My watchmen have subdued him and he is tied up. Could you please come and pick him up?"

There was a delay while the policeman called his commander to the phone. "I'm sorry, Mr. Ambassador," the commander said, but we only have one vehicle, and it has no fuel. But if you would bring the man here to the police station, we would be happy to put him in Jail."

So that's what we did. The watchmen lifted the hog-tied intruder into the trunk of my official, flag-bedecked sedan, and I drove to the station. The policemen removed him, roughing him up a bit as they carried him inside. The commander apologized for their inability to take a more active role in the matter.

I realized that in spite of the fine words of the Vienna Convention and the government's intent to assure our security, its capacity to do so was extremely limited. I reported the incident to the Foreign Ministry and to Washington, but there was no reaction other than expressions of relief that the threat level remained low.

Since the attacks on U.S. Embassies and the rise of global Islamist terrorism in the past two decades, Foreign Service security has been greatly strengthened; but we still have to rely on host governments for help that may not be available when needed.

***

The veranda in front of our residence in Bujumbura.

A party in the residence garden.

Enjoying a good story at a dinner in the residence. In spite of sometimes strained relations, we often entertained senior Burundi government officials and other leaders, as well as the diplomatic community.

A children's party at the residence swimming pool. Kim and Eva sometimes invited their friends from the French school.

***

Ham Radio Again

The house's location on a hill above Lake Tanganyika made it an excellent site for short-wave radio propagation, and the spacious grounds and tall trees provided room and support for lengthy antennas. Although the Burundi Government had a procedure for issuing ham radio licenses to foreigners, it took several meetings with the Foreign Minister, a diplomatic note, Presidential assent, and five months of patience to get my application approved.

After I was licensed, I spent much of my leisure time on assembling the station, erecting antennas, and talking to thousands of hams around the world. I was one of only two hams in Burundi, and the other, a Frenchman, was not very active. Consequently, Burundi was considered a "rare country," and other hams were eager to make contact. With the help of a ham in Chattanooga, I also used the radio for weekly chats with my parents.

Social Life, and Tuy-Cam's Role

Mid-way through the assignment, I asked my secretary to inventory social engagements for the past year, and she determined that we had attended or hosted an average of nearly five events every week. These ranged from small sit-down dinners to large official functions, including Fourth of July receptions at the residence with a guest list of nearly 500.

Many of these events were pleasant and many were tedious; but they were a useful tool for getting information and exercising influence. Those we hosted were also a lot of work, especially for the hostess.

The responsibilities of an Ambassador's spouse (in those days, almost always the wife) are considerable, and how well they are fulfilled is important to American community morale, to how well the

Ambassador and the Embassy function, and to how the Embassy is perceived by the host government and other diplomatic missions.

Tuy-Cam was active in her role as "first lady" of the Embassy, a role she came to enjoy. In her first few months at post, she organized a children's play group, a tennis group, a weekly Mahjongg game, an English class for some Burundi ladies, an exercise class, and an international cooking group. This was in addition to the numerous dinners and other functions we hosted, as well as running a household with a seven-person staff and mothering two girls rapidly approaching puberty. Her contributions were much appreciated by both the American staff and our colleagues in the diplomatic community.

Schooling for Kim and Eva was no problem in Bujumbura, as there was a large French school, and they were now bilingual. They had close French friends, with whom they spent a summer vacation in Biarritz, France. However, Kim wanted to attend high school in the United States, so for our final year in Burundi we enrolled her in Darlington Academy, a boarding school in Rome, Georgia, not far from my parents' home in Chattanooga.

A Working Lunch with President Bagaza

There was an annual meeting of all American Ambassadors to African countries scheduled in Washington in October 1983. Prior to my departure, I asked to call on President Bagaza to review the state of U.S.-Burundi relations. He responded with an invitation to lunch at the Presidential Palace with him, Foreign Minister Nzeyimana, and Minister of Public Works and Energy Nyaboya (who had been educated in the United States and served as a Presidential counselor on all things American).

The lunch lasted two hours, and the atmosphere was cordial. We discussed global Cold War events, such as the recent Soviet downing of a South Korean civilian airliner, and current African issues such as Libya's armed intervention in Chad. Then, we reviewed U.S. economic assistance projects, the imminent arrival of the first group of Peace Corps Volunteers, and the bid of an American firm on an African Development Bank-financed $40 million sugar project in Burundi. The President asked me to tell U.S. oil companies that his Government would welcome an exploration project in Burundi (based on promising geophysical research in Lake Tanganyika). Finally, he asked me to carry the message to Washington that he wanted to cooperate with the United States politically, economically, and militarily.

As I was leaving I thanked the President for my just-approved ham radio license. He said he had been interested in ham radio as a young military officer, and remarked that his subordinates thought it had something to do with "spying," but he knew this could not be the case.

This meeting was the high-water mark of U.S.-Burundi relations during my tenure. By the end of the year, problems were developing.

The Anti-Religion Campaign

In December 1983, the Government expelled seven European missionaries. They were not accused of any particular offense, and church leaders feared that this was the beginning of a new long-term policy to force out most if not all missionaries, an action that could gravely weaken the church. This fear proved to be well founded. Over the next two years, the number of missionaries in Burundi, both Catholic and Protestant, was reduced by a third.

Moreover, in late 1984 and 1985, further measures that could only be described as a deliberate anti-religion campaign were begun. First, the Government banned all religious services except on Saturday afternoons and Sundays. Moreover, several Burundi priests, pastors, and lay leaders were jailed without charges or on vague accusations of

204

"subversive" activities and for holding prayer meetings in private homes. The Seventh-Day Adventists were effectively prevented from practicing their religion and their churches were closed because they refused Government-ordered community work projects on Saturdays. (Their offers to work on Sundays or any other day were rejected.)

Following is the analysis of the anti-religion campaign that I sent to the Department. It's an example of the sort of reporting that is done by U.S. Embassies:

> The December 1983 expulsion of seven European Catholic priests turned out to be the initial move in what has developed into a campaign, accelerated in recent months, gradually to purge Burundi of foreign missionaries and to reduce the power and influence of religious organizations, particularly the Catholics -- by far the largest group, with 65% of the population -- and the Seventh-Day Adventists, an easy target due to their non-conformity.
>
> This campaign is not in the interest of Burundi for the following reasons:
>
> - Despite efforts to develop Burundi clergy and religious workers, the Catholics and other groups remain dependent on the presence of expatriates, both for religious functions and for social services. They will be seriously weakened by the departure of missionaries.
> - The churches have a more effective infrastructure throughout the country than does the Government; and that infrastructure is the most important provider of services such as health care, social assistance, and education. To the extent this infrastructure is weakened, people will experience further decline in their already low quality of life.

- While the majority Hutus (85% of the population) are normally docile, the surest way to provoke them to action against the ruling Tutsi elite is to attack their religion. The Government risks creating enemies where there are none.

- Many Government leaders are opposed to the anti-religion campaign. Its pursuit can only exacerbate those differences and weaken the Government internally.

- Finally, the Burundi economy and prospects for development are dependent on foreign largesse. To the extent the Government loses favor with foreign donors, as it will if the anti-religion campaign continues, this will lead to reduced aid levels and economic deterioration.

Why has the Government adopted such a self-defeating policy? There are several explanations:

- The concept of unity of power. Traditionally, the Burundi Mwami [king], like most African rulers, was the incarnation of all power, spiritual as well as temporal, within the state. This concept of governance still exerts a strong influence.

- The Church as instrument of colonial domination. As a recent Burundi-published history of the colonial period put it, "Missionary and colonial administrator, each in his own sphere, were agents of the same system." In the minds of many Burundi, the Church is inseparably linked with colonial exploitation and white rule.

- Missionaries as spies. Even as early as the German period, the Governor urged on his subordinates "full and entire cooperation with the missionaries, who in many cases can give the administration useful information and prevent dangerous situations." Many Burundi are convinced that this sort of relationship persists, and that the missionaries are in effect spies. Moreover, because they learn Kirundi [the local language] and associate intimately with the Hutu masses, they are a particularly dangerous sort of spy.

- Religion as promoter of Hutu uprising. In the genocide of 1972, virtually every educated Hutu was killed or fled into exile, and a generation of Hutu leadership was wiped out. The churches work primarily with the Hutu majority, and many Tutsis fear that religious groups are raising up a new generation of Hutu leaders to encadre a new uprising.

- Anti-clerical bias. Some Government leaders, including President and Mrs. Bagaza, have a strong anti-clerical bias, much like that of radical West European socialists. The President has publicly compared the Catholic Church in Burundi to that of Europe in the Middle Ages.

Many Burundi leaders do not share these attitudes. However, those who do are the ones who count in making political decisions and determining the orientation of the regime.

After digesting this report, the Department asked for more analysis of the impact of the anti-religion campaign on internal political stability and on U.S.-Burundi relations. My reply:

In this society, the threat of some sort of violent explosion as in 1972 is a constant; and in periods of heightened political tension it is naturally higher than at other times. That being said, chances of a major upheaval remain small because:

- While a new generation of Hutu leaders has developed, at least in a demographic sense, it lacks any political organization. There are no visible leaders, no organized structures, no arms and equipment, and no external support.

- Despite its growing unpopularity and internal divisions, the Government retains control of the Army. As long as this is the case, even if trouble started, it could probably be contained.

207

We can expect continuing strains in our bilateral relations so long as we stand up vigorously for our principles. At least for the short term, it is hard to see how our relations can improve and easy to see how they can further deteriorate.

The Great Pouch Crisis

All official Americans stationed at our Embassies and Consulates receive their personal mail, including small packages, through the State Department via the "diplomatic pouch." [25] Physically, these pouches are large bags made of heavy canvas, securely sealed at the top. In addition to employee personal mail, they are used for supplies not readily available outside the United States and for unclassified official correspondence. They are sent via air freight. (Classified messages and supplies are sent via a different State Department system and are accompanied by diplomatic couriers.)

Official correspondence in a diplomatic pouch is unambiguously protected by the Vienna Convention on Diplomatic and Consular Relations. Most countries, however, do not permit their diplomatic pouches to be used for personal mail, particularly packages, for official employees. Therefore, our pouches are typically larger and more numerous than those of other countries. While there is room for argument on this point, State Department lawyers construe the Vienna Convention to protect the personal mail of diplomats as "diplomatic correspondence." There have been occasional challenges to this interpretation, but we have been successful in making our view prevail, and our system has operated accordingly, worldwide, for many years.

In September 1984, 29 of these pouches, an unusually large number, arrived at the airport, and Customs officials refused to let us have them. A few days later, 20 more arrived and were similarly blocked.

---

[25] Except in special cases where there are U.S. military postal facilities.

After the Administrative Officer and DCM tried unsuccessfully to resolve the problem with Customs officials, I called on the Foreign Minister. He said that the Vienna Convention protects only "diplomatic correspondence," and that the material in these pouches could not possibly be only diplomatic correspondence and was therefore not protected. He said we must segregate diplomatic correspondence from other items, which must be declared and cleared through normal Customs procedures.

I pointed out our differing legal interpretation of the Convention, and noted that we were doing nothing different with regard to diplomatic pouches from what we had been doing in Burundi for many years and was our practice everywhere else in the world. I added that the pouches contained checks that are necessary for the Embassy's financial operations (this was before the days of electronic fund transfers), and that we would soon run out of money to pay Burundi employee salaries, rent for our houses, etc. He was unmoved.

This stand-off continued for several weeks. We learned that the decision to block the pouches had been made by President Bagaza, on the advice of security officials who suspected that we were using the pouches to bring in arms for a Hutu uprising.

I confirmed with the Department that preserving our global policy on diplomatic pouches was more important than maintaining good relations with Burundi. In subsequent meetings with the President and others, I explained that the pouches were critical to our operations and diplomatic presence in Burundi, and without them we would have to close USAID and other programs and reduce our staff to no more than half a dozen officials. I also tried to appease any serious security concerns by offering to let the Government send a representative into the Embassy to observe the opening of the pouches.

Neither pressure nor appeasement was working, so we began preparations for program closures and staff departures.

Finally, in a meeting with President Bagaza November 16, he told me we could have the pouches if we would declare the contents on Customs forms after we had received them. This posed no problem for us, and it was a face-saving way for him to back down, so I agreed.

Thus ended the great pouch crisis, and we had no further problems.

We discovered that the contents of the pouches that arrived in September and raised the paranoid concerns of the security services were mostly boxes of vegetable seeds addressed to Peace Corps. The Peace Corps Director had seen an offer from an American company of free vegetable seeds for Peace Corps Volunteers. Thinking she was requesting 100 small seed packets of the sort on sale in American garden stores and supermarkets every spring, she instead received 100 boxes, each containing 100 of those small seed packets.

The pouch crisis combined with the anti-religion campaign to sour U.S.-Burundi relations through the rest of my assignment.

Feeding the Hungry

Because of over-population and all arable land already being under cultivation, and with pre-modern agricultural technology, even in good years Burundi is at the margin of self-sufficiency in food production. In bad years, half the people are likely to be hungry; some may starve. And because of its land-locked position, with only a mostly unpaved two-lane road connecting it to the nearest seaport, more than 700 miles away, importing food is a lengthy and expensive process.

A poor harvest in the spring of 1984 foretold serious food shortages to come, probably extending to the next harvest beginning in February or March. However, hard figures were difficult to come by, because the

Government did not make a vigorous effort to collect information. This was due to poorly trained and motivated staff, plus reluctance of officials to report problems for which they might be held responsible.

Over the summer, we pushed the Government to develop more information on the shortages. At the same time we collected information on our own, drawing on field trips by our staff, contacts with religious leaders and missionaries in rural areas, and economic indicators such as market prices. By late summer, the Government recognized the problem, partially as a result of our prompting, and requested international assistance. With the information we had gathered, we were able to generate a quick decision by USAID in Washington to send 900 tons of wheat and corn.

Our food aid arrived in the Kenyan port of Mombasa in October, but it was November before the first truckloads began arriving in Bujumbura. This was barely in time to help people get through the remaining two or three months before the next harvest. Ironically, it was also at the height of the pouch crisis and in the midst of the anti-religion campaign, when U.S.-Burundi relations were at a low point. However, U.S. policy is to avoid using humanitarian aid as pressure in political disputes, and we followed that principle in this case. We realized the people most affected by the food shortages had no responsibility for causing the conflict.

***

With USAID Director George Bliss, at the unloading of one of the first trucks delivering our emergency food aid.

With one of our pouches, at a party following their release.

***

Facilitating Oil Exploration

When I arrived in Burundi, a Duke University professor and his team were completing a seismic research project in Lake Tanganyika. He invited me to spend a day on the boat, during which he told me that their findings indicated the strong possibility of large oil deposits under the lake and nearby on-shore areas. This research aroused interest among global oil companies, and a few months later, Amoco representatives visited Burundi. I briefed them on the country's political and economic situation and helped arrange meetings with President Bagaza and Energy Minister Nyaboya.

This visit developed into negotiations between Amoco and the Burundi Government, in which the Embassy served as an occasional facilitator. An exploration agreement involving an Amoco investment of between $100 and $200 million was signed in October 1984; an Amoco office was opened in Bujumbura in February 1985; and seismic studies and test drilling began the following summer.

After more than a year of work, however, the project had not found commercially significant quantities of oil, and it was quietly terminated by the end of 1986. Although ultimately unsuccessful, the project was executed as planned and without major problems, and both Amoco and the Government expressed appreciation for the Embassy's assistance in facilitating it.

Earning our Hardship Pay

Bujumbura is designated by the State Department as a maximum hardship differential post (as were all the other African posts where we served except Dakar). This means that personnel assigned there receive a bonus of 25% of their base pay. This might appear difficult to justify, in view of Bujumbura's near-perfect year-round weather, a beautiful setting between the mountains and a huge lake, and comfortable housing provided and maintained by the Embassy. On the negative side are Burundi's isolation, lack of cultural attractions, few recreational opportunities, political instability, grinding poverty, high health risks, and poor medical facilities.

We had a full-time American nurse at the Embassy, and there were a few expatriate and Burundi doctors on whom we could call for help. However, there were no hospitals in the country that were adequate by American standards. For any serious medical problem, normal practice was evacuation to Europe. In November 1983, Tuy-Cam had to be evacuated to the U.S. military hospital in Wiesbaden for a hysterectomy due to fibroids[26]. They were not cancerous, and the surgery was routine, but it was still beyond anything that could be safely done in Burundi. Having to travel for many hours to undergo major surgery, alone in a strange country, was stressful. However, staff from the Consulate General in Frankfurt facilitated travel and administrative arrangements, and as the wife of an Ambassador, she was given a private room normally reserved for general officers. The quality of her medical care was outstanding.

Other than this incident, neither Tuy-Cam nor I nor the children suffered any major medical problems in Burundi. In fact, we enjoyed good health throughout the 13 years we lived in Africa (except for my malaria attacks in Benin and Niger).

Health risks in Africa are higher than in the United States, but they can be managed.

Hosting Memphis Slim and the Johnson Mountain Boys

The State Department has for decades operated a cultural exchange program in which it sends American artists -- musicians, writers,

---

[26] "Uterine fibroids are noncancerous growths of the uterus that often appear during childbearing years." -- Mayo Clinic website.

painters, etc. -- on tours abroad to promote American culture. These are usually younger, less well known artists or fading former stars who are willing to accept a modest stipend in return for the free travel, adventure, and prestige they receive. The program is not costly, and it's thought to produce a positive return in good will, music and book sales, and American cultural influence.

We had two American musical visits of this sort during my time in Burundi. The first, in April 1984, was by Memphis Slim, an aging blues/jazz singer and piano player, accompanied by a young drummer. Slim was a leader of the emerging blues genre in the 1930s and 1940s. He was a big hit with the Burundi university students, who had read about him in a textbook on American music. People filled the street at our house the evening we had a concert there. The drummer taught Eva a beat, and Slim invited her to play drums on-stage with him.

The visit by the Johnson Mountain Boys in November 1984 was much more important to me. This was a young bluegrass band based in the Washington area that I had heard live on several occasions. I had all of their records, and played them frequently. Although one of its principal instruments, the banjo, had its origins in Africa, bluegrass was a harder sell to Burundi audiences than was Slim's blues and jazz. Nonetheless, we hosted a successful dinner/concert for the diplomatic community and a few Burundi musicians, as well as an American community party and concert. I was thrilled to serve as Master of Ceremonies for the concerts and perform a couple of songs with the band, and Tuy-Cam and I got to know its members well. Kim even developed a crush for the mandolin picker. They were not only outstanding musicians but also fine young men and good representatives of America.

The Johnson Mountain Boys invited me to tour with them when we were in the United States, and I was delighted to accept this offer during our home leave in the summer of 1985. I spent a week with them as a bluegrass "groupie" on their bus, going to bluegrass festivals and nightclubs in Maryland, Pennsylvania, and Delaware, and selling their records, caps, and tee-shirts while they were performing. We also hired them to come to our home in Arlington when I was Dean of the Senior Seminar, for a dinner/concert for the students and several senior State Department officials.

Tuy-Cam with Memphis Slim; Eva on the drums.

I joined the Johnson Mountain Boys for a song at the outdoor dinner and concert we hosted for the diplomatic corps at our house. I'm in the center, without a jacket.

***

Freeing Marcien

Following resolution of the pouch crisis in December 1984, there was a detente in U.S.-Burundi relations. The anti-religion campaign continued, but with less intensity and fewer missionary expulsions; our emergency food aid was welcomed; and the Amoco oil exploration project raised hopes for an improved future as well as stronger economic ties with the United States. Moreover, the Government began negotiations with the World Bank and International Monetary Fund for a large aid package tied to a program of structural reform that would move the country away from socialism toward free markets.

Things were going so well that in one of my mid-1985 journal entries I complained of boredom.

In late 1985, however, a Government reorganization brought to power several anti-religion and anti-American hardliners, including an especially hostile new Foreign Minister. My boredom soon ended, to be replaced by intense activity and confrontation with both the Burundi Government and the State Department.

I'll end this account of my experience as Ambassador to Burundi with the story of our cook, Marcien, who was arrested on May 12, 1986. It illustrates that diplomacy is not only about government relations, political agreements, economic links, and the like; it's also about people and their problems, and trying to do what's right.

Marcien had been the American Ambassador's cook in Bujumbura for 14 years. He was an outstanding cook and a faithful, hard-working employee. His only "offense" was being a Seventh-Day Adventist. I reported his arrest to Washington immediately, pointing out that it was probably a Government response to the recent demarches I had been instructed to make on behalf of Adventists imprisoned without charge, and that it was likely intended as retaliation for what the

Government considered to be our "meddling" in its internal affairs. I said I would try to avoid confrontation and work informally to secure his release, but I warned that we may need to apply pressure.

During the next two weeks, it became evident that our low-key efforts had not produced results and were not likely to. Moreover, we learned that Marcien was put in solitary confinement, and that he was accused of plotting to overthrow the Government. The Department, however, expressed doubt that his arrest was intended as a political gesture.

To better acquaint Department officials who didn't follow Burundi affairs with the context, and to lay groundwork for escalating our efforts, I sent the following cable:

> For the past two years the Burundi Government has conducted a campaign of increasing intensity against the Adventists. This has been part of a broader campaign against all religious groups, but the Adventists have been a special target because of their refusal to do "voluntary" community work on Saturdays. There may also be anti-Americanism involved, since the Adventists are considered to be an American church. Moreover, they are overwhelmingly Hutu, and have strong ties with their Hutu brethren in Rwanda.
>
> The American Adventist missionaries have been expelled; the U.S. Government-financed refugee health centers project administered by SAWS [Seventh-Day Adventist World Services] collapsed due to the expulsion of the American project director; the official charter of the Adventist church was revoked, making it an illegal organization; and the Adventist schools and churches were closed and/or taken over by the Government. Moreover, in a move directed at all church groups, the Government banned religious gatherings outside recognized church buildings. All of this means that

the Adventists, for all practical purposes, are prohibited from practicing their religion, even to the extent of gathering to pray in private homes.

Last fall, there were several arrests of Adventists for refusal to do Saturday work; but they were by local authorities who kept them in commune lock-ups for a few days at most. Then, in December, 10 Adventist leaders were arrested by Government security services and put in a national prison. They were not tried or even formally charged. In early May the Government arrested 75 Adventists who had assembled for Saturday afternoon prayers in a private house in Bujumbura. The women and children in the group were released, but 15 men remain in prison.

On the Department's instructions I brought our concerns to the Government's attention on several occasions. These demarches produced no results, positive or negative. The most recent demarche, however, to new Foreign Minister Nkuriyingoma, was not met with his predecessor's affable obfuscation but with a strong rejection of our right even to ask questions about imprisoned Burundi citizens.

In addition to the Adventist situation, in the past couple of months the Government has renewed the expulsion of Catholic missionaries and obliged Catholic Relief Services to end most of its activities, including a U.S. Government-financed food distribution project. Moreover, there have been nasty anti-American articles published almost daily in the Government's newspaper.

This was the context in which Marcien was arrested on May 12. He is a devout Adventist and lay leader. He has been "guilty," like his fellow believers, of refusing Saturday work and attending worship services in private homes. However, he was not arrested for any specific act such as refusal of Saturday work. Rather, a security service agent came to the Ambassador's residence and called him to the gate, in order to be able to recognize him later. Marcien told me about this and said he feared imminent arrest. That night, he was arrested at his house.

As instructed, I requested a meeting with President Bagaza, but thus far there has been no response.

Although I suppose it is possible that Marcien's arrest was unrelated to his employment [as the Department had suggested], in the context of all these other events that notion is hard to swallow. While this cannot be proved and would never be admitted by the Government, I am convinced that senior officials realized (correctly) that Marcien was providing much of the information on which my reporting on Adventists was based, and they decided to show me and the U.S. Government what would be the result of our "interference" in matters they consider to be internal affairs. Most long-term observers of the Burundi psyche, from old Belgian colonialist residents to my European diplomatic colleagues, also believe this to be the case.

When (and if) the President agrees to see me, the odds are against his agreeing to release any of the Adventists, particularly Marcien, though I will give it my best effort. If he will not release Marcien, I plan to ask him, as a personal favor and humanitarian gesture, to let me take Marcien with me to the United States when I depart. [There are special visa provisions for FSOs to bring household servants with them when assigned to the United States.] However, since I can't

220

afford to take him on for long as an employee or dependent, a more permanent arrangement, perhaps political asylum, would have to be found.

This cable convinced the State Department that we should regard Marcien's arrest as a political issue and increase our pressure. Consequently, Burundi Ambassador Kadigiri was convoked to the Department to hear our remonstrances from the Assistant Secretary for Africa. This resulted in Kadigiri's immediate recall to Bujumbura for consultations and further instructions from President Bagaza. I invited Kadigiri to my house for coffee. Following are excerpts from my report of our conversation:

> I began by discussing our concern about the imprisonment of Adventists and the Foreign Minister's heated refusal even to accept my question as to what were the charges against them. I pointed to the subsequent arrest of my cook as something which especially disturbed us, since it appeared to be an action taken in response to our demarches, and a deliberate affront to the U.S. Government and its representative in Burundi.

> Kadigiri did not deny this charge, and in fact did not even address it. Instead, he responded with a long recital of the Government's standard position: Each religion cannot be permitted to choose its own day of worship; if these people are in jail it is because they have broken the law; and our demarches represent unacceptable interference in internal Burundi affairs. He was impervious to my attempts to draw him into discussion of what my cook and the others had done to merit imprisonment or when they might be formally charged and tried. He even claimed that revelation of the charges against those imprisoned would be a violation of

221

their right to privacy. The gist of his message was: "It's none of your business."

I then raised the almost daily attacks against the United States, sometimes in particularly offensive language, that have been appearing in the Government newspaper. Could he explain the reason for this, I asked. Kadigiri repeated the position that we have heard from the Foreign Minister and others: These articles are the work of individual journalists who are free to write what they wish. He said he could understand why we were upset by such writing, but asserted that this is, after all, a matter of no great importance, and it should not affect our good bilateral relations. I told him that we take such matters seriously.

Finally, I noted my request for a meeting with the President, and asked Kadigiri if he could do anything to facilitate it. He asked what I wished to discuss with the President. I responded that I had instructions to raise the same issues that we had just discussed, including the imprisoned Adventists and especially my cook. Kadigiri expressed astonishment that we would even think about raising with the President of the Republic a matter so minor as the jailing of a domestic servant. I stated that we did not consider this to be a minor matter; that our inquiries at lower levels had been rebuffed; that we feel humanitarian concern for the welfare of a man who has worked for U.S. Ambassadors in Burundi for 14 years and to whom we consequently have a special obligation; and that because his arrest seemed to be an effort to intimidate us, an important matter of principle is involved. Kadigiri did not respond further.

Before leaving, Kadigiri said there was one subject he wished to raise with me, and that was the U.S. "promise" to assist Burundi with additional bilateral aid to facilitate the major economic reform program it was undertaking in the context of the recent agreement with the IMF and World Bank. I responded that there was no promise, and that additional U.S. aid to Burundi is entirely out of the question so long as my cook and the other Adventists remain in jail and our other human rights and political concerns about Burundi remain unrelieved. In fact, I continued, it is becoming increasingly difficult for us to maintain even current aid levels in the face of these problems. Kadigiri said that he planned to pursue this question in Washington. I encouraged him to do so, but assured him that he would receive the same response.

Since we had received no reply to my request for a meeting with President Bagaza, and the date of my permanent departure, July 11, was drawing near, I proposed to the Department that I re-cast the meeting request as a farewell call, during which I would ask for Marcien's release as a personal favor and humanitarian gesture. The Department agreed with the farewell call idea but, to my astonishment, rejected my plan to use it to make a plea for Marcien. They instructed me to make only a broader statement of our concern for human rights and religious freedom.

I responded with this message:

> I have requested a farewell call on the President and will proceed as instructed. However, I want to register some comments on those instructions.
>
> Sympathetic Burundi who know the President have told me that it is certain he will react negatively to any appeal based on general human rights principles, and that subsuming the

223

question of my cook in the more fundamental issue of religious liberty for Adventists is to virtually guarantee his indefinite imprisonment. My reading of the President, based on our previous meetings, is similar: He can be pragmatic on specific issues (e.g., releasing the pouches), but he reacts negatively to any questioning of his principles (e.g., the Government's right to refuse their entry).

Moreover, my cook's case is very different from that of the other Adventists:

- Their arrest was an assault on their religious freedom. Marcien's arrest was an attack on the right of the U.S. Government even to question Burundi Government assaults on religious freedom.
- They were arrested for an act of worship. He was arrested because he works for the U.S. Ambassador and was suspected of providing us information.
- The other Adventists are being charged with holding an unauthorized religious meeting. Marcien is considered guilty of political subversion and perhaps espionage.

These are fundamental differences. We should NOT confuse Marcien's case with the others, or, as your message instructs, "subsume his status in that of other Adventists."

Finally, I respectfully disagree with your argument that "we obviously want to see him released, but not in a way that later opens us up to the criticism that we have shaped our appeals or used our influence selectively in a basic area of human rights." This says, essentially, that if we can't obtain freedom for everyone we will seek it for no one; and that making a statement of moral principle to an audience we know in advance will reject it, is more important than getting an individual out of prison. Of course we shape our appeals and use our influence selectively in human rights matters; or at least we certainly should if we are interested in results as opposed to empty preaching.

After this message, the Department withdrew the prohibition of a personal appeal to President Bagaza on Marcien's behalf.

When I met with the President the morning of July 11, just before my departure that afternoon, he agreed to what I described as a "personal" request (as opposed to an "official" U.S. Government request) to release Marcien. Although it took two more days, he kept his word.

Burundi Postscripts

Marcien remained out of jail and worked for my successor, a political appointee who had formerly been a U.S. Senator from Texas. When the Senator, who was a wealthy man, went home, he took Marcien, his wife, and their five children, to New Braunfels and arranged a job for Marcien to cook in a retirement community. In 2001, Tuy-Cam and I visited Marcien and his family and found them to be thriving.

A year after my departure, in 1987, the Bagaza regime was overthrown in a military coup. The stated reasons for the coup were the Government's corruption and its campaign of religious persecution.

Although the new regime was better than the one it replaced, it was not able to bring about Tutsi-Hutu reconciliation, and several years of political instability ensued, culminating in civil war and mass killings beginning in 1993. Sporadic fighting continued until 2003, when a peace agreement was signed. In 2015, violent anti-government protests again erupted, and the situation remains unresolved.

The 2016 "World Happiness Report" ranked Burundi as the world's least happy country.

When I returned to Washington in July, I found that some of the senior officers in the Africa Bureau had been offended by my cables arguing the case for a vigorous effort to free Marcien. (This was not surprising.) They also thought I had not been sufficiently conciliatory in handling the pouch crisis and other contentious issues. Their lack of support, I learned, had assured the failure of my attempts to get another ambassadorship or a senior substantive job in the Department.

I was concerned about the impact this would have on my career, but I took comfort in the conviction that my analysis of the nature of the regime in Burundi was correct, and that I was right in trying to do all I could to help one of its victims with whom we had a special relationship.

With Secretary of State George Shultz and Assistant Secretary of State for Africa Chester Crocker, at a meeting in Washington of U.S. Ambassadors to African countries.

****

11.

Twilight Cruise:

Dean of the Senior Seminar, 1986-89

My new assignment was as Coordinator, and later Dean, of the Senior Seminar, the State Department's highest level training program. It was analogous to the military war colleges, although much smaller. There were 28-30 students, half of them Foreign Service Officers and the rest O-6 military officers (colonels and Navy captains), plus comparable-level civilians from national security agencies and other government departments with international responsibilities. The program lasted for an academic year, September to June.

In the Foreign Service, training is not as highly valued as in the military and some other professions, and a training assignment, whether taking it or giving it, is not viewed as career-enhancing. Although I was disappointed that I didn't get another Ambassadorship or a mainstream, policy-related job in the Department, I saw this as an interesting assignment as well as a possible bridge to post-Foreign Service work in academia. It was like what Navy officers term a "twilight cruise": a responsible, pleasant job outside the career mainstream that is likely to be a prelude to an honorable retirement.

On our return from Bujumbura, we bought a house in Arlington. It was adequate, though a come-down from the Ambassadorial residences we had occupied for the past five years. Its main attractions were good public schools for Kim and Eva, and its location only four miles distant from my new office at the Foreign Service Institute (FSI) in Rosslyn, just across the Potomac from the State Department. This enabled me to commute by jogging and walking, thus increasing my exercise time while avoiding the area's difficult rush hour traffic.

227

Revising the Curriculum

While I found the Senior Seminar to be pleasant and interesting, as I learned more about it I also found it to be unexciting and uninspiring. It was more like a post-graduate university program than the more practically useful experience I had benefitted from at the Army War College. In particular, it had no focus on leadership, even though its stated aim was to prepare participants for senior leadership roles.

I decided the curriculum needed a thorough overhaul, and in discussing it with my bosses at FSI as well as with some senior Department officials, I found support for this view. The Director of FSI, Ambassador Charlie Bray, was especially interested in adding a strong leadership development component. I made several changes as the 1986-87 session proceeded, but the program had already been set along traditional lines, and I didn't want to disrupt it with too many untested innovations. Moreover, I had no experience in running a training program, so I needed time to gather information and develop a concept for a revised curriculum.

At the end of the session in June 1987, the Senior Seminar was elevated from being a unit of the School of Professional Studies to a position immediately under the FSI Director's office. I was given the title of Dean, the same as the heads of the Schools of Professional Studies, Area Studies, and Language Studies.

One of the graduates of the 1986-87 program, Jim Purcell, a senior State Department Civil Service Officer, did not yet have an ongoing assignment. I arranged for him to be detailed as my assistant for the next four months, to help me redesign the curriculum. Jim and I first interviewed several leaders in the State Department, USAID, USIA, and the military and intelligence services to get their views on the sort of training that was most needed for new senior officers. Then, we visited the military war colleges, the Federal Executive Institute, Harvard's

Kennedy School of Government, Georgetown's School of Foreign Service, Goldman Sachs, and IBM to look for "best practices" in executive training. Finally, we threw out the old Senior Seminar curriculum and re-designed it from scratch, with a strong focus on leadership as well as "experiential learning." We defined experiential learning as movement as far as possible along the learning spectrum suggested by a Chinese proverb: *I hear and I forget; I see and I remember; I do and I understand*. There were fewer lectures and readings, and a lot more case studies, simulations, field trips, and participative projects.

The results exceeded expectations, and the "new" Senior Seminar attracted attention not only in the State Department but also in the other participating agencies and within the executive training community. This attention was reflected in laudatory articles published in the July 1988 issues of *Government Executive* and *State Magazine* (the Department's official house organ). For readers interested in details of the program and specific innovations we implemented, the text of the *State Magazine* article is at Annex 4.

***

The "wilderness lab" at the beginning of the program used exercises such as making a vehicle in which an egg could be dropped without breaking, and falling off a ladder backwards into a "support net" formed by teammates. The objective was to build trust, communications skills, and an effective learning team.

On the trip to Miami, Seminar members explored narcotics control and other port security issues with the Coast Guard.

***

Seminarians welcomed to Parris Island by Marine drill sergeant.

Visiting an LST (landing ship, tank) at Norfolk Navy Base.

Learning about Army Special Forces at Fort Bragg.

***

Performance Evaluation

Of all my time in the Foreign Service, I think my most creative contribution was as Dean of the Senior Seminar. This was recognized in the official performance evaluations by my bosses, but the most gratifying recognition was a letter jointly written and signed by all the participants in the 1988-89 session. I had recently left the Seminar job when it was written.

> Dear Jim:
>
> We missed you when we met at Harper's Ferry last week, after a day of rappelling and rock climbing. Nursing cuts and bruises, and anticipating ivy poisoning, we assembled to discuss the "philosophy of leadership" essays each of us had written. You would, as always, have had much to contribute.
>
> The evening ended with a rousingly applauded, unanimously expressed wish: that we write to you -- each and every Member of the 31st Senior Seminar -- to say how much we have valued, and how much we have benefitted from, the unique direction and spirit which you gave to this extraordinary course.
>
> As you certainly intended, we are ending this nine months together fitter, smarter, and better prepared to succeed in the important positions to which each of us aspires.
>
> We cannot conceive of a better overall framework (call it Vision!) for this course than that which you developed for it during your tenure as Dean.
>
> Specifically:
>
> 1. We believe that each Seminar Member brings uniquely rich experience to the course, and that your Seminar concept, which places upon the Members themselves the principal responsibility for developing the year's specific units and

activities, best exploits this richness. We all learned at least as much from one another as from any "outside" speaker or resource.

2. We believe that the Seminar triad emphasizing, in roughly equal parts, domestic affairs, international affairs, and leadership and managerial skills, is excellent. The horizons of each of us, in each of these regards, have expanded greatly during these nine months together.

3. We have valued the importance which you ascribed to physical stamina and fitness, and your ensuring that appropriate time would be available for this. Each of us graduates as a healthier, more vigorous individual because of your commitment to this aspect of successful leadership.

4. We feel that our growth as individuals and as leaders has demonstrated the wisdom of your commitment to experiential learning, in tandem with the academic and intellectual. The insights gained through the seven trips have been extraordinary. And each of us strongly believes that we benefited from having been able to choose, unlike some of our predecessors, whether to devote our month-long Individual Research Project to "hands-on," experiential learning, or to the more traditional research project.

As these nine months end, we are especially aware of our debt to you for what has perhaps been the essence of this 31st Senior Seminar: the bonds of friendship and mutual respect which have developed through this period. You set the tone for this from the very beginning. Through your own personal attitude, and through the standards you set, this group of 29 sometimes un-humble individuals, from 13 sometimes fractious agencies, has from the beginning shared a collegiality and mutual regard which all of us will forever cherish.

Thanks, friend.

[signed by all Seminar members]

Premature Retirement

The positive results and evaluations of the Seminar and my role as its Dean made my forced retirement from the Foreign Service, at the ripe old age of 48, all the more shocking and disappointing when it came.

Beginning in 1987, I had sought another Ambassadorial assignment to follow the Seminar job. I was able to get on five "short lists" for African posts, but the prize always eluded me. When it became clear in early 1988 that the available posts for the year had all been filled, I was forced to do some serious thinking about career prospects.

In the Foreign Service at that time, a Minister-Counselor (my rank) had five years to be promoted to Career Minister (military three-star equivalent). If you were not promoted, you could be offered a three-year "limited career extension" (LCE), or, failing that, you were forced to retire. My five years were up in September 1988. I knew that I would not be promoted to Career Minister because of the non-substantive, out-of-the-mainstream nature of my current job. There are only half a dozen promotions to Career Minister each year (out of more than 300 Minister-Counselors); and in order to get one, you need to have served as Ambassador at a large post or in a high-level job in the Department. I calculated, however, that I would be offered an LCE (as was the case for almost half of those Minister-Counselors whose five years had expired). I couldn't imagine being forcibly retired well ahead of my peers who had advanced up through the ranks more slowly than I and had thus not yet encountered the almost insurmountable Career Minister "wall."

Nonetheless, in the spring of 1988 I decided to decline an LCE and thereby become eligible for early retirement. I judged that my chances for an Ambassadorship in 1989 would be no better than they had been in 1988. Thus, in all likelihood, at the end of my time as Senior Seminar Dean I would wind up with another non-mainstream assignment, probably not as interesting as the one I had, and then be faced with retirement at 51 rather than 48. Since I had long intended to start a second career after the Foreign Service, I would have a better chance for success if I began it sooner rather than later. And with an annuity of 54% of my current pay, I figured I could find a job paying enough that, together with the annuity, my income would rise substantially.

By summer, however, I had second thoughts about my decision to retire. First, I was enjoying my work as Dean and would be happy to continue it for another year or possibly longer. Also, with an LCE there was a chance for another Ambassadorship. An important additional consideration concerned the family: Tuy-Cam wanted to stay in the Foreign Service, and while Kim would be graduating from high school in 1989, Eva would not graduate until 1991, and she didn't want to change schools. And finally, when I discussed my voluntary early retirement plan with them, my bosses -- the FSI Director, the Deputy Assistant Secretary for Personnel, and the Director General of the Foreign Service -- all urged me to stay on.

By the cut-off date for requesting non-consideration for an LCE, I decided against making the request.

A Shocking Phone Call

The news came on July 29, 1988, via a telephone call from Foreign Service Director General George Vest, whom I had gotten to know fairly well over the past two years. He had enthusiastically supported my Senior Seminar innovations, and he had encouraged me about my prospects for an Ambassadorship in 1989. I believe his expressed regret was genuine when he told me that my ranking by the Minister-Counselor promotion board was just under the cut-off line for LCEs. Consequently, he continued, I had until September 30, 1989, to retire.

The Foreign Service up-or-out system is designed to get rid of officers who are not performing as well as their peers. I knew that I had been promoted more rapidly than almost all of my peers, and I felt like I was just reaching my prime years as a professional diplomat. Forced retirement was an unwelcomed surprise.

On the other hand, only a few months previously I had almost decided to opt voluntarily for early retirement. This made sense financially and in terms of second career prospects. Such thoughts helped me emerge from the slough of despond into which I initially fell, and to begin seeing opportunities ahead rather than just problems.

The most difficult thing to accept was being forced out -- in effect, fired, regardless of the euphemisms by which the process was known. It would have been better to have jumped rather than getting pushed.

I told the FSI Director that I would stay on as Senior Seminar Dean until I found a new job or he found a replacement, but I pointed out that now my first priority would have to be the job search, not the Seminar. Because of the way I had reorganized the curriculum, with the participants mostly designing and executing their own program, this did not pose a serious problem. The Seminar continued to function with great success in spite of my occasional absences.

Job Search

My job search extended through the fall of 1988. I was a finalist and was interviewed for four serious possibilities, but none of the first three was a good fit. The fourth possibility was to be Director of International Affairs for the City of Dallas. The work looked interesting, and I was well qualified for it. Moreover, with my redneck hillbilly roots in Tennessee and Alabama, I was confident I could relate well to Texans and thrive in the Texas culture.

After I was chosen as a finalist and visited Dallas for interviews with the Mayor and private sector leaders, I concluded that if I had been asked to design my own post-Foreign Service job, this was close to what I might have come up with. It amounted to being, in effect, the municipal Foreign Minister, working with the Mayor and business and civic leaders to promote the city's international development, facilitating foreign investment, organizing trade missions and cultural exchanges, hosting important visitors, building relations with local foreign community groups, and serving as chief of protocol for the city.

Moreover, Texas would have been near the top of any list of places I would have chosen to live. And the salary would be equal to my current Foreign Service salary, so the retirement annuity would raise my income by 54%, while the cost of living in Dallas, especially for housing, was less than in Washington. Our standard of living would improve, and financing college education for Kim and Eva would no longer be a problem.

I was elated when I was called on January 17, 1989, with the news that I had been chosen for the job, and they wanted me to begin work as soon as possible. The outcome of my forced retirement had proved to be positive! And being selected from among 453 applicants for the position restored the self-confidence that had been undermined by the Foreign Service's rejection.

****

12.

Municipal Foreign Minister:

Director of International Affairs for Dallas, 1989-93

After retirement paperwork and farewells, I arrived in Dallas in March, eager to begin this new adventure on another less-traveled road: international affairs at the municipal level. Tuy-Cam stayed behind with Kim and Eva to finish the school year and to sell the house. I bought a house in North Dallas, which was a major upgrade from what we had been able to afford in Arlington, and we were moved in by June.

Internationalizing Dallas

Most cities with a strong international character are either national capitals, the focal points of politics, or seaports, the focal points of global commerce and culture. Dallas was neither. However, it was by far the largest city in the Dallas-Fort Worth "Metroplex," which, with 5.2 million people in 2000 (7.1 million in 2015) was the country's fourth most populous metropolitan statistical area (MSA). Moreover, it had Dallas-Fort Worth International Airport (DFW), the world's third busiest in terms of aircraft movements and seventh busiest in terms of passenger traffic. By the late 20th Century, great airports such as DFW were serving the internationalizing functions of seaports, directing the world's commerce and people to cities that possess them.

The DFW Metroplex, especially Dallas, was becoming one of the "command and control centers" for the global economy, ranking ninth among all cities as a headquarters for large multi-national corporations. It was home base for firms such as Exxon-Mobil, AT&T, American Airlines, Southwest Airlines, Fluor, Texas Instruments, Kimberly-Clark, J.C. Penney, and Electronic Data Systems. More than 600 foreign companies had plants and offices in the Dallas area. The population, too, had become international, with 25% foreign-born, 40% Hispanic, and substantial Chinese, Indian, and Muslim communities.

Nonetheless, Dallas was perceived as behind many of its peers, especially Houston, in terms of its international character. Moreover, mid-1980s economic declines in the oil, real estate, and banking sectors had awakened the city's political and business leadership to the need to make Dallas a more effective global competitor. Several initiatives to promote this objective were launched under Mayor Annette Strauss. She was the sister-in-law of Robert Strauss, a Democratic Party power broker who served as U.S. Trade Representative under President Carter and Ambassador to the USSR under President George H. W. Bush. The most important of these initiatives was the 1987-88 Mayor's Commission on International Development, headed by Ross Perot's principal deputy, Mort Myerson. One of its recommendations was to transform the city's Office of Protocol, which had recently been created to host foreign dignitaries, into an Office of International Affairs, a sort of municipal foreign ministry. Given increased staff and funding, this office was additionally charged with:

- Promoting expansion of global trade and foreign investment;
- Developing the city's international economic infrastructure;
- Supporting cultural and educational exchanges;
- Marketing Dallas internationally to attract global sports events, conventions, and tourism; and
- Serving as the focal point for contact with foreign government representatives, international organizations, and immigrant communities.

This was the mission for which I was recruited. I found that I had strong support from Mayor Strauss, the Chamber of Commerce, and other leaders of the city's establishment.

Office of International Affairs

The newly-created Office of International Affairs (OIA) I inherited as Director had two deputies, for protocol and special events, and an office assistant. Over the next year, we added two new deputies, for international economic development and cultural affairs, and a second office assistant, bringing the total staff to seven.

OIA was a public-private partnership. The staff were city employees, paid from the city budget, but the entire operating budget came from private funds raised by the annual Dallas Ambassadors Forum. This event brought 40-50 foreign Ambassadors from Washington to Dallas for a weekend, with free transportation provided by Delta (which had a major hub at DFW). It featured an elegant black-tie dinner-dance hosted by the Mayor, a Texas-style barbeque at South Fork Ranch (made famous in the "Dallas" TV show that was popular in the 1980s), and presentations on the city's business opportunities. Companies bought tickets for the dinner, which became one of Dallas' premier social occasions. It raised nearly $500,000 each year.

OIA also had a volunteer corps of 55 provided by the Junior League. These were accomplished young women who helped host VIP visitors and organize hospitality events such as the Ambassadors Forum.

Because the operating budget came from private funds, OIA had greater flexibility than typical city government offices. For example, in Dallas as in most cities, it would not be politically possible, even if funds were available in the regular municipal budget, to use taxpayer money to entertain foreign dignitaries and pay for foreign travel by the Mayor and OIA staff.

OIA Accomplishments

This concerted effort to promote Dallas' international development, led by the Mayor and a small city government office, and backed by local business and civic leaders, produced dividends for the city and the DFW Metroplex that were well in excess of its modest cost in public funds, which was only about $300,000 per year. Here are some of the principal accomplishments during the four years I was Director:

- **NAFTA.** Our most important initiative was to position Dallas as the economic hub and focal point of NAFTA, the North American Free Trade Agreement. I conceived this idea based on Dallas' existing role as a major center for global trade, especially with Mexico, plus its geographic position as the closest city to the population center of North America (the point about which the combined population of the United States, Mexico, and Canada is evenly distributed), and its outstanding communication infrastructure (DFW Airport, and direct road and rail links to Mexico and Canada). Mayor Strauss and the business community enthusiastically embraced the concept, and we began a campaign in 1990, two years before NAFTA was signed, to bring what was a distant vision into reality.

  With lobbying visits to Washington, Mexico City, and Toronto, we convinced the three governments to hold the first comprehensive negotiating session in Dallas, in February 1991. It brought 400 negotiators to the city for a week, along with a lot of press attention. Dallas' role as host city produced what the *Dallas Morning News* characterized as "rave reviews" from the participants. We provided everything from bargain hotel rates, to special communications facilities, to an elegant final dinner for more than 1,000 people. After the Agreement was signed in December 1992, continued lobbying and economic inducements, including free office space, resulted in the selection of Dallas as the location of one of NAFTA's three permanent administrative offices (the other two were in Mexico and Canada).

- **Trade and investment promotion.** We organized large trade and investment promotion missions, headed by the Mayor, to

241

Japan, Mexico, Italy, Australia, the Soviet Union, and Israel, and I led smaller groups to international trade fairs in Germany and France. We also hosted dozens of incoming foreign trade groups and prospective investors.

- **International infrastructure.** One of Dallas' shortcomings as an international city was lack of an international school. This was corrected by the opening of the Dallas International School, which offered a European-style curriculum in French and English. Its Director and I traveled to Paris and successfully lobbied the French government to accredit the school and support it financially. Another new initiative was appointing a dozen "Ambassadors of Dallas." These were Dallas business people temporarily resident abroad who agreed to informally represent the city and help build commercial and cultural ties. OIA also facilitated the opening of 11 new consular and trade offices in Dallas, and we supported new sister city relationships in Mexico, France, Japan, Latvia, and the Czech Republic.

- **VIP visitors.** Our highest profile visit was by Queen Elizabeth and her husband Prince Phillip. We organized a formal dinner with 300 guests as well as several events to showcase Dallas' cultural accomplishments. Other VIP visitors included five chiefs of state and 55 foreign cabinet-level officials. These visits usually included a luncheon or dinner hosted by the Mayor as well as events involving local businesses and immigrant communities with ties to the visitor's country.

Social Prominence, Media Attention, and Waning Enthusiasm

One of the greatest benefits -- and heaviest burdens -- of my job was attending frequent ceremonial and social events at the highest level of Dallas society, sometimes with the Mayor, sometimes representing the Mayor. These events included meetings of the consular corps, cultural festivities such as the annual Asian-American Fair and *Cinco de*

Mayo, meetings of foreign-American chambers of commerce, openings of new foreign businesses, national day celebrations, and almost anything else that was international in character and called for city government representation.

Some weeks I had more than a dozen events to attend, all of them with lots of good food and drink, and many were actually fun. But my exercise schedule was often disrupted, I gained a few pounds, and I began to fear for my long-term health. It was just too much of a good thing. I met many interesting people, most of them wealthy, and I became fully engaged in the city's social life. However, this was not a status that either Tuy-Cam or I sought or very much enjoyed.

I was also regularly on local TV and in the newspapers, both in the business pages because of my international economic development work, and in the social pages because of my chief of protocol role. Most of the publicity was positive, but some was not. For example, there was small-scale but vocal political opposition to NAFTA and my support for it, and I occasionally drew criticism from those who were offended by being left off the guest list for prestigious events. I didn't try to avoid public attention, but neither did I seek it. It became just another part of this inherently high-profile job.

While I continued to enjoy my work, after the first three years my enthusiasm for it began to wane. Burdens balanced rewards, and the often frantic pace grew harder to sustain.

New City Leaders and New Problems

The concept of international affairs as an integral function of municipal government was a paradigm shift not readily accepted by most City Hall career professionals, whose horizons rarely extended beyond traditional local concerns such as fire and police protection, sanitation, street repair, zoning, etc. Even though most of my interactions were with the Mayor, I was organizationally under the

City Manager. In effect, I had two bosses. At first, this was not a problem, since the City Manager supported an expanded role for OIA and valued our contributions. However, a new City Manager in 1990 had a more traditional outlook and tried to limit my access to the Mayor, halt our staff growth, and cut our budget. With strong support from business and civic leaders as well as the Mayor, I prevailed in the ensuing bureaucratic struggle, but not without wounds and enduring hard feelings that later proved problematic.

Another blow was the end of Annette Strauss' term as Mayor in 1991. She had been a great boss, and she and her husband Ted had become our good friends, bringing us into a network of city leaders. These included business executives, lawyers, bankers, philanthropists, and the owner of the Texas Rangers baseball team, George W. Bush.

Annette's replacement was Steve Bartlett, a former Republican Congressman representing a North Dallas district. I liked Steve and we got along well, but he lacked Annette's enthusiasm for internationalization. Also, he was more of a politician, in contrast to Annette's background as a cultural and philanthropic leader. Steve had ambitions beyond City Hall, perhaps to be Governor, and he focused much attention on building his political base. When the City Manager mounted another effort to cut the OIA budget and staff, he did not vigorously resist it, and we lost two of our seven positions.

I began to question my future as Director of International Affairs. Although I didn't initiate a job search, I let friends know that I might be open to attractive opportunities.

Another New Road, to Academia

One of my friends was Bill Wallace, the Senior Vice President of the Federal Reserve Bank of Dallas. In 1992, Bill had retired after a distinguished career with the Fed to become Dean of the College of Business and Public Administration at Old Dominion University in

Norfolk. One of Bill's priorities was to give the College a more international orientation. He contacted me in March 1993 to ask if I might be interested in heading a new Center for Global Business. He was familiar with my economic development work in Dallas, especially on NAFTA, and we had also discussed the Senior Seminar, so he knew about my experience in executive training. He thought I would be a good fit for the new Center.

I had long believed I would enjoy work at a university, so this looked like a great opportunity. Moreover, with my waning enthusiasm for my present job, plus its uncertain future under the city's new leadership, I was ready for a change. I flew to Norfolk for an interview and received an attractive offer, which I was quick to accept.

Farewell to Dallas

Our friends organized a warm farewell. In some ways I was reluctant to leave. It had been a good job, and we had developed close ties to Dallas and many of its people. We had become Texans, and felt at home. Moreover, I believed in the importance of my mission to help the city strengthen its international character.

I had often been interviewed by some of the *Dallas Morning News* reporters, and was well acquainted with its President and its Editorial Page Editor. I was nonetheless surprised and gratified to read the lead editorial in the paper on April 24, 1993:

WORLD MARKETPLACE
Office has strengthened Dallas' role

For years, Dallas has enjoyed describing itself as an international city. But until an office of international affairs was established at Dallas City Hall, the claim was closer to self-promotion than factual reporting.

With the appointment of James Bullington, a former United States ambassador, as the city's international affairs director in 1989, Dallas began establishing a more polished, professional approach to international affairs. Mr. Bullington, a seasoned diplomat, strived to help make Dallas competitive with other large metropolitan areas for world trade and foreign investments.

He has been closely involved in efforts to make Dallas a hub city when the North American Free Trade Agreement is finalized. And Mr. Bullington helped attract nearly a dozen consular, trade or other offices of foreign governments to Dallas during his tenure here.

Mr. Bullington's decision to resign as international affairs director is a setback for Dallas' goal to earn a bigger share of world markets. His departure in June raises new questions about this city's commitment to maintain a high profile for Dallas on the international front.

Budget cutbacks forced the office of international affairs to scale back its staff considerably in the last year. In addition, the office has not been given the priority under Mayor Steve Bartlett that it enjoyed when Annette Strauss was mayor.

The decision by Mr. Bullington to accept a post with Old Dominion University in Virginia should be a signal to the mayor and City Council. With a decision on the free trade agreement just around the corner, Dallas cannot afford to lose ground in its work to become a more sophisticated player in international competitions. The investment the city makes in its office of international affairs is small compared to the economic returns that can be anticipated.

Dallas had been a good experience. Concerns about the future of the Office of International Affairs, however, proved to be justified. Another retired FSO and former Ambassador replaced me, but within five years the office was closed as a part of city government. Its residual functions were turned over to the Dallas Council on World Affairs and the Chamber of Commerce.

Family Update

Tuy-Cam transitioned easily from the Foreign Service to Dallas, and she developed lots of friends in the neighborhood and in the international community, including the International Women's Club, the consular corps wives group, and the Dallas chapter of Ikebana International. We did not do as much home entertaining as when we were posted overseas, but our social calendar was full with my work-related events, and she joined me for many of them. Moreover, she had to take on additional family responsibilities as an active-duty grandmother.

I was pleased that Kim had chosen to go to Auburn and was accepted following her high school graduation in 1989. Everything was arranged for her to begin that fall. However, she left Dallas "to visit friends" back in Arlington, and the next we heard from her was that she had married Roy, a young Marine who turned out to be sublimely ill-suited to be a husband. The Auburn enrollment had to be aborted, and the couple moved into a poverty-level apartment in suburban Maryland. Shortly after their son Kevin was born in 1990, Roy went to sea and never returned, abandoning his wife and child. They moved into our house in Dallas, where we had plenty of room. Kim got a part-time job at the local community college and enrolled as a student. So we now had both daughters living with us, plus an infant grandson. I helped Kim arrange a divorce from Roy, and we never heard from him again.

Eva was unhappy to leave Arlington to complete her final two years of high school in Dallas. Even my gift of a new car did little to console her. After a few months, however, she made friends and did well in her new school. After graduation in 1991, she enrolled at the University of North Texas in Denton, 40 miles north of Dallas.

***

Welcoming Queen Elizabeth, left, and Philippine President Aquino, below, with Mayor Strauss.

BELOW LEFT: Welcoming President Saleh of North Yemen, who had recently signed an oil exploration agreement with a Dallas company. For chief of state visits, as chief of protocol I first boarded the aircraft, and led the visitors down the stairs to introduce the mayor, waiting on the ground. BELOW RIGHT: Meeting Governor Ann Richards, at an Austin reception for foreign consuls in Texas.

***

With the President of the Bank of Tokyo and his wife, at a reception celebrating the opening of the Bank's office in Dallas.

Mayor Bartlett, center, and the Mayor of Monterrey, Mexico, signing a partner city agreement.

****

13.

A Difficult Detour into Academia:

Old Dominion University, 1993-2000

Old Dominion University was founded in 1930 as the Norfolk campus of the College of William and Mary. It evolved into an independent public university, and had 15,000 students when I arrived in 1993 (24,000 in 2015). It has six colleges, including the College of Business and Public Administration, home of the new Center for Global Business that I was hired to create and direct. It is a typical urban commuter university, in an academic tier below the state's flagship schools (the University of Virginia, Virginia Tech, and William and Mary), but nonetheless a locally important institution. I was to have the rank and salary of full professor.

Hampton Roads, the metropolitan region in southeast Virginia around the mouth of the Chesapeake Bay, consists of Norfolk, Virginia Beach, Newport News, and several adjacent municipalities and counties. It is home to 1.7 million people. Its status as a major east coast seaport and home of the U.S. Navy's largest base as well as several other important military facilities gives Hampton Roads an international character. I thought it would be an interesting place to live and work.

The mission of my new Center was to:

- Promote infusion of a global perspective into the College's education, research, and community outreach programs;
- Help prepare graduates for leadership positions in the global economy;
- Support the international development and competitiveness of the Hampton Roads region; and
- Position ODU as a national leader in global business education among comparable metropolitan universities.

When we arrived in Norfolk on July 2 and began moving into the house we had purchased near the ODU campus, I was enthusiastic about the job and confident I could handle it.

A Shocking Resignation

My optimism turned out to be short-lived. Dean Bill Wallace, my new boss and the driving force behind creation of the Center for Global Business, invited Tuy-Cam and me to dinner on July 3 and gave us the shocking news: He had submitted his resignation as Dean. Although he would be staying on through the academic year that was just beginning (1993-94), while a search was conducted for his replacement, he would be leaving the following summer.

Bill explained that the College faculty had fiercely resisted and sabotaged the changes he tried to implement during the past two years. He said that he had not been supported by the University administration, and that he felt obliged to resign after the faculty passed a vote of no confidence in him by a large majority. Bill's wife added that she feared for his health if he stayed on to continue the struggle. Bill said he would do what he could for me, but he acknowledged that his departure put me in a difficult situation.

During the months that followed, I learned just how difficult my situation really was. I nonetheless tried to make the best of it. I sought to build good relations with the faculty, even taking 40 of them (more than half) to one-on-one lunches to explore ways I might work with them and be helpful in the internationalization mission. With only three or four exceptions, their reactions ranged from indifference to overt hostility. They made clear that I would not be able to participate in teaching or other academic activities, and that they viewed me as an unqualified and unwelcome interloper brought in by a failed Dean. Moreover, the College's Department Chairs formally proposed, in a memorandum to the University President, that my Center be abolished as a waste of money.

251

By the end of 1993, both Dean Wallace and I realized that the Center for Global Business was a non-starter.

A New Job

Meanwhile, the College's continuing education (i.e., non-academic) unit, the Institute for Management, was failing. It had long been losing money, and the College could no longer afford to subsidize it. Its Director had been unable to end these losses. Consequently, in December 1993 he was given the required six months notice that his contract would not be renewed.

Dean Wallace proposed that I take over this failing unit. If I could make it financially self-sufficient by selling more training programs, he opined, I might be able to retain my job at the University. Otherwise, he concluded, under his successor the faculty was certain to succeed in having my position abolished.

Having no viable alternative, and needing a steady income, I accepted the offer. We changed the name of the Institute to "Center for Global Business and Executive Education," in hopes of retaining at least part of my internationalizing mission by conducting some non-academic programs with a global focus, and in order to give me a platform for writing, speaking, and community service in the international arena.

Success of the New Center

Although this was not the job I had been hired to do, I accepted the challenge of becoming a university-based entrepreneur running a training business. In the six years I headed the Center, annual revenue grew from $315,000 to $987,000, and the bottom line went from a loss of $68,000 to a profit of $191,000. We offered both open enrollment certification courses (Professional Financial Planner, Oracle Database Administrator, Professional Human Resources Manager, Paralegal Certificate, etc.), and customized contract training for regional businesses, governments, and military organizations.

I didn't enjoy this work, which mostly involved marketing and administration, plus management of a staff that grew to six employees and an on-call faculty of 50 trainers, consultants, practicing professionals, and professors. However, Dean Wallace and his successor, Taylor Sims, gave me almost complete autonomy in running the Center, as long as I achieved profits (which supplemented the College's budget), so I eventually came to regard the job as tolerable.

In spite of the "Global Business" in the Center's name, few of our courses or contract programs were internationally focused. However, I was able to use my international background in doing community outreach and service activities. I became chairman of the Hampton Roads Chamber of Commerce International Business Council and a board member of the World Affairs Council. I also published newspaper and magazine articles and spoke for civic clubs and other local organizations, mostly on global affairs.

I especially enjoyed becoming a Senior Fellow at the Joint Forces Staff College, located on the Norfolk Navy Base. I gave presentations about the State Department and Foreign Service, civil-military relations, and counterinsurgency in Vietnam; and I participated in exercises and simulations, playing the role of Ambassador.

I got along well with Dean Sims, but my relations with the College faculty remained strained. They continued to exclude me from any participation in academic programs as well as their social activities, so I gradually withdrew into the professional cocoon of my Center and found other friends, in the military, government, civic, and business communities.

A Sexual Harassment Charge against my Deputy

As time went by, I grew increasingly dissatisfied with my role at the University, and I began to look for another job. Before I could find one, however, I was fired.

253

My deputy at the Center was an immigrant from the Middle East -- let's call him Karim (not his real name) -- who had recently completed his Ph.D. at ODU. Karim was an excellent salesman, and he played a key role in the Center's growth and financial success. However, in August 1999, the University's Equal Opportunity and Affirmative Action Office brought charges of sexual harassment against him.

In addition to his work at the Center, Karim had taught an undergraduate economics class. One of his former students in that class, a 27-year-old woman, said he had a sexual relationship with her. She did not charge coercion of any sort, but had sought help from the University's student counseling office when the relationship ended because, she said, it had left her emotionally distraught and unable to continue her classes. The counselor brought the case to the attention of the Equal Opportunity and Affirmative Action Office, which in turn made the sexual harassment charge. They said that any faculty member who has sexual relations with a student is presumed guilty of sexual harassment. Karim was formally notified of the charges, with a copy to me (as his supervisor) and to Dean Sims. This notification was the first I knew about the matter.

Karim, who was married, denied having sex with the woman. An investigation was conducted by the EO/AA Office, extending over several months, but insofar as I am aware, no proof or corroborating witnesses were found. Karim's (female) assistant at the Center testified that the woman had persistently pursued Karim and that he had tried to avoid her.

A Rigged Audit

In November, I was called to a meeting in Dean Sims' office with him, the Associate Dean, and the University Internal Auditor. I was informed that ODU President Jim Koch had ordered an audit of the Center because of charges made by a former instructor. The audit was to begin immediately.

The former instructor had been involved in several Center programs managed by Karim, and there had been disputes between them about pay and about Karim's use of another instructor to teach a course that this instructor regarded as "his." He charged that a major customer of the Center, the Navy Exchange Service, had stolen his copyrighted course materials and used them in one of its internal training programs, a theft for which he held the Center somehow responsible. I had previously investigated these charges and found them to be without merit.

The following day, Dean Sims told me privately that President Koch had decided Karim must be dismissed because of the accusation by the student and another unsubstantiated report of sexual misconduct that had reached Koch's office. However, Dean Sims continued, sexual harassment was notoriously difficult to prove. Therefore, he said, the audit was ordered by the President to confirm that Karim was responsible for not properly protecting the instructor's copyrighted materials and to find additional, performance-related grounds on which to fire him. The Dean told me to assist the auditors in finding these additional grounds.

My response was that if Karim were guilty of sexual harassment, he should be fired for that reason. However, his record at the Center was unblemished in terms of conduct and outstanding in terms of productivity, and I would not agree to manufacture accusations against him that were not true. A few days later, I learned from one of my few faculty friends that the Dean had told her that my refusal to find reasons to fire Karim was likely to result in my departure as well.

The audit continued for more than 10 weeks. The final report, delivered in January, 2000, contained nothing about the alleged sexual harassment. It noted the dismissed instructor's charges (although it cited no evidence to support them), and recommended that the Center maintain tighter control over instructor-developed course material. There were no accusations of theft, fraud, or waste, nor any comments about the quality of the Center's training, its customer service, or its profitability. A few minor infractions of University regulations were reported, such as our failure to use the University's sole-source caterer to provide coffee and snacks for our programs, and our failure to have our contract forms approved by the University lawyer. (We had not previously been aware of these requirements.)

By any reasonable measure, the Center was an effective, successful operation. However, even though the audit found no serious problems, its conclusions were negative, just as President Koch had directed them to be.

On January 28, 2000, Karim and I were summoned to the office of the University attorney. Dean Sims was also present. Karim was given a letter dismissing him immediately, and he was told to clear out of his office that afternoon. I was given a letter informing me that my employment would be terminated effective July 28 (consistent with University regulations requiring six months notice to faculty administrators if their contracts were not to be renewed). Although Dean Sims signed the letter, he privately told me and others that he was not in favor of my firing but was ordered to take this action by President Koch.

Liberation and Return to the Global Arena

My first reaction was to look into the possibility of legal action. I probably had a good case, since Karim sued the University and eventually received a large payoff in an out-of-court settlement. On reflection, however, I decided that I wanted to sever all connection with ODU as quickly and completely as possible, and I didn't want to get entangled in lengthy litigation. I had never been happy at the University, and I decided to regard getting fired for refusing to abandon my principles as an act of self-liberation. I'm not proud of my association with ODU, but I am proud of getting fired from it. In retrospect, I regret only that I did not leave much sooner.

So, I began to look for a new job, never again returning to the campus except to clean out my office, say goodbye to my staff, and complete paperwork related to my pension.

In reaching out to Foreign Service colleagues as part of my job search, I discovered that one of my Senior Seminar students, Chuck Baquet, was now Deputy Director of the Peace Corps. I had been inspired by Peace Corps when it was created by President Kennedy in 1961, and had I not passed the Foreign Service exam in 1962, I might well have become a Volunteer after graduating from Auburn. Moreover, I had frequent contact with Peace Corps staff and Volunteers during my Foreign Service assignments, and had thought that someday I might like to do that sort of work. And because Peace Corps limits employees to five-year terms (with exceptional extensions of no more than three years), for the purpose of avoiding creation of a bureaucracy, it has never developed a career staff, and there is high turnover and lots of employment opportunities.

I contacted Chuck, and he was helpful in moving my application through channels and assuring its serious consideration. I was interviewed and offered a job as Country Director in Niger, beginning in July with a two-week Washington orientation program.

Living in Norfolk

In spite of my professional frustration at ODU, Tuy-Cam and I found life in Norfolk reasonably pleasant. The pace was slower than in Dallas, and social obligations were much less frequent, leaving adequate time for exercise, leisure activities, and family affairs.

As usual, Tuy-Cam took the lead in our social life. At first we reached out to the ODU faculty, but with only three exceptions we were not successful in developing friendships with them. Tuy-Cam became active in a Mahjongg group composed mostly of wives of senior military officers at the Navy Base and the NATO Atlantic Command,

and we socialized primarily with them plus a few of our neighbors and people we met through the World Affairs Council and Chamber of Commerce.

I resumed contact with the group of Vietnam veterans who wrote and performed songs about the War, which had been formed by Dr. Lydia Fish, a folklorist at Buffalo (New York) State College. We did several concerts during the years I was at ODU, mostly at universities and officers clubs on military bases. Two of our memorable "gigs" were at the Smithsonian Institution in Washington and an oral history symposium on Vietnam at Hampden-Sydney College.

After graduating *magna cum laude* from the University of North Texas with a degree in psychology, Eva began graduate school at Arizona State University in Tempe. She eventually switched her focus to speech-language pathology and transferred to the University of Texas in Austin, where she received her Master's degree in Communication Disorders. She also got married to a fellow graduate student, Jeremy Gustafson, who had spent two years in The Gambia as a Peace Corps Volunteer. We attended their wedding in Flagstaff, Arizona, in August 2000, on our way from Norfolk to Niger.

Kim and Kevin came with us from Dallas to Norfolk and lived in our house. Kim got a part-time job in the ODU admissions office and enrolled as a student. She graduated with a degree in French and moved into full-time work with admissions. Soon, she began work on a Ph.D. in university administration.

Kim was busy with school, work, and an active social life, so Tuy-Cam and I assumed a co-parental role with regard to Kevin. He was an indifferent and sometimes unruly student who needed more attention than Norfolk public schools were able to provide, and we enrolled him in private schools. When I got the job in Niger, we all agreed that it would be best for him to go there with us and complete the sixth and seventh grades at the small Embassy-sponsored International School.

Tuy-Cam and I, together with Kevin, arrived in Niger in August, 2000, ready for a new adventure and eager to return to the Foreign Service lifestyle that we had so much enjoyed.

Performing Vietnam warrior songs, 1993.

Eva's wedding in Flagstaff, 2000. Left to right: Jim, Kim, Jeremy, Eva, Tuy-Cam, Stephanie (Tuy-Cam's sister), Kevin.

****

14.

Hard Core Peace Corps: Niger, 2000-2006

The six years I spent as Peace Corps Director in Niger were professionally and personally gratifying, better even than my two tours of duty in charge of U.S. Embassies. Every time I went to the Embassy in Niamey and saw the Ambassador, I was reminded of how happy I was to have my job instead of hers. This was partly because the Peace Corps experience came at the right season of my life; partly because it liberated me from a stifling academic environment; partly because I was able to operate with a great deal of independence from Peace Corps headquarters in Washington; but mostly because of the satisfaction of being able to use a lifetime of experience to support the 435 outstanding American Volunteers who served under my direction in Niger in their efforts to help some of the world's poorest people.

I wrote a book about it: *Adventures in Service with Peace Corps in Niger*, published in 2007 and available from Amazon. Here, in this memoir, I will only record some of the highlights.

Peace Corps Overview

In a campaign speech during the 1960 election, Senator Kennedy asked an audience of University of Michigan students if they would be willing to volunteer for work in developing countries. He had in mind the Cold War struggle with communism for influence in the newly independent countries then emerging from colonialism.

The students responded enthusiastically, and more than a thousand signed a petition pledging to volunteer. Stirred by the students' petition, two weeks later Kennedy formally proposed creation of what he called a "Peace Corps." He reinforced his call to national service in his inaugural address: "And so, my fellow Americans, ask not what your country can do for you, ask what you can do for your country." The establishment of Peace Corps just two months after the inauguration gave practical substance to this challenge and inspired a generation of American youth.

Peace Corps' three goals have remained unchanged since President Kennedy proclaimed them:

- Sustainable development in poor countries, with a focus on people and building local capacity.
- Better understanding of America through building relationships at the grass-roots level.
- Better American understanding of others through internationally engaged Volunteers and those they influence.

The first goal, promoting economic development, is the most well-known, but the other two, about promoting mutual understanding, have proved to be more important. Peace Corps has a useful but small role in economic development. It was never thought of as a charity; and although conceived in the context of Cold War competition for global influence, it was never intended to be a short term foreign policy tool. Rather, it was to be an instrument for building long term relationships. It was a government-sponsored people-to-people program, and part of what we would today call our "soft power."

It's important to note that Peace Corps has always been an independent agency, not part of the State Department. It has zealously guarded this separation from diplomacy and politics.

Peace Corps Today

Peace Corps grew rapidly in the 1960s, reaching a peak of 16,000 Volunteers. During this period, it was the focus of much public attention, with cover stories in *Time* and *Newsweek* as well as frequent articles in Volunteers' hometown newspapers. However, during the 1970s and 1980s, the number of Volunteers dwindled to 5,400. It began to recover under President Clinton in the 1990s, and also had strong support from the Bush 43 Administration. It peaked again at 9,200 Volunteers in 2010, but as of 2016, it has dropped back to 7,200, distributed in 65 countries.

The constraint on Volunteer numbers has always been limited funding. Peace Corps regularly has three to four times more applicants than it can afford to accept. The 2016 budget is $410 million, which, adjusted for inflation, is about the same as it has been for the past decade.

As in the 1960s, today's typical Volunteer is a recent college graduate, 22-26 years old; but 8% are over 50, with a few in their 70s and 80s. We had one married couple in Niger who were in their 50s, but the harsh living conditions and limited medical facilities made it impossible to accept Volunteers older than that.

In the early years of Peace Corps, when the modern women's liberation movement was just getting underway, two-thirds of the Volunteers were male. Today, two-thirds are female.

Volunteer recruitment is primarily via the Internet and on college campuses. The principal motivators for joining are altruism and desire for adventure.

New Volunteers are assembled in groups of 30-40 who are going to the same country. After two days of orientation, they are sent directly to the country of assignment for three months of training in the local language and survival skills they need to live among the people. In Niger, they learned Hausa or Zarma and basic understanding of Nigerien culture, plus how to deal with the Saharan heat and reduce the risk of malaria and other diseases.

Peace Corps takes care of all the Volunteers' travel, medical, and other essential expenses, and gives them a monthly allowance designed to enable them to live at the same level as the people they are working with. In Niger, they were working mostly with subsistence farmers and herders, so they only got the local currency equivalent of about $200 a month. Also, $225 per month is deposited into a fund they receive at the end of their two-year term of service, which is designed to help them re-integrate into American life.

But the most important benefits the Volunteers receive are intangible:

- A life-changing experience that shapes their future and their understanding of the world;
- The greatest adventure of a lifetime; and
- Exceptional self-confidence and maturity.

I told all the new arrivals that if they could complete two years living in a village in Niger, there is not much that subsequent life could possibly bring them that they wouldn't be able to handle. It was gratifying to watch these young people, just out of college, rapidly develop into strong adults.

Niger is a *National Geographic* sort of place, colorful and picturesque, but living there is a challenge that's outside the experience or even the imagination of almost all Americans.

Preparing for a camel race at a nomad festival near Ingall.

***

The grand mosque at Agadez, an ancient oasis town on one of the principal caravan routes across the Sahara.

Wodabe dancers at an annual nomad festival. The young men wear heavy makeup and dance to impress the girls.

***

Kim Ziropoulas with the Sarki of Konni and his court. A Sarki is the religious and cultural leader of a group of villages.

Jen Rice and her visiting father head to her village in a "bush taxi," the principal means of motorized transport in rural Niger.

***

Niger, a former French colony, lies in the center of the Sahara and is almost twice the size of Texas. It is often confused with Nigeria, a former British colony just to its south. Both countries take their name from the Niger River. Most of Niger's 17 million people live in the southern third of the country, a semi-arid region called the Sahel, which stretches across Africa from the Atlantic to the Indian Ocean. Niger's only paved highway runs from the Mali border along the Niger River to Niamey, the capital, and then eastward along the Nigerian border to Zinder, with one branch extending north to Agadez and the uranium mines at Arlit, and another leading south to the border with Benin. Most Volunteers were stationed in villages along the route of this highway. More than 90% of the population is Muslim, but not extremist.

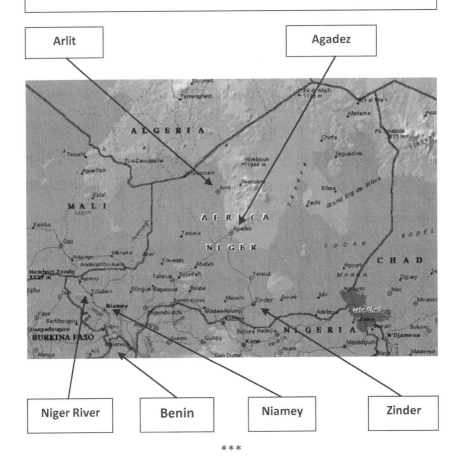

Arlit

Agadez

Niger River

Benin

Niamey

Zinder

***

Poster Country for Poverty

There are many ways to measure poverty. On an international scale, the best is the United Nations Development Program's Human Development Index, which combines per capita income with several health and social measures such as life expectancy and literacy. On this scale, in 2000 Niger ranked 174 out of 174 countries on the list. In 2016, with more countries added, it ranked 187 out of 187.

This kind of poverty does not exist in the United States or other developed countries, and unless you have spent time in a country such as Niger, you truly can't imagine what it's like.

Niger's per capita GDP is $884, compared to $50,859 in the United States. The poverty rate, defined as people living on less than $2 a day, is 90%; and the extreme poverty rate, living on less than $1.25 a day, is 44%. Here are some other grim statistics:

- One of every four children will not live to see a fifth birthday.
- 51% of children under five are malnourished.
- The adult literacy rate is 29%.
- Only 38% of primary school-age children are enrolled in school, declining to 7% at the high school level.
- Life expectancy is 48 (compared to 79 in the United States).
- There are three doctors per 100,000 people (compared to 276 in the United States).
- Less than 10% of the people have access to electricity.

Nigeriens have to endure this poverty, and foreigners living in Niger have to get used to it. This was especially challenging for the Volunteers, who lived mostly in rural villages among ordinary people and saw the sickness, the hunger, and the dying children up close.

The reasons for Niger's poverty are many, including the arid climate; environmental degradation and desertification; rapid population growth; high disease rates (malaria, AIDS, and many others); low education rates; and chronic political instability. I'll elaborate on two others: primitive technology and the low status of women.

A time traveler from 1,000 or even 2,000 years ago, if somehow magically transported to a rural Nigerien village today, would feel pretty much at home, since the way of life and technologies in use would be little changed. When I visited the Volunteers in those villages, the scenes of daily life struck me as Biblical -- living illustrations from the children's Sunday school books I had grown up with. There were bearded men in long robes praying to their God; women drawing water at the communal well and carrying it home in jars on their heads; donkeys and camels eating straw in the shade; shepherds passing by with their flocks of sheep and goats; a few skinny cows. Technologically, rural Niger was barely, if at all, connected to the modern world during the time we were there. Just before our departure in 2006, a few places were penetrated by cell phones, a technology now spreading rapidly throughout Africa.

Yet another cause of Niger's poverty is the low status accorded to women. Gender roles are strict, and women are mostly limited to field work, gardening, drawing water, food preparation, and child care. With an average of eight children per woman, the world's highest, a lot of child care is required. Female literacy is only one-third that of men; 47% of girls are married by the age of 15 and almost all are married before 18; and women between 18 and 45 are pregnant 28% of the time. In the West, we tend to think of such treatment of women as a matter of justice, but it's also an economic problem. The fact that half the population in Niger is much less productive than it could be has major implications for development prospects and the persistence of poverty.

***

Animals in a typical village in Niger.

Camel market near Konni, as a dust storm blows in from the Sahara.

***

Children pounding millet, Niger's principal food crop.

Women drawing water at a village well.

***

Peace Corps in Niger

Peace Corps sent its first Volunteers to Niger in 1962 and continued to operate there without interruption for 49 years. There are more than 3,000 Peace Corps/Niger "veterans." During my tenure, the average number of Volunteers was 120, with two groups of 35 trainees arriving each year to replace those who departed. The office support staff consisted of half a dozen Americans and 40 Nigeriens.

After three months of training, the Volunteers were sent to their posts, with one per village of 500-1,000 people (except for a few who were assigned to small regional towns). They would be "adopted" by a Nigerien family, normally that of the village chief, and they became an honorary son or daughter. They lived in houses built by the villagers, usually with mud bricks and a thatched roof, with only one room. In most cases no one in the village could speak any language but Hausa or Zarma unless there was a school, in which case the teacher could speak French. (Less than half the villages had schools.)

Under these sink-or-swim circumstances, the Volunteers quickly gained fluency in the language and integrated into village life.

Living conditions were harsh, with no electricity, telephones, running water, or toilets. Most meals were taken with villagers and consisted primarily of millet mush, an oatmeal-like grain preparation topped with sauce and vegetables. Meat was rarely served except on holidays and special occasions such as weddings. Daytime temperatures often exceeded 120F, and rarely fell below 90 except during the mid-November to mid-February "winter."

Most Volunteer projects involved transferring knowledge and skills. Here are some examples:

- School and village demonstration gardens, introducing improved seeds and irrigation techniques.

- Reclamation of desertified land and tree planting to reduce wind erosion.
- Establishment of cereal banks and credit cooperatives.
- AIDS awareness and prevention campaigns.
- Teacher training and adult literacy programs.
- Construction of village schools, clinics, and wells.

These projects reflect Peace Corps' mission of sustainable development, not charity; not just helping people, but helping people help themselves. Charity makes donors feel good and is sometimes necessary, but only development can have a lasting impact. We taught the Volunteers that development is best thought of as a process in which people are changed, not a project in which things are built. In the long run, infrastructure projects, even small ones like schools and clinics, are successful only to the extent they facilitate changes in people: new knowledge, new attitudes, new ways of doing things. And if the people being helped don't invest their own labor and resources in a project, it's unlikely to survive the departure of the donor.

The Volunteers learned these lessons of sustainable development, not just from the training but from their experience. Here's a story written by Katie Leach-Kemon for her hometown newspaper:

> Part of my job includes working with mothers to rehabilitate severely malnourished children. Since January, I have been working with a pair of twins and their mother. The twins, Amara and Boubacar, weighed only nine pounds each when they reached their first birthday.
>
> My friend Indi, a nurse at the local clinic, and I have been visiting the twins' house over the past eight months. During each visit, we discuss nutrition and hygiene with the twins' mother. Our instruction has been partially productive: The mother has been diligently preparing a protein-enriched porridge for her children, but she has yet to improve

hygiene in her household. Despite our constant reiterations about the importance of sanitation, nothing seems to change. Bowls of food left open and covered with flies, chickens eating out of cooking pots, and waste scattered throughout the yard where the children play is the scene that greets us when we visit the twins' house.

For several months, the twins have been showing signs of amelioration, like steady weight gain. Just the other day, however, I saw the twins and their mother at the clinic. Both twins were sick with vomiting and diarrhea, and their frail bodies had lost all evidence of the last eight months' progress. I am hoping that antibiotics the twins received will restore their health. I am wary, however, knowing that the unsanitary conditions in which these children live may attack their defenseless bodies with a fatal infection. While I have tried to help rehabilitate the twins as best I can, I am convinced that the only way to reduce malnutrition among young children in Niger is to encourage primary school education for girls.

Research has shown that girls' education has a direct impact on child mortality rates. In Niger, a mere 24 percent of girls attend school. Increasing school attendance among young girls seems to be the most viable approach in reducing malnutrition and child mortality. If the twins' mother had attended school, it is likely that her hygiene and feeding habits would be dramatically different. She would better understand the connection between dirt and sickness, and perhaps be more responsive to my counseling.

While the news headlines scream "CHILDREN ARE STARVING IN NIGER," the solution seems so simple. If they are starving, bring them food. End of story? Not quite. There is no "quick-fix" that will help Niger out of the hole in which it finds itself. The best way to help Niger is to work with its people and its government toward long-term goals, like increasing primary education, reducing population growth, slowing desertification, and improving access to healthcare.

Since two-thirds of the Niger Volunteers were female, many of their projects focused on women and girls. For example, one of the constraints on girls' education is that in rural villages there are only, at most, primary schools, so to go beyond the first four years of education it's necessary to send the student to live in a regional town. This is too expensive for most families. They might be able to send one child to live with relatives or friends, but this would almost always be a son, not a daughter. So the Volunteers organized a girls scholarship fund, raised money, mentored the recipients, and encouraged local women leaders to support the program.

Here are some other examples of women-focused projects:

- Campaigns to discourage precocious marriage (i.e., under the age of 18 -- many girls were married at 12 or 13).
- Condom distribution -- Niger's birth rate is among the highest in the world, and AIDS is a major threat.
- Promotion of breast feeding.
- Creation of micro-credit groups for income-generating activities.
- Organization of girls soccer teams, which had never been done in Niger.

***

Liz Cromwell at her house in Zinder.

Mike Toppe at his house in Harikanassou.

***

Virginia Emmons in the village school she organized.

Jessica Wysopal working in her demonstration garden.

***

Left: Sharon Lai with the scholarship recipient she mentored.
Right: Laura Bacon with her micro-credit group.

Amanda Goetz and village women preparing for a wedding.

***

Hard Core Peace Corps!

Within the Peace Corps community, Niger was known as "hard core Peace Corps." It was certainly one of the most difficult countries for the Volunteers, arguably the most difficult in the world. In addition to the poverty and the harsh environment, they suffered frequent sickness because of the unsanitary conditions and prevalence of disease. Yet, most of them not only endured the experience but enjoyed it, and actually took a sort of perverse pride in such hardships. For example, we received a report from Washington headquarters showing that Peace Corps/Niger was the leading program in all of Peace Corps, by far, number one in the world...for the incidence of acute diarrhea among the Volunteers. There were 221 cases per year per 100 Volunteers, well ahead of runner-up Burkina Faso, with 196. The Volunteers celebrated Peace Corps/Niger's distinction.

It was because of the challenging conditions rather than in spite of them that our Volunteers were proud of themselves and what they were doing. They considered themselves a sort of Peace Corps elite, the Navy Seals or Army Rangers of Peace Corps. This was reflected in a lower rate of early terminations and a higher rate of extensions than Peace Corps Africa-wide and worldwide averages:

2004 figures	PC/Niger	PC/Africa	PC/worldwide
Vol. attrition	4.0%	9.3%	10.1%
Vol. extension	13.7%	9.7%	8.1%

I was worried about Islamist terrorist threats to the Volunteers throughout my tenure as Country Director. There were no incidents within Niger, but the problem was growing in neighboring countries. We took what precautions we could, including removing Volunteers from remote posts near vulnerable borders. In 2011, however, the kidnapping and murder of several European tourists in Niger by Al Qaida terrorists coming from Algeria led to a decision to withdraw the

Volunteers. A continued high threat level from Islamist terrorists based in Algeria and Mali, plus attacks in southeastern Niger by the Boko Haram terrorist group from Nigeria, make resumption of Peace Corps operations in Niger unlikely in the foreseeable future.

Living in Niamey

Tuy-Cam and I did not live in a village hut like the Volunteers. We lived in Niamey, the capital, in a nice house with electricity, indoor plumbing, and air conditioning.

But many Americans thought that even Niamey was a difficult, unpleasant place. Except for the 3-month "winter," it was always intensely hot. Massive sandstorms penetrated houses, covered everything with dust, and made breathing unpleasant. Streets were mostly unpaved and littered with garbage. Blackouts and water shortages were frequent. The lack of decent hotels outside Niamey discouraged travel inside the country, and there was only one weekly flight to Europe. It was not a place many Americans wanted to live.

Children scavenging a trash pile on a street near our house in Niamey. They were often joined by goats and crows.

***

279

A typical street in downtown Niamey.

A dust storm blowing in from the Sahara.

***

The heat, the dust, the squalor, the isolation, the lack of sanitation, the threat of disease -- all of these were very real. And yet, Tuy-Cam and I enjoyed living in Niger. How could this be?

Although much of Niamey is indeed squalid, it's a city of more than a million people, and parts of it are relatively modern, even attractive. An example is the Peace Corps office, which we inherited from Exxon-Mobil after they ended an unsuccessful effort to find commercially viable oil deposits. Our house was comparable to the best houses we had in America, and it included a large yard filled with flowering bougainvillea and mango trees. We had a cook/housekeeper, a gardener, and a driver, who by local standards were well paid at $100 each per month. Fresh fruits and vegetables were plentiful (though seasonal) and often better than what you find in American supermarkets. Excellent, freshly-baked French bread was always available at 15 cents for a large *baguette*. There was local beef, mutton, and fish from the Niger River, as well as imported European food. The local beer, made at a brewery owned by Heinekens, was good, and French wine was readily available. We ate and drank well! Moreover, the Nigeriens were friendly, and there were many interesting people in the international community with whom to socialize.

But most important was the great pleasure we found in working with the remarkable young American Volunteers in our charge, and we enjoyed the frequent, almost weekly, dinners we hosted for Volunteers visiting Niamey, featuring Tuy-Cam's great food and my free cold beer. This was a dramatic change from their normal fare in the villages where they lived.

***

The Peace Corps office in Niamey.

Our house in Niamey.

***

Visiting the Volunteers

I spent a third of my time visiting Volunteers in their villages and the regional hostels we maintained to support them logistically. This involved road trips of several days, on ill-maintained roads, or sometimes just trails through the desert, via our Toyota Land Cruisers, rugged four-wheel-drive vehicles that could carry eight people plus baggage tied on top.

The villagers, impoverished as they were, often insisted on giving us a gift: some peanuts or beans recently harvested, sugar cane, a few eggs, perhaps a chicken. It would have been extremely impolite to have refused such gifts, so I tried to send them something in return, such as vegetable seeds or candy for the kids.

I especially enjoyed visiting Adam Barnes' village, because the village chief was a veteran of the French Army who had served in Vietnam in the early 1950s during France's Indochina War. We could communicate in French and tell war stories.

Two old Vietnam veterans with Adam Barnes, in his village.

***

With Zinder Volunteers in their demonstration garden.

With Joseph Adams, his village chief, and gifted chicken.

***

The Marriage Bonus

One of the reasons we so much enjoyed our time in Niger was that Tuy-Cam was able to share fully in the work, more so than in any of my previous jobs. This was a great bonus for Peace Corps and the Volunteers.

I made clear to my staff that supporting the Volunteers was my top priority. The second priority, I told them, was supporting the Volunteers. So was the third, fourth, and fifth. Everything else, especially bureaucratic requirements from Washington, was on page two of our priority list. Since nothing about Peace Corps work is classified, it was appropriate for Tuy-Cam to take a large role, and she enjoyed doing so. Also, our children were on their own and far away, so it was natural that the Volunteers, who were roughly the same age as them, would become in some ways our surrogate children.

Food is a great tool with which to build relationships with young Americans living in the African bush, where a can of sardines was a major treat. Since Tuy-Cam likes to cook and is good at it, she used this tool to great advantage. Not only did she prepare almost weekly dinners in our home for Volunteers visiting Niamey, she accompanied me on most road trips to their villages. On one-day trips, she took a good lunch for the Volunteers, and for longer trips, she brought along some ingredients and bought others at local markets to prepare dinners in regional hostels.

Tuy-Cam also supported the Volunteers in other ways, including just being a friend and surrogate mom in times of need. For example, she once stood in as mother of the bride when a pair of Volunteers got married. A gesture of support that gained her considerable fame, even in Peace Corps programs elsewhere in Africa, was a bake sale to raise money for repairs to a badly deteriorated regional hostel. (Amazingly, Peace Corps had no official funds for such repairs.)

***

Left: With Chris Hwang and the Sultan of Zinder, in his palace.
Right: Cooking dinner for Volunteers in the regional hostel at
Konni, with Carol Grimes. The miner's lamp was needed
because it was getting dark, and there was no electricity.

With Teresa Torres, in her village house.

***

Tuy-Cam's lunch for Volunteers at their hostel in Gaya.

A dinner for the Volunteers at our house in Niamey.

***

Family Update

The small American school in Niamey only went through the eighth grade, so in 2002 we enrolled Kevin in Fork Union Military Academy, a boarding school near Charlottesville. Kim now had a full-time job at Old Dominion University, so she could re-assume the principal parenting role for him. She also met (via the Internet) Steve Sibson, an Englishman who came to the United States to marry her and found work at ODU. He has proved to be a fine husband and son-in-law.

Following completion of their Master's degrees at the University of Texas, Eva and Jeremy moved to Washington. Jeremy got a job at the Urban Institute, a leading policy think tank, and Eva worked with special needs children in the District of Columbia public school system. Their first child, Dylan, was born in 2004. The following year, Jeremy became a Foreign Service Officer with the Agency for International Development, and as Tuy-Cam and I returned home from Niger in 2006, he and Eva were preparing for their first overseas assignment.

Making a Difference

President Kennedy reportedly considered Peace Corps his proudest accomplishment. President Reagan said, "Nowhere has the American tradition of voluntarism been better illustrated than through Peace Corps." President George W. Bush asked Congress to fund doubling the number of Peace Corps Volunteers, and President Obama expressed the same objective.

While Peace Corps is often seen as a proto-typically liberal initiative, with its low cost and reliance on voluntarism it's also a great example of compassionate conservatism on an international scale. It has become an American icon, a well-known American brand that's respected world-wide, and it enjoys bipartisan support in Congress.

It should be viewed not as global welfare, but as a cost-effective instrument of American soft power, our power to persuade, to influence, perhaps to inspire, as opposed to coerce. It's an inexpensive international showcase of American ideals in action, and it productively engages the willingness of Americans to serve their country through service to others.

At the end of their tours, I interviewed all the Niger Volunteers and asked them to tell me about their experience. Without exception, they found it positive and deeply transformative. They all said something like: "I received a lot more than I gave."

Likewise, while Peace Corps helps poor people in poor countries, ultimately its greatest benefits are to America and Americans.

All our foreign assistance amounts to less than 1% of the federal budget, and Peace Corps is less than 1% of our total foreign assistance. It's an important instrument of American soft power, and it's an institution of which all Americans should be proud.

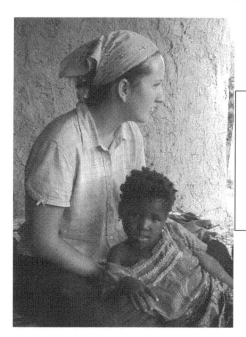

The Volunteers in Niger often developed close ties with village children. This is Ana Fereira, about two weeks after she had been posted to her village, with her new best friend.

****

289

15.

Retirement and Recall to Diplomatic Duty, 2006-14

My assignment in Niger was due to end in July 2005, but headquarters asked me to stay on for another year. While I welcomed this opportunity, Tuy-Cam was ready to leave and be nearer the children and grandchildren. Our compromise was an extension until March 2006.

We decided to retire in Williamsburg. Because of our seven years in Norfolk, we were familiar with the Hampton Roads region and knew Williamsburg to be a popular retirement destination, especially for military and federal government personnel. A small, quiet, attractive town, it offered excellent medical facilities and easy access to Kim's home in Suffolk and Eva's in Washington. Also, our long-time CIA friends Joe and Trinh Murphy had retired in Williamsburg and were urging us to join them. So during our home leave in August 2005, we bought a house in a newly-developed "active adult" community.

I found the transition into retirement to be difficult. There were some things I enjoyed, including the opportunity to travel and re-connect with family and friends. I also resumed my work as a Senior Fellow and lecturer at the Joint Forces Staff College in Norfolk; I published a book about our Peace Corps experience as well as newspaper and magazine articles; and I gave talks for local civic organizations.

But I was still bored.

During my time at ODU and in Niger, I had written several articles for *American Diplomacy*, an on-line professional journal based at the University of North Carolina and published by a group of retired FSOs in the Chapel Hill area. The long-time editor decided to step down in 2007, and the organization's board asked me to replace him. This was a volunteer, non-paying job, but I was happy to accept.

My work as *American Diplomacy* editor alleviated my boredom, as it required 20-25 hours per week, mostly sitting at my computer, plus quarterly two-day trips to Chapel Hill for board meetings. The work was interesting and suited my talents, but it eventually became routine. Also, frustrations developed in recruiting authors (who were not paid) and in mobilizing volunteer editorial assistance. I again became restless, and after two years I decided to look for something different, preferably full-time international work.

Family Matters

Being located close to both daughters enabled us to visit regularly, get better acquainted with our new sons-in-law and grandsons, and become more involved in family matters.

With her full-time job at ODU, a husband, and Kevin to look after, Kim's progress toward her Ph.D. in university administration was necessarily slow, but she was both a good student and persistent. When she became pregnant in 2007, Tuy-Cam and I feared that a new baby might end her academic career, but our concern was misplaced. Oliver was a healthy baby and Steve was a helpful father, so Kim pressed on and was awarded her degree in 2014. Her dissertation examined retention in college of veterans and active-duty military personnel using the Post-9/11 GI Bill.

Kim has remained at ODU and moved up through the ranks as an administrator. As of 2016, she is managing a successful master's program for U.S. Navy Nuclear Officers.

Unlike his mother, Kevin was not a good student. After two unsuccessful semesters at the local community college, I decided not to waste any more money on his tuition, and Kim and I agreed that he would have to find a job or enlist in the military. This was during the Great Recession and jobs were scarce, so we encouraged the latter. He chose the Navy, but found he would have to lose 30 pounds to pass the physical exam. In order to help him do so, Tuy-Cam and I had him move in with us. She became his dietician and I became his drill sergeant, making him join me for a daily 90-minute morning workout in our basement gym, plus hour-long afternoon runs (for him) and walks (for me) through the neighborhood.

Getting Kevin through the physical exam and into the Navy proved to be a year-long process. An unanticipated benefit of our diet and workouts was that I lost 25 pounds. I reached an ideal weight and have maintained it. Tuy-Cam has joined me in daily exercise, and our diet is healthy. For our age group, we are both in excellent condition.

Kevin remains in the Navy, and we hope he will make it his career.

Eva and Jeremy, together with Dylan, began their first Foreign Service assignment in Cairo in 2006. Their second son, Eli, was born in 2007. Eva worked as a speech-language therapist, first privately and then at the British International School of Maadi (a Cairo suburb). She has continued in similar jobs at international schools during subsequent assignments in New Delhi and Manila, their current (2016) post. Jeremy is advancing rapidly in USAID, and Dylan and Eli are thriving.

Expeditionary Diplomacy

My job search eventually led back to the Foreign Service. To describe how this happened, I need to begin with the concept of "expeditionary diplomacy."

In addition to supporting the development, articulation, and implementation of American foreign policy and the President's international agenda, the normal, day-to-day, core responsibilities of the State Department and Foreign Service are to:

- Represent the U.S. Government to foreign governments and international organizations, and maintain our relationships with them;

- Provide reporting and analysis on international developments impacting U.S. interests;
- Issue passports to American citizens and visas for foreigners traveling to the United States, and provide protection and welfare services for Americans living or traveling abroad; and
- Conduct "public diplomacy" programs, i.e., press and public relations and educational and cultural exchanges.

Along with these traditional responsibilities, galloping globalization in recent decades has brought new functions to our Embassies, such as intelligence activities, economic and military assistance, trade promotion, global financial management, law enforcement, communicable disease control, etc. At large Embassies, there may be 20 or 25 U.S. Government agencies represented. Until the 1960s, almost all American civilians working for the U.S. Government abroad were State Department employees; today, State employees constitute only a third of the total American staff at our Embassies and Consulates. (All U.S. Government personnel, however, are under the authority of the Ambassador, regardless of their "home" agency.)

In addition to these continuing responsibilities, focused on steady-state relationships among governments, the State Department and Foreign Service have sometimes taken on additional functions that might be described generically as conflict prevention and response operations. However, I prefer the term that emerged during the Bush 43 Administration: expeditionary diplomacy.

This term was borrowed from the military concept of an "expeditionary" force that goes abroad for a specific mission, completes it, and returns home to prepare for the next mission. These functions, which have waxed and waned over the years, include post-conflict reconstruction and stabilization operations, nation-building, counterinsurgency, the war on terrorism, disaster response, etc. For example, after World War II, large numbers of FSOs were sent to help

293

administer occupied Germany and Japan. There was another surge of this sort when hundreds of FSOs were sent to work in Vietnam, principally in counterinsurgency operations. I was one of them.

After the end of the Vietnam War in 1975 and the winding down of the Cold War in the 1980s, U.S. spending and staffing for international affairs fell sharply, and while most traditional, steady-state diplomatic responsibilities continued to be met, our capacity for expeditionary diplomacy withered. This became dramatically apparent after 9/11, when State and USAID were ineffective in meeting the needs of counterinsurgency and stabilization efforts in Iraq and Afghanistan. In response, the Bush Administration developed the concept of expeditionary diplomacy and sought to build a "civilian surge capacity." Congressional funding, however, remained insufficient.

When the Obama Administration took office in 2009, the idea of preparing for future contingencies comparable to Iraq and Afghanistan was shelved. Nonetheless, Secretary of State Clinton recognized the need to upgrade the Department's expeditionary diplomacy capacity. A policy review she mandated specified conflict response as a core State Department mission and called for a new Bureau of Conflict and Stabilization Operations (CSO), which began in 2011. It included a standby reserve component, the Civilian Response Corps, for which a few Foreign Service retirees were to be recruited.

I monitored these developments closely, and I was among the first volunteers for the new on-call reserve element.

Recall to Diplomatic Duty

In August 2011 I attended a two-week Civilian Response Corps orientation program, but this was followed by a lengthy wait. I had almost given up hope when a call came in August 2012 from Rebecca Wall, a young staff officer in the CSO Bureau, asking me to come to Washington to discuss a potential assignment as Casamance Advisor in

Senegal. I had the qualifications they were looking for – ambassadorial rank, experience in Africa and in conflict situations, and fluency in French – and I found the job attractive. It was agreed that I would start work in mid-September, with a couple of weeks in Washington and arrival in Dakar by October 1. The assignment was envisioned to be for three-six months, but it lasted for more than a year.

Tuy-Cam did not fully share my enthusiasm for a return to active duty. Content with life in Williamsburg, she felt no need for new adventures. However, she understood how deeply I wanted this one last opportunity, and she agreed once more to accompany and support me, as she had always done. Moreover, as she learned about the nature of the assignment and life in Dakar (a more modern place than any of our previous African posts), her attitude became increasingly positive. In the end, she enjoyed the experience almost as much as I did. After conclusion of the assignment, Tuy-Cam and I published a book about it: *Expeditionary Diplomacy in Action.*

***

295

The Casamance Conflict

Senegal is located on the westernmost tip of Africa, about the same latitude as the southern Caribbean. Note on the map how it is divided by The Gambia, a small former British colony extending along a river of the same name and poking like a long, bony English middle finger into the heart of Senegal, the crown jewel of the former French colonial empire in West Africa. The Casamance is that part of Senegal south of The Gambia and north of the former Portuguese colony of Guinea-Bissau. To travel from the Casamance to the political and economic heartland of Senegal, it is necessary to cross two national frontiers plus a major river that has no bridges, only a dilapidated ferry.

A low-level secessionist insurgency began in the Casamance in 1982. Unlike so many of Africa's conflicts, it is not primarily ethnic or religious. Rather, it is rooted in the geographic, economic, political, and psychological isolation of the Casamance from the rest of Senegal. Many Casamance residents feel neglected and mistreated by the national government, and a substantial number have called for independence. This is not a realistic goal, since it is strongly opposed by Senegal's government and has no international support, but nonetheless many people have been willing to fight for it.

The resulting insurgency has not been especially bloody compared to other African conflicts, but it has caused several thousand casualties and created more than 100,000 refugees. Moreover, it has crippled the Casamance economy and drained Senegal's resources, retarding the country's development, tying down its military forces, and creating political instability that might provide an opening for the rise of Islamist extremism.

Why Should We Care?

Why should Americans care about the Casamance insurgency? There are several reasons:

- Senegal has been among the most important of the African countries since the colonial period when it was the capital of French West Africa. It remains a regional transportation hub and commercial center as well as a political and cultural leader, especially among former French colonies.

- It is also one of the few African countries NOT to have experienced a military coup or other violent change of government; and it has become a stable democracy.

- Senegal's population is 90% Muslim but not extremist, and most Senegalese are pro-American. Its government has been among our closest African and Islamic community friends. Senegal sent a battalion to participate in the First Gulf War in 1990-91, and it served as the forward logistics base for U.S. anti-Ebola operations in West Africa in 2014-15.

- Senegal has one of the most professional armies in Africa, and it has been a major contributor to a dozen UN peacekeeping operations. We want those contributions to continue and grow; and we also want Senegal to participate in countering global Islamist extremism.

For these reasons, we have invested large amounts of economic and military aid in Senegal, and we have developed close diplomatic, intelligence, military, and economic cooperation with its government. We want Senegal to succeed and to continue its role as an important American partner.

President Macky Sall

A new Senegalese President, Macky Sall, was elected in 2012. He had campaigned on a promise to launch a Casamance peace initiative, and he welcomed international assistance for it. At the same time, there was an uprising for peace by Casamance civil society, with women's groups, student associations, and war victims organizations marching in the streets to call for an end to the conflict. There were also growing signs of war-weariness among the rebels, including expressions of willingness to negotiate with the Senegalese government.

We Offer Help

With the creation of the new Bureau of Conflict and Stabilization Operations (CSO) in 2011, the State Department had an organizational structure, dedicated resources, and a policy in place for expeditionary diplomacy, at least on a small scale. CSO staff members, especially Rebecca Wall, recognized an opportunity to promote our interests and those of our friend and partner Senegal by supporting President Sall's Casamance peace initiative. Rebecca and some CSO colleagues sold this idea to Secretary Clinton, and during her visit to Dakar in July 2012 she offered President Sall our help. He accepted, and I was selected for the job.

Reflecting on her experience as Secretary of State, Hilary Clinton said she had learned that an important part of global diplomacy is "just being there." The Casamance engagement illustrates this point. I was surprised by the extraordinary warmth of the welcome I received in Senegal, not only by President Sall and senior government officials, but also by ordinary people. The day my appointment as Casamance Advisor was publicly announced and I appeared briefly on the national TV news, on returning to my hotel I found that a dozen of the staff -- desk clerks, chamber maids, etc. -- had gathered to express thanks and tell me how happy they were that I had come. I heard similar comments from many other Senegalese in the following days. This had nothing to do with me personally, but it indicated the importance people attached to what my appointment represented: the engagement of the U.S. government to support President Sall's peace initiative, not just with words but with actions, including assigning a former American Ambassador to Dakar as Casamance Advisor.

This was a cost-effective project. It consisted of me, a part-time deputy I recruited in Dakar (another retired senior FSO, Sue Patrick, who was already there as the wife of the USAID Mission Director), and an officer (Rebecca) to manage the project in the CSO Bureau. We also obtained a $1 million program budget from Defense Department funds made available to the State Department for conflict prevention and stabilization. This demonstrated U.S. political engagement and provided useful assistance, but it didn't imply any military commitment or suggest an American "global policeman" role.

Mobilizing U.S. and International Community Support

There were no additional U.S. resources available for Casamance-related projects. However, our aid programs for Senegal were large, and it was possible to move funding from lower priority projects and less important regions to the Casamance. For example, we relocated a road construction project previously planned for northern Senegal, and we fast-tracked from 2015 to 2013 a military training program to strengthen the Senegalese Army's de-mining capability.

More important than these small augmentations in U.S. Casamance-related assistance was successful mobilization of support for the Casamance peace initiative from our allies (France, Canada, Japan, South Korea, Germany, etc.) and especially from the World Bank, the European Union, and United Nations development-related agencies. All this required was for me to call on the Dakar representatives of these countries and organizations and explain what we, the United States, were doing. Their analysis of the opportunity presented by President Sall's initiative -- to end a conflict that had long been undermining everyone's efforts to promote economic development and stability in Senegal -- was much the same as ours. Their response to my briefings was most often to express appreciation for U.S. leadership and ask how they could help. The European Union soon joined us in taking a leadership role.

Facilitating Negotiations and Lobbying The Gambia

In early 2013, the leader of the largest rebel faction, César Badiate, sent word that he wanted to meet with me. With the agreement of the Senegalese Government, with which he had recently broken off negotiations, I accepted in principle but insisted on the prior release of a dozen Senegalese mine clearance workers his fighters were holding hostage in order to stop demining operations. I told him the U.S. Government would regard him as an international terrorist if he continued to hold hostages, and I would not be permitted to meet with someone we considered a terrorist. After a month, he released them unharmed.

César would not come to an area controlled by the Government, and I couldn't go to his base camp in the Casamance (which could be interpreted as U.S. recognition of a rebel movement), so we agreed to meet in Sao Domingos, a small town in Guinea-Bissau just over Senegal's southern border. Logistics for the meeting were arranged by the International Committee of the Red Cross (ICRC), with help from a senior Casamance political leader and the Catholic Archbishop of Dakar, who agreed to send along his deputy to help guarantee my security. We were driven in ICRC jeeps to the dilapidated Sao Domingos city hall, where César and 20 of his lieutenants were awaiting us. The atmosphere was relaxed, and the four-hour meeting ended with everyone holding hands in a large circle while the Archbishop's deputy prayed for peace. I hosted a lunch for the group at a nearby inn, and we parted cordially.

Soon, negotiations between César and the Senegal Government were resumed, and an agreement was reached that permitted demining activities to proceed.

Negotiations with the other principal rebel faction, headed by Salif Sadio, were held in Rome with the mediation of Sant'Egidio, a Catholic lay organization that has successfully helped end conflicts in Algeria,

Mozambique, and elsewhere in Africa. We contributed $100,000 of our DOD-funded CSO Casamance budget to Sant'Egidio to support their mediation role. Also, at the request of Sant'Egidio and the Sadio rebel faction, I made two trips to Rome to participate in negotiations.

Another Casamance-related diplomatic trip was to The Gambia. Its president, Yahya Jammeh, an Army captain who took power in a 1994 coup, has a long history of providing sanctuary and arms for Casamance rebels, as well as facilitating their narcotics and illegal timber trafficking (for a cut of the profits). With my visit, I wanted to let him know we were supporting President Sall's Casamance peace initiative, and we would highly value his cooperation with it. On the other hand, I indicated that we would be highly pissed off -- that's a technical diplomatic term that goes a step beyond an expression of "grave concern" -- if he did anything to derail it.

Jammeh refrained from making serious mischief, and I believe our diplomacy contributed to this outcome.

The Conflict Fades Away

Most insurgencies don't end with signed agreements; they just fade away. That has been happening with the Casamance conflict. As of 2016, a *de facto* ceasefire that became apparent in 2012, shortly after my arrival, remains in effect, and negotiations continue between the Senegal Government and the rebels. Some insurgents have agreed to enter the Government's "disarmament, demobilization, and re-insertion" process, and refugees have begun to return to their former homes. There has been a surge in development aid (mostly from the World Bank, European Union, and UN). It includes an African Development Bank project to construct a bridge on the Gambia River, which will help alleviate the root cause of the conflict by better connecting the Casamance with the rest of Senegal.

Another important indication that peace is returning is the government's willingness to send forces outside the country to help combat Islamist extremism. In 2013, Senegal sent a battalion to join the French-led operation in Mali that blocked the threatened takeover of that country by a jihadist group. Also, in 2015 Senegal joined a Saudi-led coalition battling Iranian-backed rebels in Yemen. These decisions have raised Senegal's profile in the struggle within the Muslim community between moderates and Islamist extremists. This is a positive development for U.S. foreign policy that was facilitated by the Casamance peace initiative.

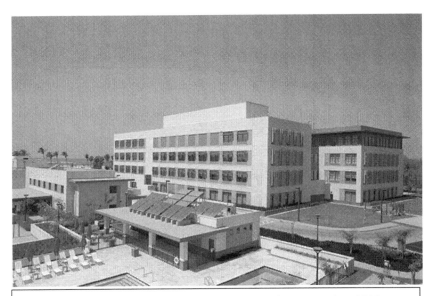

The new U.S. Embassy in Dakar, completed in December 2012.

***

Chairing a meeting of the Casamance international donors group in Dakar. CSO Casamance project officer Rebecca Wall is to my right.

Meeting with refugees from the Casamance in The Gambia. U.S. Ambassador to The Gambia Ned Alford is to my right.

***

Tuy-Cam accompanied me on visits to Ziguinchor, provincial capital of the Casamance. This is at our hotel.

Meeting with leaders of the mine victims association in Ziguinchor. They and other civil society leaders organized demonstrations for an end to the conflict.

***

César Badiate, leader of the largest Casamance rebel faction.

The road into Sao Domingos, a small town in Guinea-Bissau where I met with César and his lieutenants.

Meeting some ex-rebels at a government DDR (disarmament, demobilization, re-insertion) camp that we helped to equip.

***

Living in Dakar

Living in Dakar was pleasant for Tuy-Cam and me. We were first in an apartment hotel that was adequate but in a high-crime downtown area near the port and not convenient to the new Embassy building that was opened in December 2012. At that time, we moved into an extended-stay apartment in the Radisson Blu Hotel, in a more modern part of the city and closer to the new Embassy. The hotel is built into a bluff overlooking the Atlantic on the *corniche*, the principal thoroughfare along the coast between downtown and the airport. Its apartment wing had just been completed, and we were the apartment's first occupants. We made daily use of the hotel's fitness facility, and we often took walks along the *corniche*.

The Radisson Blu hotel in Dakar, where we lived in an extended stay apartment for most of our time in Senegal.

Although most of Senegal is rural and poor, Dakar is a bustling, cosmopolitan, mostly modern city of 2.5 million with lots of good restaurants. Tuy-Cam even found a few Chinese-owned Asian stores where she could buy ingredients for Vietnamese cooking. We liked the Senegalese people and made some friends, including the Senegalese Director of National Intelligence, who was President Sall's designee to head the Casamance peace initiative and my principal interlocutor. He and his wife and twin daughters were our house guests in Williamsburg in late 2013.

Several of the staff at the U.S. Embassy in Dakar were especially supportive and hospitable, including the CIA Station Chief, the FBI Legal Attaché and Deputy Attaché and their spouses, the Marine Attaché, and the USAID Mission Director and his wife (my deputy and successor). Thanks to them, we enjoyed an active social life.

A highlight of our time in Dakar was a visit by Eva and family on their way from home leave in the United States to their post in New Delhi.

By the summer of 2013, we decided it was time to return home. I had developed arthritic problems that needed attention, and Tuy-Cam wanted to be closer to family and friends. We left in late September and moved back to our house in Williamsburg. Sue Patrick, my deputy, replaced me, but because of her husband's retirement she only stayed on until December. A recently retired Ambassador with extensive Africa experience, Mark Boulware, was chosen to become the new Casamance Advisor. I accompanied him to Dakar in January 2014 and spent three weeks orienting him on the project and introducing him to the people I worked with. He stayed on for 10 more months, until everyone involved agreed that ongoing U.S. support for maintaining the peace that had been achieved in the Casamance could be handled by the regular staff of the U.S. Embassy.

Policy Conclusions of an Old Expeditionary Diplomat

Although the Casamance project was a minor sideshow in U.S. foreign policy, it illustrates two important principles:

- First, U.S. leadership and active engagement are vital to effectively address many global issues. This may be unfair and unfortunate, and it often raises questions: Why can't such problems be handled by the UN? Why don't our European allies, the former colonial powers, do more? Why can't the countries in the region resolve their own conflicts? These are legitimate questions, and the issues they suggest need to be addressed; but the reality remains that other governments and people often look to Uncle Sam to identify problems and opportunities and build coalitions to deal with them.

- Second, the concept of expeditionary diplomacy offers an alternative to "imperial overstretch," or trying to act as a global policeman; and, at the other extreme, ignoring smaller conflicts and doing nothing until they grow, threaten important interests, and require costly, large-scale, perhaps military, intervention.

Theodore Roosevelt was one of our most successful practitioners of expeditionary diplomacy, for example in his mediation of the war between Russia and Japan, for which he was awarded the Nobel Peace Prize. He used what he described as an old African proverb to characterize his foreign policy: "Speak softly and carry a big stick." That's still good advice. We need both military power and soft power, including an effective diplomatic capacity, to protect American interests in a dangerous world.

In deciding when to use our instruments of national power, whether military or diplomatic, and when to follow the principle of our 18th Century founders to "avoid foreign entanglements," we need to heed the wisdom in a popular country song by Kenney Rogers: "You've got to know when to hold 'em, know when to fold 'em, know when to walk away, and know when to run." The same message was conveyed in the soul-stirring, inspiring words of the Obama Doctrine: "Don't do stupid shit!"

It's true that there are many global problems in which our interest is less than existential and the deck is stacked against us. Of course we need to avoid such slippery slopes. But any foreign intervention involves some risk, so the expeditionary diplomat is necessarily a gambler. In most cases, however, we are better off working persistently to shape events rather than waiting for events to shape us. We just have to pay attention to the odds, play our cards with professional skill, and recognize that inaction can often be the greatest risk of all.

Unfortunately, the effort to re-build the State Department's expeditionary diplomacy capacity that was begun under President George W. Bush and continued -- albeit in a less ambitious form -- by Secretary of State Clinton in the first term of the Obama Administration, became stalled after 2012, far short of its goals. The continuing problem has been well stated by retired Marine General Tony Zinni: "The other agencies of government needed to resolve crises are anemic in comparison with our military....Our State Department, USAID, and other critically needed agencies are underfunded, undermanned, and poorly structured for the tasks we need them to accomplish....We've allowed the military to become too easy to use and other agencies too hard to use."[27]

****

---

[27] Zinni, Anthony, *Before the First Shots are Fired*, p. 229, p. 107.

16.

Re-Retirement and Journey's End: 2014-?

Shortly after our return from Dakar, in early 2014 Tuy-Cam and I moved into Patriots Colony, a continuing care retirement community in Williamsburg. It was founded by retired career military officers, who constitute about 80% of the residents; but career federal government civilians, particularly those from national security-related agencies, are also welcomed. We have a lot in common with these aging warriors, most of whom served in Vietnam, and we expect to spend the rest of our days here.

We are healthy, happy, and content, and we enjoy close ties with our daughters and their families as well as with new friends and old, here and around the world.

Professionally, the Casamance assignment was the most satisfying of my career. It was pure diplomacy, at a senior level, advancing U.S. interests in long-term peace and stability by helping a friendly country end a bloody insurgency. Because of its expeditionary nature, there were clear objectives, measurable progress, and an end state in view when I left. And it was especially fitting as a bookend to my first and most memorable Foreign Service assignment, to Vietnam as a junior expeditionary diplomat helping fight a counterinsurgency war.

I would welcome another short-term diplomatic job, but since there are many younger, recently-retired FSOs competing for such assignments, I don't expect one. Writing, speaking, service as a Joint Forces Staff College Senior Fellow, and volunteer work keep me sufficiently busy. I no longer feel the need to seek yet another less-traveled road to explore.

Theodore Roosevelt said that "life's greatest good fortune is to work hard at work worth doing." I feel fortunate to have had a career in the

Foreign Service and international affairs, with lots of hard work and exciting adventures in my life-long journey along less-traveled roads. I also had the great good fortune of finding Tuy-Cam, my companion on that journey, and meeting lots of good friends along the way.

Since my college days I've had an interest in philosophy and some of life's deeper questions, and I've done quite a bit of reflection about them. I've concluded that the purpose of life is living, and its only destination is the end of the journey.

What a journey it has been!

Celebrating my 75th birthday in our villa at Patriots Colony, 2015.

****

Annex 1.
Genealogy Notes

Nicholas Bullington (b. 1605) arrived in the first permanent English settlement in North America, Jamestown (founded 1607), in 1623. He is documented in the *U.S. and Canada Passenger and Immigration Lists* and *The American Genealogical-Biographical Index*.

It seems unusual that Nicholas arrived alone at the age of 17 or 18, with no family members. He may have been from an adventuresome family that somehow got separated in immigrating to the New World. English spelling in this era was highly variable, and it is plausible that Nicholas was a son of John Billington (1576-1630), who with his wife and two sons arrived in Plymouth on the Mayflower in 1620.[28] They came from Lincolnshire.

If Nicholas is not John Billington's son, another possible home in England is Bullington parish and village in Hampshire, southwest of London near Winchester, which Tuy-Cam and I visited in 2007. Today, Bullington village consists of two dozen houses, half a dozen farms, a parish church, and the Bullington Cross Inn, where we had an excellent lunch; but there are no longer any Bullingtons living there. We also toured the "Bullington house," a substantial manor house which the current owner told us dates mostly from the 18th Century, though he thinks some parts were originally built earlier. Bullington village is an example of the southern English countryside at its most picturesque.

In 1624, Nicholas Bullington was recorded as living on "the Maine," i.e., the mainland adjacent to the colony's original site on Jamestown

---

[28] At least two family trees posted on Ancestry.com for John Billington's wife, Elinor Bradford Newton, show that they had another son, named Nicholas and born in 1605. However, I haven't been able to verify the original source of this information.

Island (in the James River). His 1624 marriage to Cynthia Clarke is documented in *U.S. and International Marriage Records, 1560-1900*. They soon moved to Varina Parish, Henrico County, which is located further up the James River southeast of present-day Richmond. They produced seven children who survived to adulthood, including my ancestor Robert (1632-1688). He was the first of four successive Robert Bullingtons in my family line.

Robert II (1687-1739) was born in Henrico County, but moved to Pittsylvania County, just north of Danville. Both his son Robert III (1725-1777) and grandson Robert IV (1750-1811) were born and died there. Robert IV is listed as a corporal in the *U.S. Revolutionary War Rolls*, but I have not located any details about his military service.

Robert IV's son John W. (1773-1832) and grandson Henderson A. (1809-1860) were also born in Pittsylvania County; but John W. and his family, including young Henderson, moved on to Lauderdale County in northwest Alabama sometime in the early years of the 19th Century.

Henderson was married in 1836 to Elizabeth Sanderson in Limestone County, and the couple settled there in Pleasant Grove, along Elk River near its juncture with the Tennessee River. They had six children, including John Douglas (1845-1899). John had 10 children, including my grandfather, Mack Richard Bullington (1881-1960). He married my grandmother, Ida Tidwell, in 1907. They initially lived on a farm in the small community of Oxford, Limestone County, where their two children were born: my uncle James Irvin (1908-1995) and my father Iris Nell (1910-1997). In 1919 the family moved to a 40-acre farm on the outskirts of Athens, the Limestone County seat.

Other Ancestors

My paternal grandmother's family, the **Tidwells**, can also be traced back to early Colonial times. The first of the line in America, Richard Tidwell (1635-1692), came from Staffordshire to Virginia in 1657,

313

where he had land on the Potomac River in Westmoreland County, near present-day Alexandria. The family remained in northern Virginia until Richard's great-grandson John Robert Tidwell (1740-1796) moved to South Carolina, sometime before 1774. John Robert's son Isaac (1766-1815) moved to Tennessee about 1810. His grandson, Silas Edd, born 1824, was a private in the 32nd Tennessee Infantry, and died of pneumonia in 1862 in a Federal prisoner of war camp in St. Louis.

Silas Edd's son William V. Tidwell moved to Alabama and married Elizabeth Lentz in Limestone County in 1881. They settled in the Pleasant Grove community (near the Bullingtons) and had nine children who survived to adulthood, including my grandmother Ida (1883-1967).

The family of my maternal grandfather, the **Justices**, can be traced back to Kinnekulle, Sweden, from whence his ancestor Johan Gustafson (1623-1682) arrived in New Sweden (now Delaware) in 1643. He moved to Philadelphia, where his name evolved to Johan Justason and eventually to John Justes. His son Mounce (1659-1749) changed the spelling to Justice. Mounce's son Peter (1700-1763) was born in Philadelphia, but sometime after 1728 moved to Virginia, where his son Moses (1735-1802) was born. Moses' son, Moses Jr. (1760-1829), moved on to North Carolina; and his son, Abraham Justice (1790-1859) continued westward to Morgan County, Tennessee. Abraham's grandson, my grandfather James Fred Justice (1888-1978) was born in Wartburg, Morgan County. As a young man, his job as a switchman with Southern Railroad took him to Chattanooga, where he married my grandmother, Jessie Florence West (1891-1976). Except for a brief stay in Tuscaloosa, Alabama, they remained in Chattanooga, where my mother, Esther Elizabeth (1917-2003), and her sister Frances (1919-2012) were born.

The family of my maternal grandmother, Jessie **West**, can only be traced back as far as John West (1732-1776) of North Carolina. He was a soldier in the Revolutionary War, and was probably killed fighting with Patriot forces against Loyalists at the Battle of Moore's Creek Bridge in North Carolina, February 27, 1776. His grandson, William P. West, moved to Cherokee County, in the Smoky Mountains on the Tennessee line. William's grandson, my great-grandfather Jerome Napoleon West (1857-1947), moved down from the Smokies to Chattanooga, where he worked in a factory. He and his wife, Sarah Elizabeth, had 10 children, including my grandmother Jessie.[29]

****

---

[29] The most important source of my information on the Bullington family is a book by Lilla Bullington Brackeen, *All in Our Family*, published in Decatur, Alabama, in 1976. She was the daughter of my grandfather's brother Joseph. She had a serious interest in genealogy and did extensive research. Her husband, Louis O. Brackeen, was the Director of Public Affairs at Auburn when I was a student there.

Tom Bullington, son of my grandfather's brother Clifford, also published a family book: *Cross the River*, Fayetteville, Tennessee, 1993. Unlike Lilla's book, it is not based on genealogical research but is focused on material submitted by the Bullingtons of Limestone County and their progeny. I drew on it for some information about them as well as pictures.

The Internet, particularly Ancestry.com, is the source of virtually all my information about the Tidwell, Justice and West families, as well as some additional details and confirmation of Lilla's research on the Bullingtons.

Annex 2.
Freedom Riders Editorial
Auburn *Plainsman* - May 24, 1961
Written the week after I became editor, at age 20.

AN EDITORIAL
A CHOICE—REALITY OR ANARCHY

WE ARE NOW seeing the violent, vehement, vociferous death throes of segregation. The die-hard, bitter-enders are having their say. They speak through riot, through lead pipes, through floggings, through destruction, through ignorance, and through lawlessness in support of their narrow, senseless view of hallowed, almighty, and apparently decadent Southern custom and tradition. In Montgomery last weekend they spoke particularly loud.

And the horrifying, revolting thing about it is that the vast majority of the people of this state let them have their way. If they have not supported the hatred and bigotry and violence directly, they have winked at it and covertly supported it by their silence and refusal to act—all of them, our politicians, from the governor on down, our law officers, our preachers, our educators, our newspaper editors, and our common ordinary citizens who have laughed and cursed and joked at the "smart niggers" and "nigger lovers."

Alabama has been sowing the wind, and now she is left to reap the whirlwind.

Nor can we blame this violence on "outside interference" and "agitators" as most Alabamians wishfully try to do. To attempt this is the worst possible sophistry and insipid rationalization. If we are to try to shift the blame to the Freedom Riders, we should logically go even deeper into the heart of the matter and blame it on Abraham Lincoln who freed the slaves in the first place. Or perhaps on the framers of the Constitution who said that all men are created equal, or on the first slave trader, or perhaps even on God, who presumably created man with a capacity for bigotry, prejudice and hate.

(continued next page)

No, we cannot blame the Freedom Riders. They are known to be dedicated to passive resistance—they do not strike back when attacked or return curse for curse and hate for hate. Their motive is admittedly a test designed to dramatize a moral issue, just as the recent sit-ins brought out lunch counter discrimination and succeeded in ending much of it. They have law and morality on their side. The blame must lie squarely on the shoulders of the white supremacist bigots of the state of Alabama and the people who actively or tacitly help them.

"The old order changeth, and giveth place to the new." Alabama may not like it, but the old order is changing, and it must change. Integration is coming; doggedly, persistently, and ever stronger, it is coming.

Southerners run in fear, they wail, they react with violence, but still it comes. They scream of States Rights, they organize White Citizen's Councils, they use economic pressure to keep the Negro "in his place," and it still comes. It is inevitable, and those who think it is not are either miserably stupid or living in self-delusion.

People who can adapt to the new order will weather the storm—they may not like it because of years of custom, but they will have the good sense and moderation to accept the inevitability of change in the social order and work to make that change one for the better. We have already seen what people who cannot adapt to the new order will do. Perhaps they will do more of it in their last ditch efforts to preserve prejudice, ignorance, and bias.

One way or another, these people must be stopped. If possible they should be stopped through the influence of newspapers, preachers, and other leaders and citizens of good will and good sense. If such leaders do not have the courage and foresight to speak out on this question, and keep the ostrich-like attitude they have exhibited in the past, then even more federal action will be necessary. We cannot continue to tolerate such flagrant instances of man's inhumanity to man as have taken place all across the state in past weeks.

Soon, integration will come to Auburn. We cannot degrade our name and the name of our school, as the name of Alabama has already been degraded, by allowing violence and hatred and stupidity to accompany this step in the onward march of integration. We hope that this will be poor spawning ground for such action.

****

Annex 3.
A Call to Leadership
Speech by J. R. Bullington
Sigma Pi Province Workshop
Old Dominion University, November 1, 2014

My first significant leadership role was at Auburn, as editor of the student newspaper, *The Plainsman*; and I soon had other leadership responsibilities as a young Foreign Service Officer in Vietnam during the War. But until I was nearly 40, when the State Department sent me for a year of training at the U.S. Army War College, I never realized that leadership was something that could be consciously learned, a skill that you needed to study and practice and try to get better at.

After that foundational training at the Army War College, I continued to study leadership at the Federal Executive Institute and at Harvard, and I put what I learned into practice in jobs as U.S. Ambassador and Peace Corps Director. And finally I was called on to teach leadership, as Dean of the State Department's senior level training program and, after I retired from the Foreign Service, as director of a program for business and government executives here at ODU.

I hope I can influence you young men of Sigma Pi to get an earlier start than I did on <u>consciously</u> developing your leadership skills.

What Leadership Isn't

Leadership is rarely taught – and even more rarely taught well – in most of our schools and colleges. Consequently, lots of misperceptions and wrong notions surround it, and one of the first things you need to learn about leadership is what it isn't.

In Shakespeare's *Henry IV,* the Welch sorcerer Owen Glendower says, "I can call spirits from the vasty deep." To which Hotspur, a man with real leadership challenges, replies, "Why, so can I, or so can any man; <u>but will they come when you do call for them?</u>"

This quote emphasizes that leadership isn't magic, and more importantly, it's not <u>command</u>, not even in very hierarchical organizations such as the military. All thoughtful veterans will tell you that stripes on your sleeve or stars on your collar may make you a unit's <u>commander</u>, but they can't make you an effective <u>leader</u>. That status must be earned. If it's not, your subordinates may <u>not</u> come when you do call for them.

Some think that leadership is mainly about <u>power</u>, being able to require others to do your bidding. Now, it's true that with sufficient power you can get people to do what you want, but power doesn't make you a leader. A story about my Uncle Ozro back in North Alabama that illustrates this point.

> Uncle Ozro was the wayward child of a simple, religious family of country folk, and among his many weaknesses was an inordinate love of hunting. When he was supposed to be working on the farm, he was usually out hunting instead. This one particular day, he'd been walking up and down the red clay hills of north Alabama since the crack of dawn, but hadn't seen a thing to shoot his shotgun at. Along about sundown he was downright frustrated as he walked out of the woods and came into this cotton field where there was an old farmer out plowing behind a big red mule. This was the 1940s, and we still used mules in those days. Uncle Ozro decided he'd take out his frustration on the old farmer, so he walked up to him and asked, "Farmer, can you dance?" The farmer said, "Why no, I can't dance. We don't believe in dancing in my church." Uncle Ozro said, "I bet you can dance!" BLAM! He shot down at the farmer's feet, and the farmer danced a little jig. "My, my, that 'uz a mighty good dance, farmer. I'd like to see you do it again." BLAM! The farmer danced another fine jig. Uncle Ozro laughed and

started walking away, but he didn't get more'n a few feet when the farmer hollered out and said, "Hunter, 'at there's a double-barrel shotgun ya got, ain't it." Uncle Ozro said, "Yeah, it's a double-barrel Remington, a fine gun!" The farmer said, "You fired twice, didn't ya." "Yeah, 'at's right, I fired two times." Then the old farmer reached down inside his overalls and drew out this great long horse pistol, pointed it right at Uncle Ozro's head, and he said, "Hunter, have you ever kissed a big red mule's ass?" Uncle Ozro said, "No sir, but I've wanted to all my life!"

Now, both Uncle Ozro and the farmer brought about some extraordinary action, and exercised a sort of power, but I wouldn't call either of them a leader. Leaders <u>have</u> power, but leadership isn't the <u>same</u> as power.

And finally, leadership isn't <u>management</u>. Now, management skills are important, and good managers are valuable people – but they aren't necessarily good leaders. Here are some of the differences:

The manager:	The leader:
Administers	Innovates
Maintains	Develops
Focuses on structure	Focuses on people
Relies on control	Inspires commitment
Asks how, and when	Asks what, and why
Keeps an eye on the bottom line	Keeps an eye on the horizon
Does things right	Does the right things

Principles of Leadership

What, then, is leadership?

President Eisenhower defined it as "The art of getting someone to do something you want done <u>because he wants to do it</u>."

It can also be thought of as the ability to move people beyond mere compliance with requirements, to <u>commitment</u> to doing all they can to achieve the organization's goals.

But more important than definitions of leadership are practical principles you can use in leading businesses or bureaucracies, military operations or charity drives, families or fraternities. All of these principles I'm going to suggest are easy to understand but difficult to truly live by – that's why <u>great</u> leaders are rare. But by applying these principles, even imperfectly, all of us can become better leaders, competent leaders, successful leaders.

1. The first principle is to develop a vision.

This may seem obvious, because as the Cheshire Cat told Alice, "If you don't know your destination, any road will get you there."

What <u>is</u> a leader's vision? Here's an excellent example from our Sigma Pi fraternity brother Jay Jacobs, Auburn's Athletic Director. He recently told an interviewer that his vision is for Auburn to have the <u>pre-eminent athletics department in the nation</u>. He said, "...great organizations need a big vision to accomplish great things. That's why our vision statement is so ambitious." He went on to list some specific, measurable goals, and said, "We talk about those goals every day, and we focus our energy and resources on achieving them. If we can be successful in those areas, we <u>will</u> be the pre-eminent athletics department in the nation." I'd say Brother Jay is well on the way to achieving that vision! A national football championship in 2010, missing another in the 2013 national championship game by only 13 seconds, and we're currently at number three in the national rankings. And watch out for our revitalized basketball program in the next couple of years!

How do you develop a leadership vision? You need to aim high, well beyond your easy grasp; and you need to make it personal, a sort of internal compass that guides your daily actions. But ultimately there is no formula, no checklist. It might be a sudden inspiration, but much more likely is that it only happens after lots of study, analysis, consultation, reflection, and plain hard work.

2. The second principle is: communicate, communicate, communicate.

Studies of executive performance have shown that the number one cause of leadership failure is poor communication. Vision without action is just a daydream, and communication is the <u>indispensable link</u> between vision and action. A leader needs to develop strong communication skills, written, verbal, and by means of example, in order to translate vision into action.

This too should be obvious, even if it may be difficult to achieve. But what's less obvious is that the communication must be two-way. Leaders have to connect to their followers, listen to them, learn from them, draw strength and inspiration from them. Leaders should be guided by the maxim: "Seek first to understand, and then to be understood."

3. Know yourself, and know your people.

The injunction that marked the entrance to the ancient Greek oracle at Delphi, *know yourself*, is more than a platitude – for a leader, it's practical advice. Why? One important reason is that all of us have weaknesses, and as leaders we need to recognize those weaknesses and rely on subordinates to help compensate for them.

I learned both from psychological profiles like Myers-Briggs and from some unfortunate experiences that one of my many weaknesses is thinking abstractly to the exclusion of noticing practical details. So, when as Ambassador I was able to choose my deputy from among several nominees, I didn't choose the one most highly recommended, who had experience and characteristics that looked a lot like my own, but the one with a successful background as an administrative officer, who seemed likely to be strong where I was weak.

Beyond offsetting your own weaknesses, what should a leader look for in choosing subordinates and filling positions? I've discovered that degrees, credentials, grades, past job titles, and such are not very important. What you should look for are <u>qualities</u> such as integrity, energy, intelligence, judgment, creativity, and the like. This requires getting to know your people, and know them well.

And after you choose people for a job, never, never try to re-engineer them to suit the work, but if necessary re-structure the work to suit the people. As business guru Peter Drucker advised, "Put people where their strengths can produce the most results, and their weaknesses are irrelevant."

4. Take care of yourself; stay fit.

This is of course good advice for anyone, but why is it especially important for a leader? Because fitness is about more than health — it's about self-confidence and energy and stamina. The very adjectives we use to describe leadership in a positive way — <u>strong</u> leadership, <u>dynamic</u> leadership, <u>vigorous</u> leadership, <u>forceful</u> leadership, <u>active</u> leadership — these all suggest that leadership has an important physical component. Moreover, studies confirm that a high energy level is characteristic of virtually all successful leaders. Now, our energy <u>limits</u> are probably set by our genes; but we can all maximize how close we come to those limits through fitness and exercise.

Several years ago, I served as a sort of drill sergeant for my overweight grandson, to get him in good enough shape to pass the physical exam for joining the Navy. During one of our workouts, trying to encourage him I told him what I would do if I had my life to live over. While the list would be long, at the top of it would be to get fit while young and stay that way.

When I was an Auburn student I was fat, I smoked cigarettes, and my most vigorous exercise was one-arm beer can lifts from the table to my lips. (Not much weight was involved, but I got in an enormous amount of repetitions!) I finally began to change my ways and try to get physically fit in my late 30s, and when I did, I could tell, and others could tell, that I became a better leader.

5. Take care of your people.

General Colin Powell, who was Secretary of State as well as an outstanding military officer, is in my opinion one of our greatest contemporary practitioners of the art of leadership. He said:

> *Organization doesn't really accomplish anything. Plans don't accomplish anything either. Theories of management don't much matter. Endeavors succeed or fail because of the people involved.*

Leaders must support and be loyal to their subordinates in order to earn their support and loyalty. A fundamental goal of every leader should be to create an environment where the best, the brightest, the most creative people are attracted, retained, and above all empowered to contribute all they are capable of contributing. This means not just seeing that they are compensated adequately and treated fairly, but also sharing information widely, delegating necessary authority, involving subordinates in decision-making, and seeking out feedback (not just accepting it, but actively seeking it out).

6. Embrace change.

Leadership at its core is about change, and leaders need to not just accept change but to embrace it, to promote it, to guide it in the right direction, for change will surely come, whether we want it or not. If you don't lead it by the hand, it's likely to jump up and grab you by the throat.

Charles Darwin had this profound insight: "It is not the strongest of the species that survive, nor the most intelligent, but the ones most responsive to change."

This is as true in business and government and education and all other fields of endeavor as it is in biology. Our world is changing ever more rapidly, and we have to change along with it. Yet, change <u>always</u> evokes resistance, often fierce resistance, and leaders are needed to overcome that resistance. Leaders aren't really needed to maintain the status quo – managers can do that.

7. The final leadership principle I want to suggest is to <u>establish trust</u>.

This is the bottom line, the principle I hope you'll remember best: <u>The central ingredient in leadership, its most important and fundamental element, is the capacity to generate and sustain trust</u>. People will follow to the death those they trust completely; they simply will not follow those they don't trust.

How, then, do you establish trust?

Applying the principles I've just discussed is a good start: Develop and communicate a vision with worthy goals, know yourself and know your people, stay fit and energetic, support and empower your team, embrace change.

But building trust involves qualities that come from the heart as well as the head, that involve belief as well as reason. These qualities include moral clarity and a keen sense of right and wrong. They include passion – as St. Augustine put it, "In you must <u>burn</u> what you want to ignite in others." They include integrity and standing by your values under pressure. They include commitment to service. They include a willingness to put yourself at risk – Think of the statue of the new second lieutenant outside the Army infantry school at Fort Benning, leaning forward, with his fist in the air, and the inscription at its base that says "Follow me!" He's not saying go there, and do this, but leading from the front. "Follow me!"

And the qualities that help build trust include perseverance, the sort of refusal to accept defeat that enables a team to come back from being down 24-0 on the road in a hostile stadium and still win the game, as Auburn did against Alabama on its way to the national championship in 2010.

Never Give In!

Winston Churchill is one of the great leaders I've looked to as a hero since I studied about him and read some of his books during my student days at Auburn. He became Prime Minister of Great Britain in 1940, when Hitler's armies had overrun almost all of Europe, and Britain was left to stand alone against the Nazi tide. A new age of darkness seemed about to envelop all of Western civilization, and few thought the British could hold out. But with the force of his leadership Churchill rallied his countrymen, gained their trust, turned back the Germans in the Battle of Britain, and went on to help guide the Allies to victory in World War II.

In October 1941, before America had entered the war on Britain's side, and when the outlook for Britain was still grim, Churchill was asked to give a speech at Harrow, his old high school. His message to the students was brief and simple: "Never give in," he said. "Never, never, never give in!" All of the people who were there that day were moved, and never forgot those simple words, not because of their eloquence, but because of the eloquent life and stirring example of the great leader who spoke them.

I don't know if there's a future Churchill among you young men of Sigma Pi. I hope there is, because our country desperately needs some Churchillian-quality leadership. But even if you don't become great leaders of the nation, I fully expect that all of you will have opportunities to lead in business, in government, in politics, in your profession, in your family. I urge you to seize these opportunities. Begin <u>now</u> to develop your leadership skills. <u>Seek out</u> leadership roles in academic projects, in sports teams, in Sigma Pi. And never, never, <u>never</u> give in.

****

Annex 4

SENIOR SEMINAR:
What a Difference the Years Make!
By Pat McNees
State Magazine, July, 1988

Members of the latest Senior Seminar (they graduated on June 10) had a year that Dwight Eisenhower and John Foster Dulles probably didn't envision when they instructed Ambassador Loy Henderson to launch the first seminar 30 years ago. These 14 men and women from State, with an equal number from other Government agencies, had an unusual curriculum -- which they helped shape. It included, in addition to the usual Senior Seminar subjects, courses in physical fitness and a taste of inner-city community service. And at a three-day "wilderness lab" on the Chesapeake Bay, near Annapolis, as the seminar began, they got to know each other by working through a series of physical challenges designed to get people talking to each other, to develop the group as a learning team and to promote an open learning environment. For the State Department people, at least, said James Bullington, dean of the seminar (he's a former ambassador to Burundi), this was "pretty touchie-feelie stuff."

For most of its three decades, the Senior Seminar -- considered by many to be the *creme de la creme* of executive development programs for senior federal career officials -- was more akin to an advanced graduate seminar. "This year we made a lot of changes," said Mr. Bullington, "and I think it's more exciting. Now it's experientially oriented, designed to engage members physically and psychologically as well as intellectually. Thanksgiving week, for example, the Seminar members went out and took minimum-wage or volunteer jobs -- working in soup kitchens and homeless shelters and old folks' homes -- and came back and talked and wrote about their experiences." He added: "The Seminar was also more self-directed. The members were primarily responsible for determining the content. And another thing that was new was the emphasis on leadership and executive development. In prior years there was very little of that."

The dean said he sees health and fitness as an integral part of executive development. "You need stamina and good health simply to feel good, to be out in front. If you feel good about yourself, you're more likely to project an aura of competence and an attitude of 'follow me, guys!' The fitness training is optional, but with some subtle and not-so-subtle peer pressure, participation was nearly 100%."

Who attended

Although run by the Foreign Service Institute, the nine-month Seminar is very much an interdepartmental affair. It included participants from the Departments of Agriculture and Commerce, as well as USIA, AID, the National Security Agency, the Army, Navy, Air Force, Marines, Coast Guard, Secret Service, Federal Bureau of Investigation and Central Intelligence Agency.

The Seminar is very selective: participants are chosen from the top ranks of the Senior Foreign and Civil Services. "I can't tell you how the other agencies decide," said Mr. Bullington, "but I can speak for State. The lists of people who are being promoted into the Senior Foreign Service are rank-ordered, and the members of the Seminar are selected from the top of that rank-ordered list. Participants tend to be in their 40s -- generally, people with 20 years in the Service. We get women (this year there were four), but at these levels men still tend to predominate."[30]

Essentially, the Seminar is for personnel who are ready to move from senior management to leadership positions -- from positions that

---

[30] It was only in the 1970s and 80s that large numbers of women began to enter the Foreign Service and move to senior levels.

require enforcing, explaining and defending policy to positions that may also require shaping or changing it. "The Seminar provides officers who've crossed the senior threshold an opportunity to step away from the cycles of crisis and reaction, to reflect on the issues that face this nation and the skills they'll need to resolve them," Mr. Bullington said.

The curriculum

As part of the leadership training, in late September the new members went on a two-day retreat to Harper's Ferry, WVA, for a planning session at which they designed their curriculum for the rest of the year, based on what they had decided together they needed most to learn. Members had been told that the curriculum should be designed to cover three broad areas:

- Leadership and executive development (to help improve skills they would need in demanding, top-level positions).
- Domestic affairs (to give an understanding of the domestic institutions, issues and conditions that influence foreign relations).
- National security and foreign policy (to help them understand major issues and how policies are developed).

The members decided on specific subjects in these areas, focusing on domestic issues in the first half of the course, national security and foreign policy in the second half, and leadership and executive development throughout. They apportioned time to these subjects, in one- to five-day study units, and assigned individuals or small groups to be responsible for the detailed programming of each unit (e.g., selecting and arranging for speakers). They also chose committees to program the group's seven field trips -- which included visits to New York, Detroit, Miami, Atlanta, San Antonio, El Paso, Winona MN, Mexico City, and a number of armed forces bases.

Need for executive training

Executive development and management training were given high priority, but Mr. Bullington's first efforts were met with skepticism. He explained, "It wasn't so much a resistance to new training approaches but skepticism that 'management training' would work. What was called 'executive development' had been tried in the Senior Seminar some years ago, and elsewhere at State, and it hadn't worked."

Yet it was clear senior officers needed something in this area. Dee Hanh-Rollins, a professional trainer who helped the Foreign Service Institute revise its training curriculum, explained, "Up to the managerial and leadership level, State rewards individual achievement. Then all of a sudden officers are cast into a position of responsibility that requires management and leadership skills. In the past, the Department has thought: 'Well, you learn it on the job' -- but that just hasn't happened."

On the 12th floor of the Foreign Service Institute's main building in Rosslyn, the Seminar members heard from a wide range of experts -- academics, public officials, journalists, economists, business and labor leaders, and representatives of interest groups -- often on both sides of contentious issues. For example, they heard both Sarah Melendez and Linda Chavez on bilingual education, and both union workers and trade representatives on the textile industry. Other speakers included Haynes Johnson and Leon Dash of the *Washington Post* and David Shipler of the *New York Times*, two speakers from Greenpeace, the environmental organization, Richard Scammon on political polling, Herbert Stein on the budget deficit, Mayor Andrew Young of Atlanta, and General Brent Scowcroft, the former presidential national security adviser. Between major presentations, the members gave "brown bag lunch" talks on the areas of their own expertise.

Professional trainers conducted sessions on leadership skills such as public speaking, negotiating, and dealing with the press. Four weeks were set aside in February for individual projects: a research paper, a tour as diplomat-in-residence at a small college remote from Washington, or a work experience on Capitol Hill, in state or local government, or in business or industry. For example, Pat Langford, who had been consul general in Bangkok, spent her four weeks teaching at Southern University, an all-black school in Baton Rouge.

Physical activity

Throughout the year, health and fitness experts talked to Seminar members about nutrition, stress management, and how to maintain the good health and stamina an executive needs. And at the start of the year a fitness expert gave everybody a mini-physical exam to determine levels of cholesterol and body fat, and encouraged them all to set fitness goals. The members set aside Tuesday and Thursday afternoons for the gym, and to do physical training at Arlington Hall, a military facility a couple of miles from Rosslyn (where the new Foreign Service Institute facilities will eventually be built). Some jogged, some swam, some used weights or rode stationary bicycles. The fitness expert helped them with individual problems.

At the "wilderness lab" early in September, the idea was to see one's regular behavior patterns in a new setting. In one exercise, all of the members of a small group were blindfolded and handed part of one 250-foot rope. Participants had no idea whether they were holding the end of the rope or the middle; they knew only that, together, they were to shape that rope into a four-cornered square, within a certain time limit. Clear communication was crucial in this exercise.

In another exercise, individuals had to climb up four steps on a ladder, then fall off backward into the support net formed by their team-mates, standing in two lines with their arms interlocked. This was an exercise in trust-building, in getting comfortable with other people supporting you, in stretching yourself psychologically so you could begin to trust people you don't know.

The field trips

As to the field trips, for officers who have been posted abroad for much of their career, these trips are vivid re-entry experiences. For Bill Brew, who came to the Seminar from a four-year stint as economic counselor in Israel, the trip to Detroit -- where he visited Ford and the United Auto Workers by day, then rode in police patrol cars until midnight -- was "impressionistic, sure; and it's only a day or two, but you do get a pretty good sense of what people are thinking about."

The impact of the Thanksgiving week experiences was profound. Some members got their families involved, and several decided to continue community service work. Dick Combs, who had been deputy chief of mission in Moscow, worked in a shelter for the homeless in northern Virginia. He wrote in his report: "The main surprise about the residents was their youth. I had expected to find mostly old folks. In fact, the average age was between 25 and 35. The next surprise was their diversity: some were hooked on drugs and spent what little money they could accumulate on their habit; some were alcoholics; some were mentally incompetent; some were just down on their luck. One unfortunate man, for example, knew no English, had been disowned by his American-citizen relative, had broken his leg and was awaiting money from his relatives in Latin America for the trip home. Still others were married couples living in their automobiles or vans and needing a bed and bath. The homeless at this shelter were not suffering from unemployment. Most could find work. But they could qualify only for low-paying employment that was insufficient to enable them to acquire permanent housing in Fairfax County.... Overall, I was depressed by the evident intractability of the homeless problem I saw, yet encouraged by the skill and determination of the shelter staff to chip away at reducing it."

Like many Seminar members, Douglas Watson, who had been administrative counselor in Islamabad, found the units on domestic issues to be both important and frustrating. "I ended up very

333

frustrated with our continuing failure to provide the kind of education in our primary and secondary systems that will enable the nation to remain strong," he said. He found the three most intractable domestic problems to be education, the nation's increasing drug problem (particularly as it affects inner-city kids), and "this permanent underclass which we've allowed to develop in our society. Whether it's in Appalachia or in the urban ghetto, it's remote from those of us who are participating more fully in the economic and social system, so we're more complacent about it than we have any logical right to be."

Different flavors

Summing up, Ms. Langford said: "It's been a wonderful experience. I feel as it I've been dangled from a string and dipped in 99 different wonderful coatings, everything from chocolate to raspberry, I came into it knowing I would learn a lot. I'm leaving it amazed at how much more I learned than I thought I would."

Made in the USA
Middletown, DE
31 December 2018